Get the eBook FREE!
(PDF, ePub, Kindle, and liveBook all included)

We believe that once you buy a book from us, you should be able to read it in any format we have available. To get electronic versions of this book at no additional cost to you, purchase and then register this book at the Manning website.

Go to https://www.manning.com/freebook and follow the instructions to complete your pBook registration.

That's it!
Thanks from Manning!

grokking
Deep Learning

grokking
Deep Learning

Andrew W. Trask

MANNING
SHELTER ISLAND

For online information and ordering of this and other Manning books, please visit
www.manning.com. The publisher offers discounts on this book when ordered in
quantity. For more information, please contact

Special Sales Department
Manning Publications Co.
20 Baldwin Road, PO Box 761
Shelter Island, NY 11964
Email: orders@manning.com

 Manning Publications Co.   Development editor: Christina Taylor
        20 Baldwin Road   Review editor: Aleksandar Dragosavljevic
        Shelter Island, NY 11964 Production editor: Lori Weidert
                                  Copyeditor: Tiffany Taylor
                                  Proofreader: Sharon Wilkey
                                  Technical proofreader: David Fombella Pomball
                                  Typesetter: Dennis Dalinnik
                                  Cover designer: Leslie Haimes

ISBN: 9781617293702
Printed in the United States of America

• •

*To Mom. You sacrificed so much time in your life to bless Tara and me with education.
I hope you see your work behind this book.*

*And to Dad. Thank you for loving us so much and for taking the time to teach me
programming and technology at such a young age. I wouldn't be doing this without you.*

It is a great honor to be your son.

contents

preface

Grokking Deep Learning is the product of a monumental three years of effort. To get to the book you hold in your hand, I wrote at least twice the number of pages you see here. Half-a-dozen chapters were rewritten from scratch three or four times before they were ready to publish, and along the way important chapters were added that weren't part of the original plan.

More significantly, I arrived at two decisions early on that make *Grokking Deep Learning* uniquely valuable: this book requires no math background beyond basic arithmetic, and it doesn't rely on a high-level library that might hide what is going on. In other words, anyone can read this book and understand how deep learning really works. To accomplish this, I had to invent new ways to describe and teach the core ideas and techniques without falling back on advanced mathematics or sophisticated code that someone else wrote.

My goal in writing *Grokking Deep Learning* was to create the lowest possible barrier to entry to the practice of deep learning. You don't just read the theory; you'll discover it yourself. To help you get there, To help you get there, I wrote a lot of code and did my best to explain it in the right order so that the code snippets required for the working demos all made sense.

This knowledge, combined with all the theory, code, and examples you'll explore in this book, will make you much faster at iterating through experiments. You'll have quick successes and better job opportunities, and you'll even learn about more-advanced deep learning concepts more rapidly.

In the last three years, I not only authored this book, but also entered a PhD program at Oxford, joined the team at Google, and helped spearhead OpenMined, a decentralized artificial intelligence platform. This book is the culmination of years of thinking, learning, and teaching.

There are many other resources for learning deep learning. I'm glad that you came to this one.

acknowledgments

I'm exceedingly grateful for everyone who has contributed to the production of *Grokking Deep Learning*. First and foremost, I'd like to thank the amazing team at Manning: Bert Bates, who taught me how to write; Christina Taylor, who patiently kept me going for three years; Michael Stephens, whose creativity has allowed the book to have great success even before publication; and Marjan Bace, whose encouragement in the midst of delays made all the difference.

Grokking Deep Learning wouldn't be what it is without the immense contributions of early readers through email, Twitter, and GitHub. I feel greatly indebted to Jascha Swisher, Varun Sudhakar, Francois Chollet, Frederico Vitorino, Cody Hammond, Mauricio Maroto Arrieta, Aleksandar Dragosavljevic, Alan Carter, Frank Hinek, Nicolas Benjamin Hocker, Hank Meisse, Wouter Hibma, Joerg Rosenkranz, Alex Vieira, and Charlie Harrington for all your help refining the text and the online code repository.

I'd like to thank the reviewers who took time to read the manuscript at various stages in development: Alexander A. Myltsev, Amit Lamba, Anand Saha, Andrew Hamor, Cristian Barrientos, Montoya, Eremey Valetov, Gerald Mack, Ian Stirk, Kalyan Reddy, Kamal Raj, Kelvin D. Meeks, Marco Paulo dos Santos Nogueira, Martin Beer, Massimo Ilario, Nancy W. Grady, Peter Hampton, Sebastian Maldonado, Shashank Gupta, Tymoteusz Wołodźko, Kumar Unnikrishnan, Vipul Gupta, Will Fuger, and William Wheeler.

I'm also grateful to Mat and Niko at Udacity, who included the book in Udacity's Deep Learning Nanodegree, which greatly aided in early awareness of the book among young deep learning practitioners.

I must thank Dr. William Hooper, who let me wander into his office and bug him about computer science, who made an exception to let me into his (already full) Programming 1 class, and who inspired me to pursue a career in deep learning. I am exceedingly thankful for all the patience you had with me starting out. You have blessed me immensely.

Finally, I'd like to thank my wife for being so patient with me during all the nights and weekends spent working on the book, for copyediting the entire text several times herself, and for creating and debugging the online GitHub code repository.

about this book

Grokking Deep Learning was written to help give you a foundation in deep learning so that you can master a major deep learning framework. It begins by focusing on the basics of neural networks and then switches its focus to provide an in-depth look at advanced layers and architectures.

Who should read this book

I've intentionally written this book with what I believe is the lowest barrier to entry possible. No knowledge of linear algebra, calculus, convex optimization, or even machine learning is assumed. Everything from those subjects that's necessary to understand deep learning will be explained as we go. If you've passed high school mathematics and hacked around in Python, you're ready for this book.

Roadmap

This book has 16 chapters:

- Chapter 1 focuses on why should you learn deep learning, and what you'll need to get started.

- Chapter 2 starts to dig deep in fundamental concepts, such as machine learning, parametric and nonparametric models, and supervised and unsupervised learning. It also introduces the "predict, compare, learn" paradigm that will continue through the following chapters.

- Chapter 3 will walk you through using simple networks to make a prediction, as well as provide your first look at a neural network.

- Chapter 4 will teach you how to evaluate the predictions made in chapter 3 and identify errors to help train models in the next step.

- Chapter 5 focuses on the *learn* part of the "predict, compare, learn" paradigm. Using an in-depth example, this chapter walks through the learning process.

- In chapter 6, you'll build your first "deep" neural network, code and all.

- Chapter 7 focuses on the 10,000-foot view of neural networks and works to simplify your mental picture.

- Chapter 8 introduces overfitting, dropout, and batch gradient descent, and teaches you how to classify your dataset within the new network you just built.

- Chapter 9 teaches activation functions and how to use them when modeling probabilities.

- Chapter 10 introduces convolutional neural networks, highlighting the usability of structure to counter overfitting.

- Chapter 11 dives into natural language processing (NLP) and provides foundational vocabulary and concepts in the deep learning field.

- Chapter 12 discusses recurrent neural networks, a state-of-the-art approach in nearly every sequence-modeling field, and one of the most popular tools used in the industry.

- Chapter 13 will fast-track you on how to build a deep learning framework from scratch by becoming a power user of deep learning frameworks.

- Chapter 14 uses your recurrent neural network to tackle a more challenging task: language modeling.

- Chapter 15 focuses on privacy in data, introducing basic privacy concepts such as federated learning, homomorphic encryption, and concepts related to differential privacy and secure multiparty computation.

- Chapter 16 will give you the tools and resources you need to continue your deep learning journey.

About the Code conventions and downloads

All code in the book is presented in a `fixed-width font like this` to separate it from ordinary text. Code annotations accompany some of the listings, highlighting important concepts.

You can download the code for the examples in the book from the publisher's website at www.manning.com/books/grokking-deep-learning, or from https://github.com/iamtrask/grokking-deep-learning.

Book forum

Purchase of *Grokking Deep Learning* includes free access to a private web forum run by Manning Publications, where you can make comments about the book, ask technical questions, and receive help from the author and from other users. To access the forum, go to https://forums.manning.com/forums/grokking-deep-learning. You can also learn more about Manning's forums and the rules of conduct at https://forums.manning.com/forums/about.

Manning's commitment to our readers is to provide a venue where a meaningful dialogue between individual readers and between readers and the author can take place. It isn't a commitment to any specific amount of participation on the part of the author, whose contribution to the forum remains voluntary (and unpaid). We suggest you try asking the author some challenging questions lest his interest stray! The forum and the archives of previous discussions will be accessible from the publisher's website as long as the book is in print.

about the author

Andrew Trask is the founding member of Digital Reasoning's machine learning lab, where deep learning approaches to natural language processing, image recognition, and audio transcription are being researched. Within several months, Andrew and his research partner exceeded best published results in sentiment classification and part-of-speech tagging. He trained the world's largest artificial neural network with over 160 billion parameters, the results of which he presented with his coauthor at The International Conference on Machine Learning. Those results were published in the *Journal of Machine Learning*. He is currently the product manager of text and audio analytics at Digital Reasoning, responsible for driving the analytics roadmap for the Synthesys cognitive computing platform, for which deep learning is a core competency.

grokking
Deep Learning

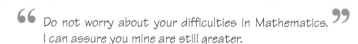

In this chapter

- Why you should learn deep learning

- Why you should read this book

- What you need to get started

> 66 Do not worry about your difficulties in Mathematics. 99
> I can assure you mine are still greater.
>
> —Albert Einstein

Welcome to *Grokking Deep Learning*

You're about to learn some of the most valuable skills of the century!

I'm very excited that you're here! You should be, too! Deep learning represents an exciting intersection of machine learning and artificial intelligence, and a very significant disruption to society and industry. The methods discussed in this book are changing the world all around you. From optimizing the engine of your car to deciding which content you view on social media, it's everywhere, it's powerful, and, fortunately, it's fun!

Why you should learn deep learning

It's a powerful tool for the incremental automation of intelligence.

From the beginning of time, humans have been building better and better tools to understand and control the environment around us. Deep learning is today's chapter in this story of innovation.

Perhaps what makes this chapter so compelling is that this field is more of a *mental* innovation than a *mechanical one*. Much like its sister fields in machine learning, deep learning seeks to *automate intelligence* bit by bit. In the past few years, it has achieved enormous success and progress in this endeavor, exceeding previous records in computer vision, speech recognition, machine translation, and many other tasks.

This is particularly extraordinary given that deep learning seems to use *largely the same brain-inspired algorithm* (neural networks) for achieving these accomplishments across a vast number of fields. Even though deep learning is still an actively developing field with many challenges, recent developments have lead to tremendous excitement: perhaps we've discovered not just a great tool, but a window into our own minds.

Deep learning has the potential for significant automation of skilled labor.

There's a substantial amount of hype around the potential impacts of deep learning if the current trend of progress is extrapolated at varying speeds. Although many of these predictions are overzealous, I believe one merits your consideration: job displacement. I think this claim stands out from the rest because even if deep learning's innovations stopped *today*, there would already be an incredible impact on skilled labor around the globe. Call-center operators, taxi drivers, and low-level business analysts are compelling examples where deep learning can provide a low-cost alternative.

Fortunately, the economy doesn't turn on a dime; but in many ways we're already past the point of concern, given the current power of the technology. It's my hope that you (and people you know) will be enabled by this book to transition from perhaps one of the industries facing disruption into an industry ripe with growth and prosperity: deep learning.

It's fun and creative. You'll discover much about what it is to be human by trying to simulate intelligence and creativity.

Personally, I got into deep learning because it's fascinating. It's an amazing intersection between human and machine. Unpacking exactly what it means to think, to reason, and to create is enlightening, engaging, and, for me, inspiring. Consider having a dataset filled with every painting ever painted, and then using that to teach a machine how to paint like Monet. Insanely, it's possible, and it's mind-bogglingly cool to see how it works.

Will this be difficult to learn?

How hard will you have to work before there's a "fun" payoff?

This is my favorite question. My definition of a "fun" payoff is the experience of witnessing something that I built *learning*. There's something amazing about seeing a creation of your hands do something like that. If you also feel this way, then the answer is simple. A few pages into chapter 3, you'll create your first neural network. The only work involved until then is reading the pages between here and there.

After chapter 3, you may be interested to know that the *next* fun payoff occurs after you've memorized a small snippet of code and proceeded to read to the midway of chapter 4. Each chapter will work this way: memorize a small code segment from the previous chapter, read the next chapter, and then experience the payoff of a new learning neural network.

Why you should read this book

It has a uniquely low barrier to entry.

The reason you should read this book is the same reason I'm writing it. I don't know of another resource (book, course, large blog series) that teaches deep learning *without assuming advanced knowledge of mathematics* (a college degree in a mathy field).

Don't get me wrong: there are really good reasons for teaching it using math. Math is, after all, a language. It's certainly more *efficient* to teach deep learning using this language, but I don't think it's absolutely necessary to assume advanced knowledge of math in order to become a skilled, knowledgeable practitioner who has a firm understanding of the "how" behind deep learning.

So, why should you learn deep learning using this book? Because I'm going to assume you have a high school–level background in math (and that it's rusty) and *explain everything else you need to know as we go along*. Remember multiplication? Remember x-y graphs (the squares with lines on them)? Awesome! You'll be fine.

It will help you understand what's *inside* a framework (Torch, TensorFlow, and so on).

There are two major groups of deep learning educational material (such as books and courses). One group is focused around how to use popular frameworks and code libraries like Torch, TensorFlow, Keras, and others. The other group is focused around teaching deep learning itself, otherwise known as the *science under the hood* of these major frameworks.

Ultimately, learning about *both* is important. It's like if you want to be a NASCAR driver: you need to learn both about the particular model of car you're driving (the framework) and about driving (the science/skill). But just learning about a framework is like learning about the pros and cons of a Generation 6 Chevrolet SS before you know what a stick shift is. This book is about teaching you what deep learning is so you can then be prepared to learn a framework.

All math-related material will be backed by intuitive analogies.

Whenever I encounter a math formula in the wild, I take a two-step approach. The first is to translate its methods into an intuitive *analogy* to the real world. I almost never take a formula at face value: I break it into *parts*, each with a story of its own. That will be the approach of this book, as well. Anytime we encounter a math concept, I'll offer an alternative analogy for what the formula is actually doing.

> Everything should be made as simple as possible, but not simpler.
> —Attributed to Albert Einstein

Everything after the introduction chapters is "project" based.

If there's one thing I hate when learning something new, it's having to question whether what I'm learning is useful or relevant. If someone is teaching me everything there is to know about a hammer without actually taking my hand and helping me drive in a nail, then they're not really teaching me how to use a hammer. I know there will be dots that aren't connected, and if I'm thrown out into the real world with a hammer, a box of nails, and a bunch of two-by-fours, I'll have to do some guesswork.

This book is about giving you the wood, nails, and hammer *before* telling you what they do. Each lesson is about picking up the tools and building stuff with them, explaining how things work as we go. This way, you won't leave with a list of facts about the various deep learning tools you'll work with; you'll have the ability to use them to solve problems. Furthermore, you'll understand the most important part: when and why each tool is appropriate for each problem you want to solve. It is with this knowledge that you'll be empowered to pursue a career in research and/or industry.

What you need to get started

Install Jupyter Notebook and the NumPy Python library.

My absolute favorite place to work is in Jupyter Notebook. One of the most important parts of learning deep learning (for me) is the ability to stop a network while it's training and tear apart absolutely every piece to see what it looks like. This is something Jupyter Notebook is incredibly useful for.

As for NumPy, perhaps the most compelling case for why this book leaves nothing out is that we'll be using only a single matrix library. In this way, you'll understand *how* everything works, not just how to call a framework. This book teaches deep learning from absolute scratch, soup to nuts.

Installation instructions for these two tools can be found at http://jupyter.org for Jupyter and http://numpy.org for NumPy. I'll build the examples in Python 2.7, but I've tested them for Python 3 as well. For easy installation, I also recommend the Anaconda framework: https://docs.continuum.io/anaconda/install.

Pass high school mathematics.

Some mathematical assumptions are out of depth for this book, but my goal is to teach deep learning assuming that you understand only basic algebra.

Find a personal problem you're interested in.

This might seem like an optional "need" to get started. I guess it could be, but seriously, I highly, highly recommend finding one. Everyone I know who has become successful at this stuff had some sort of problem they were trying to solve. Learning deep learning was just a "dependency" to solving some other interesting task.

For me, it was using Twitter to predict the stock market. It's just something I thought was really fascinating. It's what drove me to sit down and read the next chapter and build the next prototype.

And as it turns out, this field is *so new*, and is changing *so fast*, that if you spend the next couple of years chasing one project with these tools, you'll find yourself becoming one of the leading experts in that *particular problem* faster than you might think. For me, chasing this idea took me from barely knowing anything about programming to a research grant at a hedge fund applying what I learned, in around 18 months! For deep learning, having a problem you're fascinated with that involves using one dataset to predict another is the key catalyst! Go find one!

You'll probably need some Python knowledge

Python is my teaching library of choice, but I'll provide a few others online.

Python is an amazingly intuitive language. I think it just might be the most widely adopted and intuitively readable language yet constructed. Furthermore, the Python community has a passion for simplicity that can't be beat. For these reasons, I want to stick with Python for all the examples (Python 2.7 is what I'm working in). In the book's downloadable source code, available at www.manning.com/books/grokking-deep-learning and also at https://github.com/iamtrask/Grokking-Deep-Learning, I provide all the examples in a variety of other languages online.

How much coding experience should you have?

Scan through the Python Codecademy course (www.codecademy.com/learn/python). If you can read the table of contents and feel comfortable with the terms mentioned, you're all set! If not, then take the course and come back when you're done. It's designed to be a beginner course, and it's very well crafted.

Summary

If you've got a Jupyter notebook in hand and feel comfortable with the basics of Python, you're ready for the next chapter! As a heads-up, chapter 2 is the last chapter that will be mostly dialogue based (without building something). It's designed to give you an awareness of the high-level vocabulary, concepts, and fields in artificial intelligence, machine learning, and, most important, deep learning.

fundamental concepts: how do machines learn? | 2

. . . .

In this chapter

- What are deep learning, machine learning, and artificial intelligence?

- What are parametric models and nonparametric models?

- What are supervised learning and unsupervised learning?

- How can machines learn?

. . . .

Machine learning will cause every successful IPO win in five years.

—Eric Schmidt, Google executive chairman, keynote speech, Cloud Computing Platform conference, 2016

What is deep learning?

Deep learning is a subset of methods for machine learning.

Deep learning is a subset of machine learning, which is a field dedicated to the study and development of machines that can learn (sometimes with the goal of eventually attaining general artificial intelligence).

In industry, deep learning is used to solve practical tasks in a variety of fields such as computer vision (image), natural language processing (text), and automatic speech recognition (audio). In short, deep learning is a subset of *methods* in the machine learning toolbox, primarily using *artificial neural networks*, which are a class of algorithm loosely inspired by the human brain.

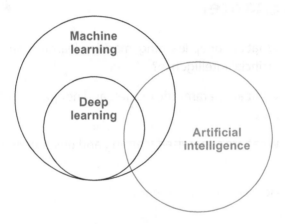

Notice in this figure that not all of deep learning is focused around pursuing generalized artificial intelligence (sentient machines as in the movies). Many applications of this technology are used to solve a wide variety of problems in industry. This book seeks to focus on teaching the fundamentals of deep learning behind both cutting-edge research and industry, helping to prepare you for either.

What is machine learning?

 A field of study that gives computers the ability to learn without being explicitly programmed.

—Attributed to Arthur Samuel

Given that deep learning is a subset of machine learning, what is machine learning? Most generally, it is what its name implies. Machine learning is a subfield of computer science wherein *machines learn* to perform tasks for which they were *not explicitly programmed*. In short, machines observe a pattern and attempt to imitate it in some way that can be either direct or indirect.

Machine ~= Monkey see,
learning   monkey do

I mention direct and indirect imitation as a parallel to the two main types of machine learning: *supervised* and *unsupervised*. Supervised machine learning is the direct imitation of a pattern between two datasets. It's always attempting to take an input dataset and transform it into an output dataset. This can be an incredibly powerful and useful capability. Consider the following examples (*input* datasets in bold and *output* datasets in italic):

- Using the **pixels** of an image to detect the *presence* or *absence of a cat*

- Using the **movies you've liked** to predict more *movies you may like*

- Using someone's **words** to predict whether they're *happy* or *sad*

- Using weather sensor **data** to predict the *probability of rain*

- Using car engine **sensors** to predict the optimal tuning *settings*

- Using news **data** to predict tomorrow's stock *price*

- Using an input **number** to predict a *number* double its size

- Using a raw **audio file** to predict a *transcript* of the audio

These are all supervised machine learning tasks. In all cases, the machine learning algorithm is attempting to imitate the pattern between the two datasets in such a way that it can *use one dataset to predict the other*. For any of these examples, imagine if you had the power to predict the *output* dataset given only the **input** dataset. Such an ability would be profound.

Supervised machine learning

Supervised learning transforms datasets.

Supervised learning is a method for transforming one dataset into another. For example, if you had a dataset called Monday Stock Prices that recorded the price of every stock on every Monday for the past 10 years, and a second dataset called Tuesday Stock Prices recorded over the same time period, a supervised learning algorithm might try to use one to predict the other.

If you successfully trained the supervised machine learning algorithm on 10 years of Mondays and Tuesdays, then you could predict the stock price on any Tuesday in the future given the stock price on the immediately preceding Monday. I encourage you to stop and consider this for a moment.

Supervised machine learning is the bread and butter of applied artificial intelligence (also known as narrow AI). It's useful for taking *what you know* as input and quickly transforming it into *what you want to know*. This allows supervised machine learning algorithms to extend human intelligence and capabilities in a seemingly endless number of ways.

The majority of work using machine learning results in the training of a supervised classifier of some kind. Even unsupervised machine learning (which you'll learn more about in a moment) is typically done to aid in the development of an accurate supervised machine learning algorithm.

For the rest of this book, you'll be creating algorithms that can take input data that is observable, recordable, and, by extension, *knowable* and transform it into valuable output data that requires logical analysis. This is the power of supervised machine learning.

Unsupervised machine learning

Unsupervised learning groups your data.

Unsupervised learning shares a property in common with supervised learning: it transforms one dataset into another. But the dataset that it transforms into is *not previously known or understood.* Unlike supervised learning, there is no "right answer" that you're trying to get the model to duplicate. You just tell an unsupervised algorithm to "find patterns in this data and tell me about them."

For example, *clustering a dataset into groups* is a type of unsupervised learning. Clustering transforms a sequence of *datapoints* into a sequence of *cluster labels*. If it learns 10 clusters, it's common for these labels to be the numbers 1–10. Each datapoint will be assigned to a number based on which cluster it's in. Thus, the dataset turns from a bunch of datapoints into a bunch of labels. Why are the labels numbers? The algorithm doesn't tell you what the clusters are. How could it know? It just says, "Hey scientist! I found some structure. It looks like there are groups in your data. Here they are!"

I have good news! This idea of clustering is something you can reliably hold onto in your mind as the definition of unsupervised learning. Even though there are many forms of unsupervised learning, *all forms of unsupervised learning can be viewed as a form of clustering.* You'll discover more on this later in the book.

Check out this example. Even though the algorithm didn't tell what the clusters are named, can you figure out how it clustered the words? (Answer: 1 == cute and 2 == delicious.) Later, we'll unpack how other forms of unsupervised learning are also just a form of clustering and why these clusters are useful for supervised learning.

Parametric vs. nonparametric learning

Oversimplified: Trial-and-error learning vs. counting and probability

The last two pages divided all machine learning algorithms into two groups: supervised and unsupervised. Now, we're going to discuss another way to divide the same machine learning algorithms into two groups: parametric and nonparametric. So, if we think about our little machine learning cloud, it has two settings:

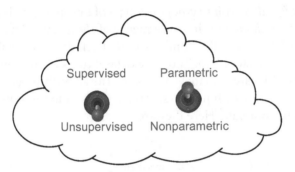

As you can see, there are really four different types of algorithms to choose from. An algorithm is either unsupervised or supervised, and either parametric or nonparametric. Whereas the previous section on supervision is about the *type of pattern* being learned, parametricism is about the way the learning is *stored* and often, by extension, the *method for learning*. First, let's look at the formal definitions of parametricism versus nonparametricism. For the record, there's still some debate around the exact difference.

A parametric model is characterized by having a fixed number of parameters, whereas a nonparametric model's number of parameters is *infinite* (determined by data).

As an example, let's say the problem is to fit a square peg into the correct (square) hole. Some humans (such as babies) just jam it into all the holes until it fits somewhere (parametric). A teenager, however, may count the number of sides (four) and then search for the hole with an equal number (nonparametric). Parametric models tend to use trial and error, whereas nonparametric models tend to count. Let's look closer.

Supervised parametric learning

Oversimplified: Trial-and-error learning using knobs

Supervised parametric learning machines are machines with a fixed number of knobs (that's the parametric part), wherein learning occurs by turning the knobs. Input data comes in, is processed based on the angle of the knobs, and is transformed into a *prediction*.

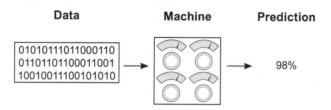

Learning is accomplished by turning the knobs to different angles. If you're trying to predict the probability that the Red Sox will win the World Series, then this model would first take data (such as sports stats like win/loss record or average number of toes per player) and make a prediction (such as 98% chance). Next, the model would observe whether or not the Red Sox actually won. After it knew whether they won, the learning algorithm would *update the knobs* to make a more accurate prediction the next time it sees the *same or similar input data*.

Perhaps it would "turn up" the "win/loss record" knob if the team's win/loss record was a good predictor. Inversely, it might "turn down" the "average number of toes" knob if that datapoint wasn't a good predictor. This is how parametric models learn!

Note that the entirety of what the model has learned can be captured in the positions of the knobs at any given time. You can also think of this type of learning model as a search algorithm. You're "searching" for the appropriate knob configuration by trying configurations, adjusting them, and retrying.

Note further that the notion of trial and error isn't the formal definition, but it's a common (with exceptions) property to parametric models. When there is an arbitrary (but fixed) number of knobs to turn, some level of searching is required to find the optimal configuration. This is in contrast to nonparametric learning, which is often count based and (more or less) adds new knobs when it finds something new to count. Let's break down supervised parametric learning into its three steps.

Step 1: Predict

To illustrate supervised parametric learning, let's continue with the sports analogy of trying to predict whether the Red Rox will win the World Series. The first step, as mentioned, is to gather sports statistics, send them through the machine, and make a prediction about the probability that the Red Sox will win.

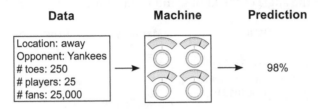

Step 2: Compare to the truth pattern

The second step is to compare the prediction (98%) with the pattern you care about (whether the Red Sox won). Sadly, they lost, so the comparison is

Pred: 98% > **Truth**: 0%

This step recognizes that if the model had predicted 0%, it would have perfectly predicted the upcoming loss of the team. You want the machine to be accurate, which leads to step 3.

Step 3: Learn the pattern

Adjusting sensitivity by turning knobs

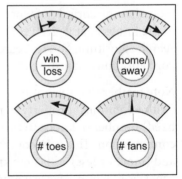

This step adjusts the knobs by studying both how *much* the model missed by (98%) and what the input data *was* (sports stats) at the time of prediction. This step then turns the knobs to make a more accurate prediction given the input data.

In theory, the next time this step saw the same sports stats, the prediction would be lower than 98%. Note that each knob represents the *prediction's sensitivity to different types of input data*. That's what you're changing when you "learn."

Unsupervised parametric learning

Unsupervised parametric learning uses a very similar approach. Let's walk through the steps at a high level. Remember that unsupervised learning is all about grouping data. Unsupervised *parametric* learning uses knobs to group data. But in this case, it usually has several knobs for each group, each of which maps the input data's affinity to that particular group (with exceptions and nuance—this is a high-level description). Let's look at an example that assumes you want to divide the data into three groups.

Home or away	# fans
home	**100k**
away	50k
home	**100k**
home	**99k**
away	50k
away	*10k*
away	*11k*

In the dataset, I've identified three clusters in the data that you might want the parametric model to find. They're indicated via formatting as **group 1**, group 2, and *group 3*. Let's propagate the first datapoint through a trained unsupervised model, as shown next. Notice that it maps most strongly to **group 1**.

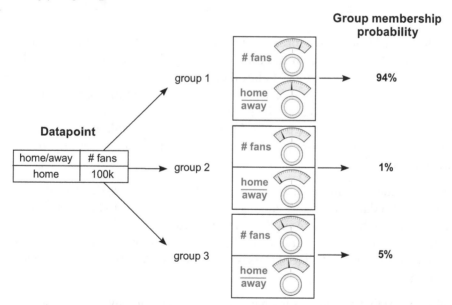

Each group's machine attempts to transform the input data to a number between 0 and 1, telling us the *probability that the input data is a member of that group*. There is a great deal of variety in how these models train and their resulting properties, but at a high level they adjust parameters to transform the input data into its subscribing group(s).

Nonparametric learning

Oversimplified: Counting-based methods

Nonparametric learning is a class of algorithm wherein the number of parameters is based on data (instead of predefined). This lends itself to methods that generally count in one way or another, thus increasing the number of parameters based on the number of items being counted within the data. In the supervised setting, for example, a nonparametric model might count the number of times a particular color of streetlight causes cars to "go." After counting only a few examples, this model would then be able to predict that *middle* lights always (100%) cause cars to go, and *right* lights only sometimes (50%) cause cars to go.

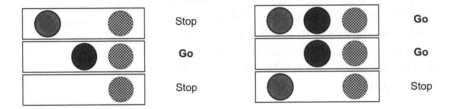

Notice that this model would have three parameters: three counts indicating the number of times each colored light turned on and cars would go (perhaps divided by the number of total observations). If there were five lights, there would be five counts (five parameters). What makes this simple model *nonparametric* is this trait wherein the number of parameters changes based on the data (in this case, the number of lights). This is in contrast to parametric models, which start with a set number of parameters and, more important, can have more or fewer parameters purely at the discretion of the scientist training the model (regardless of data).

A close eye might question this idea. The parametric model from before seemed to have a knob for each input datapoint. Most parametric models still have to have some sort of *input* based on the number of classes in the data. Thus you can see that there is a *gray area* between parametric and nonparametric algorithms. Even parametric algorithms are somewhat influenced by the number of classes in the data, even if they aren't explicitly counting patterns.

This also illuminates that *parameters* is a generic term, referring only to the set of numbers used to model a pattern (without any limitation on how those numbers are used). Counts are parameters. Weights are parameters. Normalized variants of counts or weights are parameters. Correlation coefficients can be parameters. The term refers to the set of numbers used to model a pattern. As it happens, deep learning is a class of parametric models. We won't discuss nonparametric models further in this book, but they're an interesting and powerful class of algorithm.

Summary

In this chapter, we've gone a level deeper into the various flavors of machine learning. You learned that a machine learning algorithm is either supervised or unsupervised and either parametric or nonparametric. Furthermore, we explored exactly what makes these four different groups of algorithms distinct. You learned that supervised machine learning is a class of algorithm where you learn to predict one dataset given another and that unsupervised learning generally groups a single dataset into various kinds of clusters. You learned that parametric algorithms have a fixed number of *parameters* and that nonparametric algorithms adjust their number of parameters based on the dataset.

Deep learning uses neural networks to perform both supervised and unsupervised prediction. Until now, we've stayed at a conceptual level as you got your bearings in the field as a whole and your place in it. In the next chapter, you'll build your first neural network, and all subsequent chapters will be *project based*. So, pull out your Jupyter notebook, and let's jump in!

introduction to neural prediction: forward propagation | 3

·· ··· ···· ····

In this chapter

- A simple network making a prediction

- What is a neural network, and what does it do?

- Making a prediction with multiple inputs

- Making a prediction with multiple outputs

- Making a prediction with multiple inputs and outputs

- Predicting on predictions

···

> 66 I try not to get involved in the business of prediction. 99
> It's a quick way to look like an idiot.
>
> —Warren Ellis comic-book writer,
> novelist, and screenwriter

Step 1: Predict

This chapter is about prediction.

In the previous chapter, you learned about the paradigm *predict, compare, learn*. In this chapter, we'll dive deep into the first step: *predict*. You may remember that the predict step looks a lot like this:

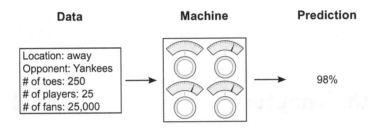

In this chapter, you'll learn more about what these three different parts of a neural network prediction look like under the hood. Let's start with the first one: the data. In your first neural network, you're going to predict one datapoint at a time, like so:

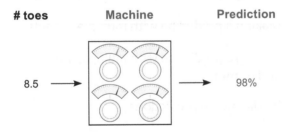

Later, you'll find that the number of datapoints you process at a time has a significant impact on what a network looks like. You might be wondering, "How do I choose how many datapoints to propagate at a time?" The answer is based on whether you think the neural network can be accurate with the data you give it.

For example, if I'm trying to predict whether there's a cat in a photo, I definitely need to show my network all the pixels of an image at once. Why? Well, if I sent you only one pixel of an image, could you classify whether the image contained a cat? Me neither! (That's a general rule of thumb, by the way: always present enough information to the network, where "enough information" is defined loosely as how much a human might need to make the same prediction.)

Let's skip over the network for now. As it turns out, you can create a network only after you understand the shape of the input and output datasets (for now, *shape* means "number of columns" or "number of datapoints you're processing at once"). Let's stick with a single prediction of the likelihood that the baseball team will win:

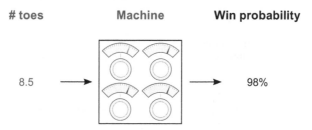

Now that you know you want to take one input datapoint and output one prediction, you can create a neural network. Because you have only one input datapoint and one output datapoint, you're going to build a network with a single knob mapping from the input point to the output. (Abstractly, these "knobs" are actually called *weights*, and I'll refer to them as such from here on out.) So, without further ado, here's your first neural network, with a single weight mapping from the input "# toes" to the output "win?":

As you can see, with one weight, this network takes in one datapoint at a time (average number of toes per player on the baseball team) and outputs a single prediction (whether it thinks the team will win).

A simple neural network making a prediction

Let's start with the simplest neural network possible.

❶ An empty network

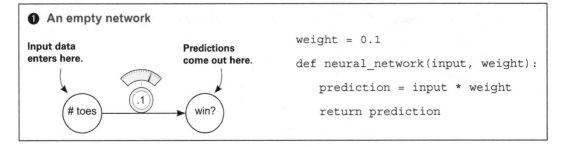

Input data
enters here.

Predictions
come out here.

```
weight = 0.1

def neural_network(input, weight):

    prediction = input * weight

    return prediction
```

❷ Inserting one input datapoint

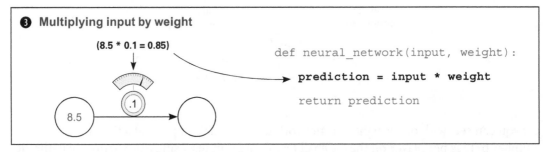

Input data
(# toes)

```
number_of_toes = [8.5, 9.5, 10, 9]

input = number_of_toes[0]

pred = neural_network(input,weight)

print(pred)
```

❸ Multiplying input by weight

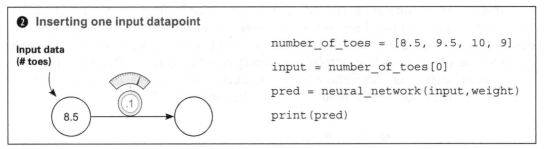

(8.5 * 0.1 = 0.85)

```
def neural_network(input, weight):

    prediction = input * weight

    return prediction
```

❹ Depositing the prediction

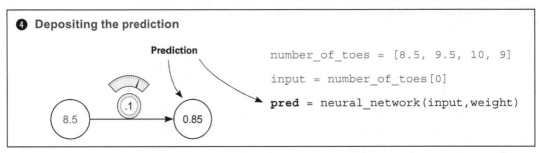

Prediction

```
number_of_toes = [8.5, 9.5, 10, 9]

input = number_of_toes[0]

pred = neural_network(input,weight)
```

What is a neural network?

Here is your first neural network.

To start a neural network, open a Jupyter notebook and run this code:

```
weight = 0.1

def neural_network(input, weight):

    prediction = input * weight

    return prediction
```

The network

Now, run the following:

```
number_of_toes = [8.5, 9.5, 10, 9]

input = number_of_toes[0]

pred = neural_network(input,weight)
print(pred)
```

How you use the network to predict something

You just made your first neural network and used it to predict! Congratulations! The last line prints the prediction (pred). It should be 0.85. So what is a neural network? For now, it's one or more *weights* that you can multiply by the *input* data to make a *prediction*.

What is input data?

It's a number that you recorded in the real world somewhere. It's usually something that is easily knowable, like today's temperature, a baseball player's batting average, or yesterday's stock price.

What is a prediction?

A *prediction* is what the neural network tells you, *given the input data*, such as "given the temperature, it is **0%** likely that people will wear sweatsuits today" or "given a baseball player's batting average, he is **30%** likely to hit a home run" or "given yesterday's stock price, today's stock price will be **101.52**."

Is this prediction always right?

No. Sometimes a neural network will make mistakes, but it can learn from them. For example, if it predicts too high, it will adjust its weight to predict lower next time, and vice versa.

How does the network learn?

Trial and error! First, it tries to make a prediction. Then, it sees whether the prediction was too high or too low. Finally, it changes the weight (up or down) to predict more accurately the next time it sees the same input.

What does this neural network do?

It multiplies the input by a weight. It "scales" the input by a certain amount.

In the previous section, you made your first prediction with a neural network. A neural network, in its simplest form, uses the power of *multiplication*. It takes an input datapoint (in this case, 8.5) and *multiplies* it by the weight. If the weight is 2, then the neural network will *double the input*. If the weight is 0.01, then the network will *divide* the input by 100. As you can see, some weight values make the input *bigger*, and other values make it *smaller*.

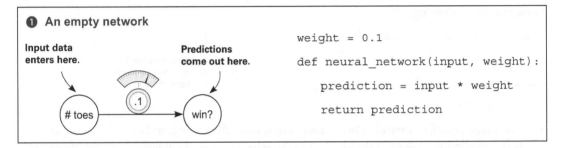

The interface for a neural network is simple. It accepts an `input` variable as *information* and a `weight` variable as *knowledge* and outputs a `prediction`. Every neural network you'll ever see works this way. It uses the *knowledge* in the weights to interpret the *information* in the input data. Later neural networks will accept larger, more complicated `input` and `weight` values, but this same underlying premise will always ring true.

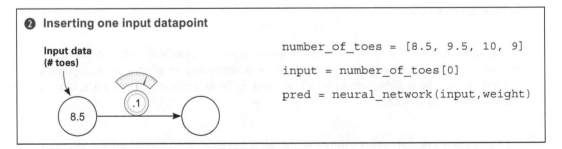

In this case, the information is the average number of toes on a baseball team before a game. Notice several things. First, the neural network does *not* have access to any information except one instance. If, after this prediction, you were to feed in `number_of_toes[1]`, the network wouldn't remember the prediction it made in the last timestep. A neural network knows only what you feed it as input. It forgets everything else. Later, you'll learn how to give a neural network a "short-term memory" by feeding in multiple inputs at once.

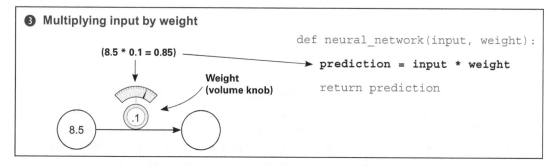

③ Multiplying input by weight

(8.5 * 0.1 = 0.85)

Weight
(volume knob)

```
def neural_network(input, weight):

    prediction = input * weight

    return prediction
```

Another way to think about a neural network's weight value is as a measure of *sensitivity* between the input of the network and its prediction. If the weight is very high, then even the tiniest input can create a really large prediction! If the weight is very small, then even large inputs will make small predictions. This sensitivity is akin to *volume*. "Turning up the weight" amplifies the prediction relative to the input: weight is a volume knob!

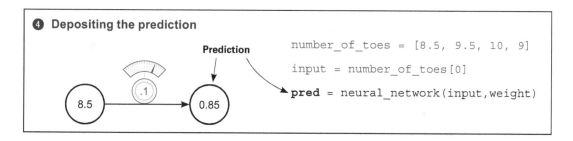

④ Depositing the prediction

Prediction

```
number_of_toes = [8.5, 9.5, 10, 9]

input = number_of_toes[0]

pred = neural_network(input, weight)
```

In this case, what the neural network is really doing is applying a *volume knob* to the `number_of_toes` variable. In theory, this volume knob can tell you the likelihood that the team will win, based on the average number of toes per player on the team. This may or may not work. Truthfully, if the team members had an average of 0 toes, they would probably play terribly. But baseball is much more complex than this. In the next section, you'll present multiple pieces of information at the same time so the neural network can make more-informed decisions.

Note that neural networks don't predict just positive numbers—they can also *predict negative numbers* and even take *negative numbers as input*. Perhaps you want to predict the probability that people will wear coats today. If the temperature is –10 degrees Celsius, then a negative weight will predict a high probability that people will wear their coats.

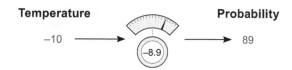

Temperature   **Probability**

–10   89

(–8.9)

Making a prediction with multiple inputs
Neural networks can combine intelligence from multiple datapoints.

The previous neural network was able to take one datapoint as input and make one prediction based on that datapoint. Perhaps you've been wondering, "Is the average number of toes really a good predictor, all by itself?" If so, you're onto something. What if you could give the network more information (at one time) than just the average number of toes per player? In that case, the network should, in theory, be able to make more-accurate predictions. Well, as it turns out, a network can accept multiple input datapoints at a time. Take a look at the next prediction:

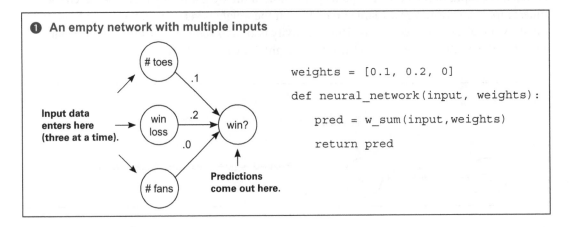

❶ **An empty network with multiple inputs**

```
weights = [0.1, 0.2, 0]

def neural_network(input, weights):

    pred = w_sum(input,weights)

    return pred
```

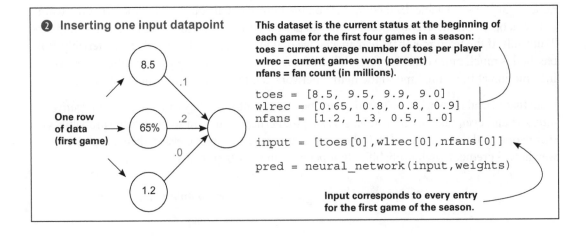

❷ **Inserting one input datapoint**

This dataset is the current status at the beginning of each game for the first four games in a season:
toes = current average number of toes per player
wlrec = current games won (percent)
nfans = fan count (in millions).

```
toes  = [8.5, 9.5, 9.9, 9.0]
wlrec = [0.65, 0.8, 0.8, 0.9]
nfans = [1.2, 1.3, 0.5, 1.0]

input = [toes[0],wlrec[0],nfans[0]]

pred = neural_network(input,weights)
```

Input corresponds to every entry
for the first game of the season.

❸ Performing a weighted sum of inputs

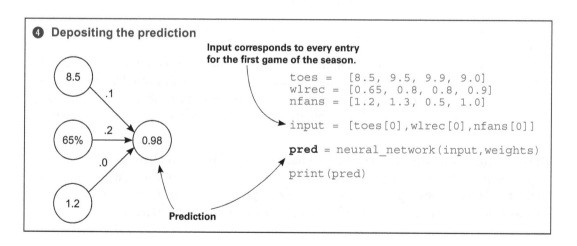

```
def w_sum(a,b):

    assert(len(a) == len(b))

    output = 0

    for i in range(len(a)):
        output += (a[i] * b[i])

    return output


def neural_network(input, weights):

    pred = w_sum(input,weights)

    return pred
```

Inputs		Weights		Local predictions		
(8.50	*	0.1)	=	0.85	= toes prediction
(0.65	*	0.2)	=	0.13	= wlrec prediction
(1.20	*	0.0)	=	0.00	= fans prediction

toes prediction + wlrec prediction + fans prediction = final prediction

     0.85   +   0.13   +   0.00   =   0.98

❹ Depositing the prediction

Input corresponds to every entry
for the first game of the season.

```
toes =  [8.5, 9.5, 9.9, 9.0]
wlrec = [0.65, 0.8, 0.8, 0.9]
nfans = [1.2, 1.3, 0.5, 1.0]

input = [toes[0],wlrec[0],nfans[0]]

pred = neural_network(input,weights)

print(pred)
```

Prediction

Multiple inputs: What does this neural network do?

It multiplies three inputs by three knob weights and sums them. This is a weighted sum.

At the end of the previous section, you came to realize the limiting factor of your simple neural network: it was only a volume knob on one datapoint. In the example, that datapoint was a baseball team's average number of toes per player. You learned that in order to make accurate predictions, you need to build neural networks that can *combine multiple inputs at the same time*. Fortunately, neural networks are perfectly capable of doing so.

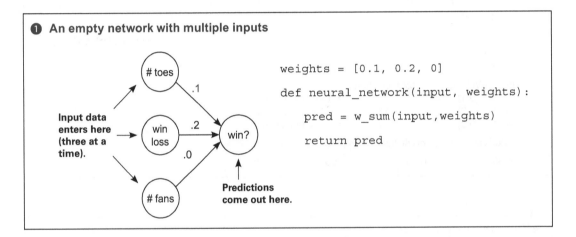

① **An empty network with multiple inputs**

```
weights = [0.1, 0.2, 0]

def neural_network(input, weights):

    pred = w_sum(input,weights)

    return pred
```

This new neural network can accept *multiple inputs at a time* per prediction. This allows the network to combine various forms of information to make better-informed decisions. But the fundamental mechanism for using weights hasn't changed. You still take each input and run it through its own volume knob. In other words, you multiply each input by its own weight.

The new property here is that, because you have multiple inputs, you have to sum their respective predictions. Thus, you multiply each input by its respective weight and then sum all the local predictions together. This is called a *weighted sum of the input*, or a *weighted sum* for short. Some also refer to the weighted sum as a *dot product*, as you'll see.

A relevant reminder

The interface for the neural network is simple: it accepts an `input` variable as information and a `weights` variable as knowledge, and it outputs a prediction.

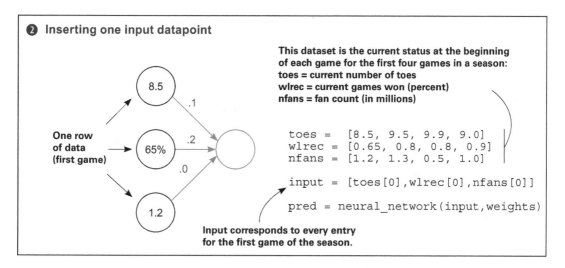

❷ **Inserting one input datapoint**

This dataset is the current status at the beginning of each game for the first four games in a season:
toes = current number of toes
wlrec = current games won (percent)
nfans = fan count (in millions)

One row of data (first game)

8.5
65%
1.2

.1
.2
.0

```
toes  =  [8.5, 9.5, 9.9, 9.0]
wlrec =  [0.65, 0.8, 0.8, 0.9]
nfans =  [1.2, 1.3, 0.5, 1.0]

input = [toes[0],wlrec[0],nfans[0]]

pred = neural_network(input,weights)
```

Input corresponds to every entry for the first game of the season.

This new need to process multiple inputs at a time justifies the use of a new tool. It's called a *vector*, and if you've been following along in your Jupyter notebook, you've already been using it. A vector is nothing other than a *list of numbers*. In the example, `input` is a vector and `weights` is a vector. Can you spot any more vectors in the previous code? (There are three more.)

As it turns out, vectors are incredibly useful whenever you want to perform operations involving groups of numbers. In this case, you're performing a weighted sum between two vectors (a dot product). You're taking two vectors of equal length (`input` and `weights`), multiplying each number based on its position (the first position in `input` is multiplied by the first position in `weights`, and so on), and then summing the resulting output.

Anytime you perform a mathematical operation between two vectors of equal length where you pair up values according to their position in the vector (again: position 0 with 0, 1 with 1, and so on), it's called an *elementwise* operation. Thus *elementwise addition* sums two vectors, and *elementwise multiplication* multiplies two vectors.

Challenge: Vector math

Being able to manipulate vectors is a cornerstone technique for deep learning. See if you can write functions that perform the following operations:

- `def elementwise_multiplication(vec_a, vec_b)`
- `def elementwise_addition(vec_a, vec_b)`
- `def vector_sum(vec_a)`
- `def vector_average(vec_a)`

Then, see if you can use two of these methods to perform a dot product!

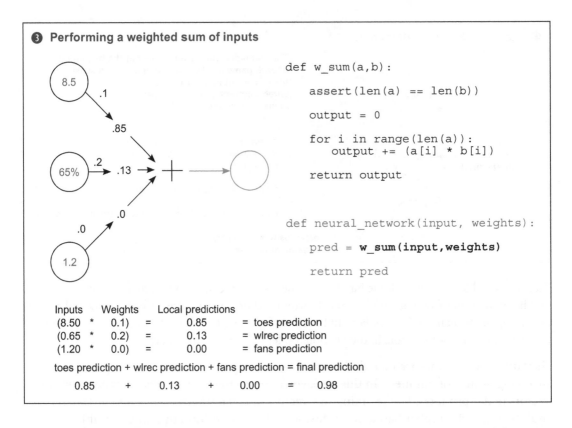

❸ **Performing a weighted sum of inputs**

```
def w_sum(a,b):
    assert(len(a) == len(b))
    output = 0
    for i in range(len(a)):
        output += (a[i] * b[i])
    return output


def neural_network(input, weights):
    pred = w_sum(input,weights)
    return pred
```

Inputs   Weights   Local predictions
(8.50 *   0.1)   =   0.85   = toes prediction
(0.65 *   0.2)   =   0.13   = wlrec prediction
(1.20 *   0.0)   =   0.00   = fans prediction

toes prediction + wlrec prediction + fans prediction = final prediction
    0.85   +   0.13   +   0.00   =   0.98

The intuition behind how and why a dot product (weighted sum) works is easily one of the most important parts of truly understanding how neural networks make predictions. Loosely stated, a dot product gives you a *notion of similarity* between two vectors. Consider these examples:

```
a = [ 0, 1, 0, 1]          w_sum(a,b) = 0
b = [ 1, 0, 1, 0]          w_sum(b,c) = 1
c = [ 0, 1, 1, 0]          w_sum(b,d) = 1
d = [.5, 0,.5, 0]          w_sum(c,c) = 2
e = [ 0, 1,-1, 0]          w_sum(d,d) = .5
                           w_sum(c,e) = 0
```

The highest weighted sum (w_sum(c,c)) is between vectors that are exactly identical. In contrast, because a and b have no overlapping weight, their dot product is zero. Perhaps the most interesting weighted sum is between c and e, because e has a negative weight. This negative weight canceled out the positive similarity between them. But a dot product between e and itself would yield the number 2, despite the negative weight (double negative turns positive). Let's become familiar with the various properties of the dot product operation.

Sometimes you can equate the properties of the dot product to a logical AND. Consider a and b:

```
a = [ 0,  1,  0,  1]
b = [ 1,  0,  1,  0]
```

If you ask whether both a[0] AND b[0] have value, the answer is no. If you ask whether both a[1] AND b[1] have value, the answer is again no. Because this is *always* true for all four values, the final score equals 0. Each value fails the logical AND.

```
b = [ 1,  0,  1,  0]
c = [ 0,  1,  1,  0]
```

b and c, however, have one column that shares value. It passes the logical AND because b[2] *and* c[2] have weight. This column (and only this column) causes the score to rise to 1.

```
c = [ 0,  1,  1,  0]
d = [.5,  0, .5,  0]
```

Fortunately, neural networks are also able to model partial ANDing. In this case, c and d share the same column as b and c, but because d has only 0.5 weight there, the final score is only 0.5. We exploit this property when modeling probabilities in neural networks.

```
d = [.5,  0, .5,  0]
e = [-1,  1,  0,  0]
```

In this analogy, negative weights tend to imply a logical NOT operator, given that any positive weight paired with a negative weight will cause the score to go down. Furthermore, if both vectors have negative weights (such as w_sum(e,e)), then the neural network will perform a *double negative* and add weight instead. Additionally, some might say it's an OR after the AND, because if any of the rows show weight, the score is affected. Thus, for w_sum(a,b), if (a[0] AND b[0]) OR (a[1] AND b[1]), and so on, then w_sum(a,b) returns a positive score. Furthermore, if one value is negative, then that column gets a NOT.

Amusingly, this gives us a kind of crude language for reading weights. Let's read a few examples, shall we? These assume you're performing w_sum(input,weights) and the "then" to these if statements is an abstract "then give high score":

```
weights = [ 1,  0,  1] => if input[0] OR input[2]
weights = [ 0,  0,  1] => if input[2]
weights = [ 1,  0, -1] => if input[0] OR NOT input[2]
weights = [ -1,  0, -1] => if NOT input[0] OR NOT input[2]
weights = [ 0.5,  0,  1] => if BIG input[0] or input[2]
```

Notice in the last row that weight[0] = 0.5 means the corresponding input[0] would have to be larger to compensate for the smaller weighting. And as I mentioned, this is a *very* crude approximate language. But I find it immensely useful when trying to picture in my head what's going on under the hood. This will help you significantly in the future, especially when putting networks together in increasingly complex ways.

Given these intuitions, what does this mean when a neural network makes a prediction? Roughly speaking, it means the network gives a high score of the inputs based on *how similar they are to the weights*. Notice in the following example that nfans is completely ignored in the prediction because the weight associated with it is 0. The most sensitive predictor is wlrec because its weight is 0.2. But the dominant force in the high score is the number of toes (ntoes), not because the weight is the highest, but because the input combined with the weight is by far the highest.

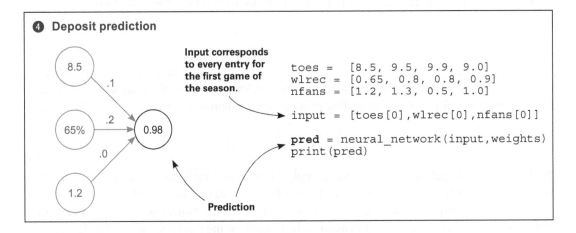

Here are a few more points to note for further reference. You can't shuffle weights: they have specific positions they need to be in. Furthermore, both the value of the weight *and* the value of the input determine the overall impact on the final score. Finally, a negative weight will cause some inputs to reduce the final prediction (and vice versa).

Multiple inputs: Complete runnable code

The code snippets from this example come together in the following code, which creates and executes a neural network. For clarity, I've written everything out using basic properties of Python (lists and numbers). But a better way exists that we'll begin using in the future.

Previous code

```
def w_sum(a,b):
    assert(len(a) == len(b))
    output = 0
    for i in range(len(a)):
        output += (a[i] * b[i])
    return output
weights = [0.1, 0.2, 0]
def neural_network(input, weights):
    pred = w_sum(input,weights)
    return pred
toes = [8.5, 9.5, 9.9, 9.0]
wlrec = [0.65, 0.8, 0.8, 0.9]
nfans = [1.2, 1.3, 0.5, 1.0]
input = [toes[0],wlrec[0],nfans[0]]
pred = neural_network(input,weights)
print(pred)
```

Input corresponds to every entry for the first game of the season.

There's a Python library called NumPy, which stands for "numerical Python." It has very efficient code for creating vectors and performing common functions (such as dot products). Without further ado, here's the same code in NumPy.

NumPy code

```
import numpy as np
weights = np.array([0.1, 0.2, 0])
def neural_network(input, weights):
    pred = input.dot(weights)
    return pred
toes = np.array([8.5, 9.5, 9.9, 9.0])
wlrec = np.array([0.65, 0.8, 0.8, 0.9])
nfans = np.array([1.2, 1.3, 0.5, 1.0])
input = np.array([toes[0],wlrec[0],nfans[0]])
pred = neural_network(input,weights)
print(pred)
```

Input corresponds to every entry for the first game of the season.

Both networks should print out 0.98. Notice that in the NumPy code, you don't have to create a w_sum function. Instead, NumPy has a dot function (short for "dot product") you can call. Many functions you'll use in the future have NumPy parallels.

Making a prediction with multiple outputs

Neural networks can also make multiple predictions using only a single input.

Perhaps a simpler augmentation than multiple inputs is multiple outputs. Prediction occurs the same as if there were three disconnected single-weight neural networks.

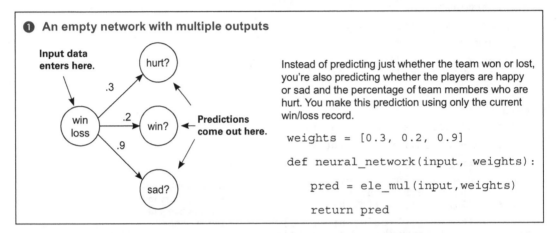

❶ An empty network with multiple outputs

Input data enters here.

hurt?

.3

win loss

.2

win?   ← **Predictions come out here.**

.9

sad?

Instead of predicting just whether the team won or lost, you're also predicting whether the players are happy or sad and the percentage of team members who are hurt. You make this prediction using only the current win/loss record.

```
weights = [0.3, 0.2, 0.9]

def neural_network(input, weights):

    pred = ele_mul(input,weights)

    return pred
```

The most important comment in this setting is to notice that the three predictions are completely separate. Unlike neural networks with multiple inputs and a single output, where the prediction is undeniably connected, this network truly behaves as three independent components, each receiving the same input data. This makes the network simple to implement.

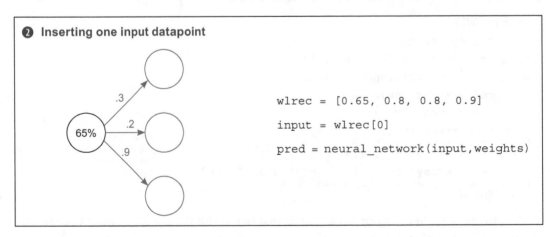

❷ Inserting one input datapoint

.3

65%

.2

.9

```
wlrec = [0.65, 0.8, 0.8, 0.9]

input = wlrec[0]

pred = neural_network(input,weights)
```

❸ Performing elementwise multiplication

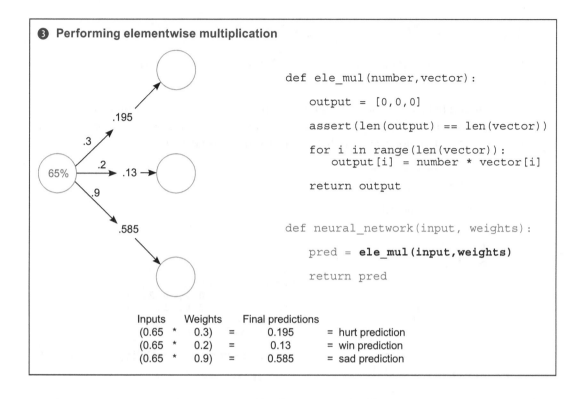

```
def ele_mul(number,vector):
    output = [0,0,0]
    assert(len(output) == len(vector))
    for i in range(len(vector)):
        output[i] = number * vector[i]
    return output


def neural_network(input, weights):
    pred = ele_mul(input,weights)
    return pred
```

Inputs		Weights		Final predictions	
(0.65	*	0.3)	=	0.195	= hurt prediction
(0.65	*	0.2)	=	0.13	= win prediction
(0.65	*	0.9)	=	0.585	= sad prediction

❹ Depositing predictions

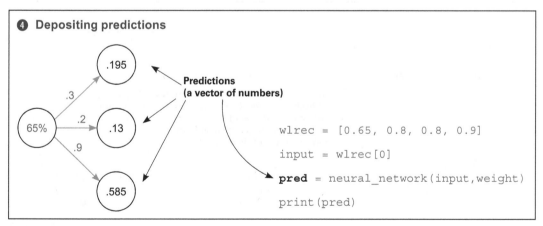

Predictions (a vector of numbers)

```
wlrec = [0.65, 0.8, 0.8, 0.9]
input = wlrec[0]
pred = neural_network(input,weight)
print(pred)
```

Predicting with multiple inputs and outputs

Neural networks can predict multiple outputs given multiple inputs.

Finally, the way you build a network with multiple inputs or outputs can be combined to build a network that has both multiple inputs *and* multiple outputs. As before, a weight connects each input node to each output node, and prediction occurs in the usual way.

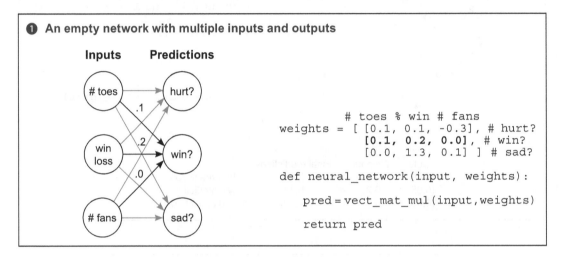

❶ An empty network with multiple inputs and outputs

Inputs   Predictions

```
                              # toes % win # fans
                 weights = [ [0.1, 0.1, -0.3], # hurt?
                             [0.1, 0.2, 0.0], # win?
                             [0.0, 1.3, 0.1] ] # sad?

                 def neural_network(input, weights):

                     pred = vect_mat_mul(input,weights)

                     return pred
```

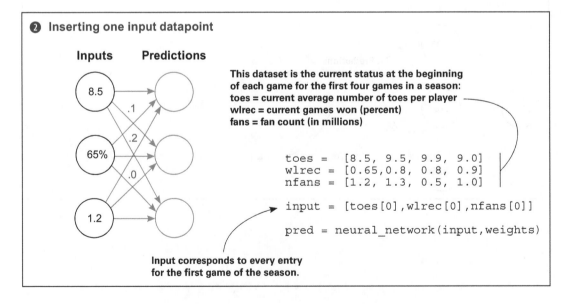

❷ Inserting one input datapoint

Inputs   Predictions

This dataset is the current status at the beginning of each game for the first four games in a season:
toes = current average number of toes per player
wlrec = current games won (percent)
fans = fan count (in millions)

```
                 toes  = [8.5, 9.5, 9.9, 9.0]
                 wlrec = [0.65,0.8, 0.8, 0.9]
                 nfans = [1.2, 1.3, 0.5, 1.0]

                 input = [toes[0],wlrec[0],nfans[0]]

                 pred = neural_network(input,weights)
```

Input corresponds to every entry
for the first game of the season.

❸ For each output, performing a weighted sum of inputs

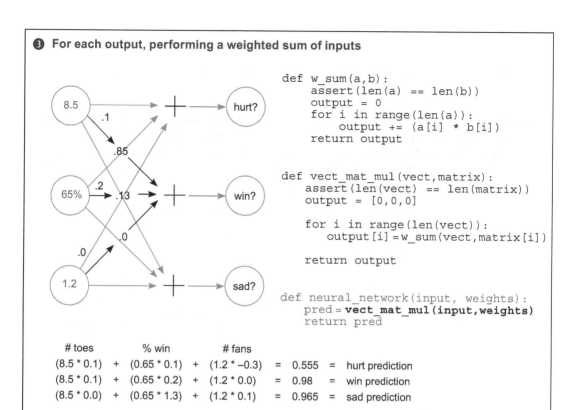

```
def w_sum(a,b):
    assert(len(a) == len(b))
    output = 0
    for i in range(len(a)):
        output += (a[i] * b[i])
    return output


def vect_mat_mul(vect,matrix):
    assert(len(vect) == len(matrix))
    output = [0,0,0]

    for i in range(len(vect)):
        output[i] = w_sum(vect,matrix[i])

    return output


def neural_network(input, weights):
    pred = vect_mat_mul(input,weights)
    return pred
```

# toes		% win		# fans				
(8.5 * 0.1)	+	(0.65 * 0.1)	+	(1.2 * –0.3)	=	0.555	=	hurt prediction
(8.5 * 0.1)	+	(0.65 * 0.2)	+	(1.2 * 0.0)	=	0.98	=	win prediction
(8.5 * 0.0)	+	(0.65 * 1.3)	+	(1.2 * 0.1)	=	0.965	=	sad prediction

❹ Depositing predictions

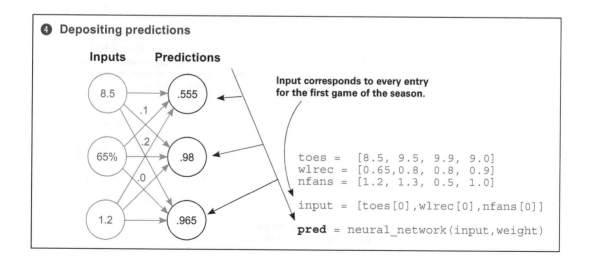

Inputs   **Predictions**

Input corresponds to every entry for the first game of the season.

```
toes  = [8.5, 9.5, 9.9, 9.0]
wlrec = [0.65,0.8, 0.8, 0.9]
nfans = [1.2, 1.3, 0.5, 1.0]

input = [toes[0],wlrec[0],nfans[0]]

pred = neural_network(input,weight)
```

Multiple inputs and outputs: How does it work?

It performs three independent weighted sums of the input to make three predictions.

You can take two perspectives on this architecture: think of it as either three weights coming out of each input node, or three weights going into each output node. For now, I find the latter to be much more beneficial. Think about this neural network as three independent dot products: three independent weighted sums of the input. Each output node takes its own weighted sum of the input and makes a prediction.

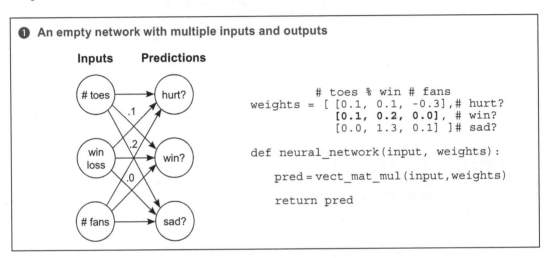

❶ An empty network with multiple inputs and outputs

Inputs   Predictions

```
                    # toes % win # fans
weights = [ [0.1, 0.1, -0.3],# hurt?
            [0.1, 0.2, 0.0], # win?
            [0.0, 1.3, 0.1] ]# sad?

def neural_network(input, weights):

    pred = vect_mat_mul(input,weights)

    return pred
```

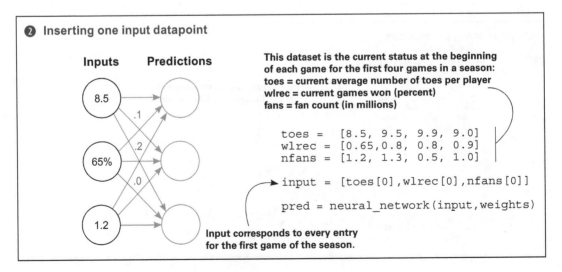

❷ Inserting one input datapoint

Inputs   Predictions

This dataset is the current status at the beginning of each game for the first four games in a season:
toes = current average number of toes per player
wlrec = current games won (percent)
fans = fan count (in millions)

```
toes  = [8.5, 9.5, 9.9, 9.0]
wlrec = [0.65,0.8, 0.8, 0.9]
nfans = [1.2, 1.3, 0.5, 1.0]

input = [toes[0],wlrec[0],nfans[0]]

pred = neural_network(input,weights)
```

Input corresponds to every entry for the first game of the season.

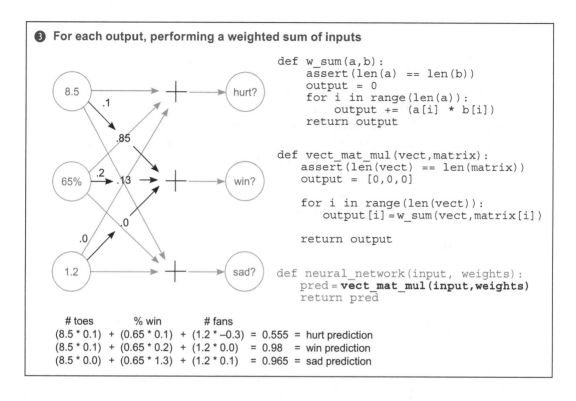

❸ For each output, performing a weighted sum of inputs

```
def w_sum(a,b):
    assert(len(a) == len(b))
    output = 0
    for i in range(len(a)):
        output += (a[i] * b[i])
    return output

def vect_mat_mul(vect,matrix):
    assert(len(vect) == len(matrix))
    output = [0,0,0]

    for i in range(len(vect)):
        output[i] = w_sum(vect,matrix[i])

    return output

def neural_network(input, weights):
    pred = vect_mat_mul(input,weights)
    return pred
```

```
     # toes        % win        # fans
(8.5 * 0.1) + (0.65 * 0.1) + (1.2 * -0.3)  = 0.555  = hurt prediction
(8.5 * 0.1) + (0.65 * 0.2) + (1.2 * 0.0)   = 0.98   = win prediction
(8.5 * 0.0) + (0.65 * 1.3) + (1.2 * 0.1)   = 0.965  = sad prediction
```

As mentioned earlier, we're choosing to think about this network as a series of weighted sums. Thus, the previous code creates a new function called vect_ mat_mul. This function iterates through each row of weights (each row is a vector) and makes a prediction using the w_sum function. It's literally performing three consecutive weighted sums and then storing their predictions in a vector called output. A lot more weights are flying around in this one, but it isn't that much more advanced than other networks you've seen.

I want to use this *list of vectors* and *series of weighted sums* logic to introduce two new concepts. See the weights variable in step 1? It's a list of vectors. A list of vectors is called a *matrix*. It's as simple as it sounds. Commonly used functions use matrices. One of these is called *vector-matrix multiplication*. The series of weighted sums is exactly that: you take a vector and perform a dot product with every row in a matrix.* As you'll find out in the next section, NumPy has special functions to help.

---

* If you're experienced with linear algebra, the more formal definition stores/processes weights as column vectors instead of row vectors. This will be rectified shortly.

Predicting on predictions

Neural networks can be stacked!

As the following figures make clear, you can also take the output of one network and feed it as input to another network. This results in two consecutive vector-matrix multiplications. It may not yet be clear why you'd predict this way; but some datasets (such as image classification) contain patterns that are too complex for a single-weight matrix. Later, we'll discuss the nature of these patterns. For now, it's sufficient to know this is possible.

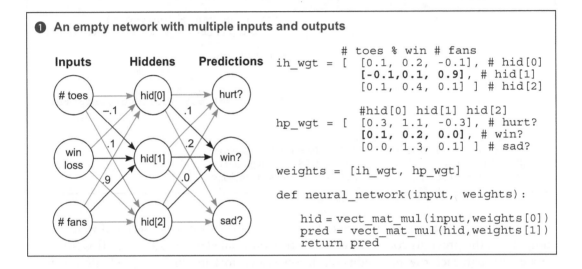

❶ An empty network with multiple inputs and outputs

```
             # toes % win # fans
ih_wgt = [ [0.1, 0.2, -0.1], # hid[0]
           [-0.1,0.1, 0.9], # hid[1]
           [0.1, 0.4, 0.1] ] # hid[2]

         #hid[0] hid[1] hid[2]
hp_wgt = [ [0.3, 1.1, -0.3], # hurt?
           [0.1, 0.2, 0.0], # win?
           [0.0, 1.3, 0.1] ] # sad?

weights = [ih_wgt, hp_wgt]

def neural_network(input, weights):

    hid = vect_mat_mul(input,weights[0])
    pred = vect_mat_mul(hid,weights[1])
    return pred
```

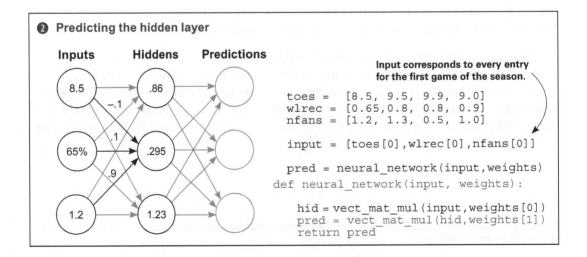

❷ Predicting the hidden layer

Input corresponds to every entry for the first game of the season.

```
toes =  [8.5, 9.5, 9.9, 9.0]
wlrec = [0.65,0.8, 0.8, 0.9]
nfans = [1.2, 1.3, 0.5, 1.0]

input = [toes[0],wlrec[0],nfans[0]]

pred = neural_network(input,weights)
def neural_network(input, weights):

    hid = vect_mat_mul(input,weights[0])
    pred = vect_mat_mul(hid,weights[1])
    return pred
```

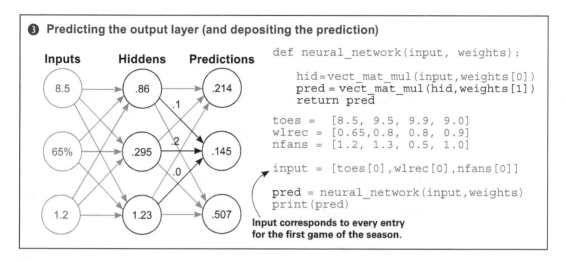

The following listing shows how you can do the same operations coded in the previous section using a convenient Python library called NumPy. Using libraries like NumPy makes your code faster and easier to read and write.

NumPy version

```python
import numpy as np

# toes % win # fans
ih_wgt = np.array([
            [0.1, 0.2, -0.1], # hid[0]
            [-0.1,0.1, 0.9], # hid[1]
            [0.1, 0.4, 0.1]]).T # hid[2]


# hid[0] hid[1] hid[2]
hp_wgt = np.array([
            [0.3, 1.1, -0.3], # hurt?
            [0.1, 0.2, 0.0], # win?
            [0.0, 1.3, 0.1] ]).T # sad?

weights = [ih_wgt, hp_wgt]

def neural_network(input, weights):

    hid = input.dot(weights[0])
    pred = hid.dot(weights[1])
    return pred


toes =  np.array([8.5, 9.5, 9.9, 9.0])
wlrec = np.array([0.65,0.8, 0.8, 0.9])
nfans = np.array([1.2, 1.3, 0.5, 1.0])

input = np.array([toes[0],wlrec[0],nfans[0]])

pred = neural_network(input,weights)
print(pred)
```

A quick primer on NumPy

NumPy does a few things for you. Let's reveal the magic.

So far in this chapter, we've discussed two new types of mathematical tools: vectors and matrices. You've also learned about different operations that occur on vectors and matrices, including dot products, elementwise multiplication and addition, and vector-matrix multiplication. For these operations, you've written Python functions that can operate on simple Python `list` objects.

In the short term, you'll keep writing and using these functions to be sure you fully understand what's going on inside them. But now that I've mentioned NumPy and several of the big operations, I'd like to give you a quick rundown of basic NumPy use so you'll be ready for the transition to NumPy-only chapters. Let's start with the basics again: vectors and matrices.

You can create vectors and matrices in multiple ways in NumPy. Most of the common techniques for neural networks are listed in the previous code. Note that the processes for creating a vector and a matrix are identical. If you create a matrix with only one row, you're creating a vector. And, as in mathematics in general, you create a matrix by listing (rows, columns). I say that only so you can remember the order: rows come first, columns come second. Let's see some operations you can perform on these vectors and matrices:

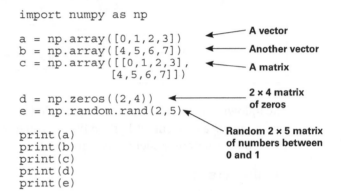

```
import numpy as np

a = np.array([0,1,2,3])          A vector
b = np.array([4,5,6,7])          Another vector
c = np.array([[0,1,2,3],         A matrix
              [4,5,6,7]])

d = np.zeros((2,4))              2 x 4 matrix
e = np.random.rand(2,5)          of zeros

print(a)                         Random 2 x 5 matrix
print(b)                         of numbers between
print(c)                         0 and 1
print(d)
print(e)
```

Output

```
[0 1 2 3]
[4 5 6 7]
[[0 1 2 3]
 [4 5 6 7]]
[[ 0.  0.  0.  0.]
 [ 0.  0.  0.  0.]]
[[ 0.22717119  0.39712632
0.0627734   0.08431724
0.53469141]
 [ 0.09675954  0.99012254
0.45922775  0.3273326
0.28617742]]
```

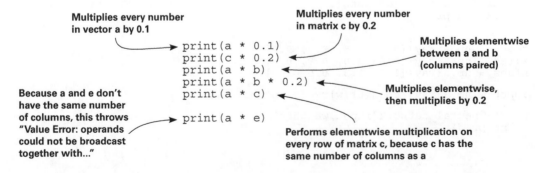

Multiplies every number in vector a by 0.1

Multiplies every number in matrix c by 0.2

```
print(a * 0.1)
print(c * 0.2)
print(a * b)
print(a * b * 0.2)
print(a * c)

print(a * e)
```

Multiplies elementwise between a and b (columns paired)

Multiplies elementwise, then multiplies by 0.2

Because a and e don't have the same number of columns, this throws "Value Error: operands could not be broadcast together with..."

Performs elementwise multiplication on every row of matrix c, because c has the same number of columns as a

Go ahead and run all of the previous code. The first bit of "at first confusing but eventually heavenly" magic should be visible. When you multiply two variables with the `*` function, NumPy automatically detects what kinds of variables you're working with and tries to figure out the operation you're talking about. This can be mega-convenient but sometimes makes NumPy code a bit hard to read. Make sure you keep track of each variable type as you go along.

The general rule of thumb for anything elementwise (+, -, *, /) is that either the two variables must have the *same* number of columns, or one of the variables must have only one column. For example, `print(a * 0.1)` multiplies a vector by a single number (a scalar). NumPy says, "Oh, I bet I'm supposed to do vector-scalar multiplication here," and then multiples the scalar (0.1) by every value in the vector. This looks exactly the same as `print(c * 0.2)`, except NumPy knows that `c` is a matrix. Thus, it performs scalar-matrix multiplication, multiplying every element in `c` by 0.2. Because the scalar has only one column, you can multiply it by anything (or divide, add, or subtract).

Next up: `print(a * b)`. NumPy first identifies that they're both vectors. Because neither vector has only one column, NumPy checks whether they have an identical number of columns. They do, so NumPy knows to multiply each element by each element, based on their positions in the vectors. The same is true with addition, subtraction, and division.

`print(a * c)` is perhaps the most elusive. `a` is a vector with four columns, and `c` is a (2 × 4) matrix. Neither has only one column, so NumPy checks whether they have the same number of columns. They do, so NumPy multiplies the vector `a` by each row of `c` (as if it were doing elementwise vector multiplication on each row).

Again, the most confusing part is that all of these operations look the same if you don't know which variables are scalars, vectors, or matrices. When you "read NumPy," you're really doing two things: reading the operations and keeping track of the *shape* (number of rows and columns) of each operation. It will take some practice, but eventually it becomes second nature. Let's look at a few examples of matrix multiplication in NumPy, noting the input and output shapes of each matrix.

```
a = np.zeros((1,4))
b = np.zeros((4,3))

c = a.dot(b)     ◄──────────── Vector of length 4
print(c.shape)   ◄
                              Matrix with
                              4 rows and
Output                        3 columns

(1,3)
```

There's one golden rule when using the `dot` function: if you put the `(rows,cols)` description of the two variables you're "dotting" next to each other, neighboring numbers should always be the same. In this case, you're dot-producing (1,4) with (4,3). It works fine and outputs (1,3). In terms of variable shape, you can think of it as follows, regardless of whether you're dotting vectors or matrices: their *shape* (number of rows and columns) must line up. The columns of the left matrix must equal the rows on the right, such that `(a,b).dot(b,c) = (a,c)`.

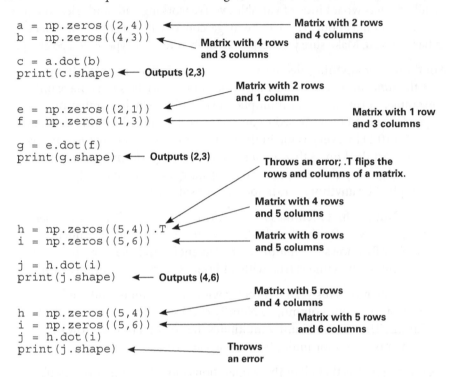

```
a = np.zeros((2,4))          ◄─────────────── Matrix with 2 rows
b = np.zeros((4,3))          ◄──            and 4 columns
                                Matrix with 4 rows
c = a.dot(b)                    and 3 columns
print(c.shape)  ◄── Outputs (2,3)
                                         Matrix with 2 rows
                                         and 1 column
e = np.zeros((2,1))     ◄──
f = np.zeros((1,3))     ◄──────────────        Matrix with 1 row
                                               and 3 columns
g = e.dot(f)
print(g.shape)  ◄── Outputs (2,3)
                                    Throws an error; .T flips the
                                    rows and columns of a matrix.

                                    Matrix with 4 rows
                                    and 5 columns
h = np.zeros((5,4)).T  ◄──
i = np.zeros((5,6))    ◄──          Matrix with 6 rows
                                    and 5 columns
j = h.dot(i)
print(j.shape)   ◄── Outputs (4,6)
                                    Matrix with 5 rows
                                    and 4 columns
h = np.zeros((5,4))  ◄──
i = np.zeros((5,6))  ◄──            Matrix with 5 rows
j = h.dot(i)                        and 6 columns
print(j.shape)  ◄──          Throws
                             an error
```

Summary

To predict, neural networks perform repeated weighted sums of the input.

You've seen an increasingly complex variety of neural networks in this chapter. I hope it's clear that a relatively small number of simple rules are used repeatedly to create larger, more advanced neural networks. The network's intelligence depends on the weight values you give it.

Everything we've done in this chapter is a form of what's called *forward propagation*, wherein a neural network takes input data and makes a prediction. It's called this because you're *propagating* activations *forward* through the network. In these examples, *activations* are all the numbers that are *not* weights and are unique for every prediction.

In the next chapter, you'll learn how to set weights so your neural networks make accurate predictions. Just as prediction is based on several simple techniques that are repeated/stacked on top of each other, *weight learning* is also a series of simple techniques that are combined many times across an architecture. See you there!

introduction to neural learning: gradient descent | 4

In this chapter

- Do neural networks make accurate predictions?

- Why measure error?

- Hot and cold learning

- Calculating both direction and amount from error

- Gradient descent

- Learning is just reducing error

- Derivatives and how to use them to learn

- Divergence and alpha

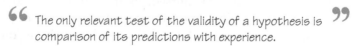

" The only relevant test of the validity of a hypothesis is comparison of its predictions with experience. "

—Milton Friedman, *Essays in Positive Economics*
(University of Chicago Press, 1953)

Predict, compare, and learn

In chapter 3, you learned about the paradigm "predict, compare, learn," and we dove deep into the first step: *predict*. In the process, you learned a myriad of things, including the major parts of neural networks (nodes and weights), how datasets fit into networks (matching the number of datapoints coming in at one time), and how to use a neural network to make a prediction.

Perhaps this process begged the question, "How do we set weight values so the network predicts accurately?" Answering this question is the main focus of this chapter, as we cover the next two steps of the paradigm: *compare* and *learn*.

Compare

Comparing gives a measurement of how much a prediction "missed" by.

Once you've made a prediction, the next step is to evaluate how well you did. This may seem like a simple concept, but you'll find that coming up with a good way to measure error is one of the most important and complicated subjects of deep learning.

There are many properties of measuring error that you've likely been doing your whole life without realizing it. Perhaps you (or someone you know) amplify bigger errors while ignoring very small ones. In this chapter, you'll learn how to mathematically teach a network to do this. You'll also learn that error is always positive! We'll consider the analogy of an archer hitting a target: whether the shot is too low by an inch or too high by an inch, the error is still just 1 inch. In the neural network *compare* step, you need to consider these kinds of properties when measuring error.

As a heads-up, in this chapter we evaluate only one simple way of measuring error: *mean squared error*. It's but one of many ways to evaluate the accuracy of a neural network.

This step will give you a sense for how much you missed, but that isn't enough to be able to learn. The output of the *compare* logic is a "hot or cold" type signal. Given some prediction, you'll calculate an error measure that says either "a lot" or "a little." It won't tell you why you missed, what direction you missed, or what you should do to fix the error. It more or less says "big miss," "little miss," or "perfect prediction." What to do about the error is captured in the next step, *learn*.

Learn

Learning tells each weight how it can change to reduce the error.

Learning is all about *error attribution*, or the art of figuring out how each weight played its part in creating error. It's the blame game of deep learning. In this chapter, we'll spend many pages looking at the most popular version of the deep learning blame game: *gradient descent*.

At the end of the day, it results in computing a number for each weight. That number represents how that weight should be higher or lower in order to reduce the error. Then you'll move the weight according to that number, and you'll be finished.

Compare: Does your network make good predictions?

Let's measure the error and find out!

Execute the following code in your Jupyter notebook. It should print `0.3025`:

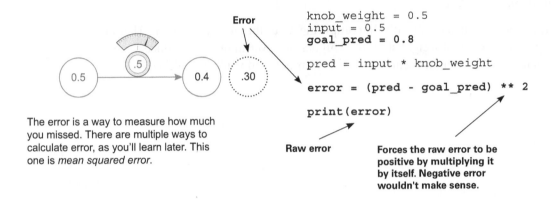

Error

Raw error

Forces the raw error to be positive by multiplying it by itself. Negative error wouldn't make sense.

```
knob_weight = 0.5
input = 0.5
goal_pred = 0.8

pred = input * knob_weight

error = (pred - goal_pred) ** 2

print(error)
```

The error is a way to measure how much you missed. There are multiple ways to calculate error, as you'll learn later. This one is *mean squared error*.

What is the goal_pred variable?

Much like `input`, `goal_pred` is a number you recorded in the real world somewhere. But it's usually something hard to observe, like "the percentage of people who *did* wear sweatsuits," given the temperature; or "whether the batter *did* hit a home run," given his batting average.

Why is the error squared?

Think about an archer hitting a target. When the shot hits 2 inches too high, how much did the archer miss by? When the shot hits 2 inches too low, how much did the archer miss by? Both times, the archer missed by only 2 inches. The primary reason to *square* "how much you missed" is that it forces the output to be *positive*. (`pred - goal_pred`) could be negative in some situations, *unlike actual error*.

Doesn't squaring make big errors (>1) bigger and small errors (<1) smaller?

Yeah … It's kind of a weird way of measuring error, but it turns out that *amplifying* big errors and *reducing* small errors is OK. Later, you'll use this error to help the network learn, and you'd rather it *pay attention* to the big errors and not worry so much about the small ones. Good parents are like this, too: they practically ignore errors if they're small enough (breaking the lead on your pencil) but may go nuclear for big errors (crashing the car). See why squaring is valuable?

Why measure error?

Measuring error simplifies the problem.

The goal of training a neural network is to make correct predictions. That's what you want. And in the most pragmatic world (as mentioned in the preceding chapter), you want the network to take input that you can easily calculate (today's stock price) and predict things that are hard to calculate (tomorrow's stock price). That's what makes a neural network useful.

It turns out that changing `knob_weight` to make the network correctly predict `goal_prediction` is *slightly* more complicated than changing `knob_weight` to make `error == 0`. There's something more concise about looking at the problem this way. Ultimately, both statements say the same thing, but trying to *get the error to 0* seems more straightforward.

Different ways of measuring error *prioritize error differently.*

If this is a bit of a stretch right now, that's OK, but think back to what I said earlier: by *squaring* the error, numbers that are less than 1 get *smaller*, whereas numbers that are greater than 1 get *bigger*. You're going to change what I call *pure error* (`pred - goal_pred`) so that bigger errors become *very* big and smaller errors quickly become irrelevant.

By measuring error this way, you can *prioritize* big errors over smaller ones. When you have somewhat large pure errors (say, 10), you'll tell yourself that you have *very* large error ($10**2 ==$ 100); and in contrast, when you have small pure errors (say, 0.01), you'll tell yourself that you have *very* small error ($0.01**2 == 0.0001$). See what I mean about prioritizing? It's just modifying what you *consider to be error* so that you amplify big ones and largely ignore small ones.

In contrast, if you took the *absolute value* instead of squaring the error, you wouldn't have this type of prioritization. The error would just be the positive version of the pure error—which would be fine, but different. More on this later.

Why do you want only *positive* error?

Eventually, you'll be working with millions of `input -> goal_prediction` pairs, and we'll still want to make accurate predictions. So, you'll try to take the *average error* down to 0.

This presents a problem if the error can be positive and negative. Imagine if you were trying to get the neural network to correctly predict two datapoints—two `input -> goal_prediction` pairs. If the first had an error of 1,000 and the second had an error of −1,000, then the *average error* would be *zero*! You'd fool yourself into thinking you predicted perfectly, when you missed by 1,000 each time! That would be really bad. Thus, you want the error of *each prediction* to always be *positive* so they don't accidentally cancel each other out when you average them.

What's the simplest form of neural learning?

Learning using the hot and cold method.

At the end of the day, learning is really about one thing: adjusting `knob_weight` either up or down so the error is reduced. If you keep doing this and the error goes to 0, you're done learning! How do you know whether to turn the knob up or down? Well, you try *both up and down* and see which one reduces the error! Whichever one reduces the error is used to update `knob_weight`. It's simple but effective. After you do this over and over again, eventually error == 0, which means the neural network is predicting with perfect accuracy.

> ### Hot and cold learning
> *Hot and cold learning* means wiggling the weights to see which direction reduces the error the most, moving the weights in that direction, and repeating until the error gets to 0.

❶ An empty network

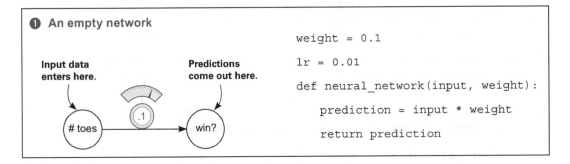

Input data enters here.

Predictions come out here.

```
weight = 0.1

lr = 0.01

def neural_network(input, weight):

    prediction = input * weight

    return prediction
```

❷ PREDICT: Making a prediction and evaluating error

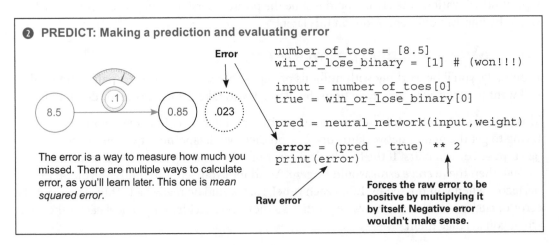

Error

The error is a way to measure how much you missed. There are multiple ways to calculate error, as you'll learn later. This one is *mean squared error*.

Raw error

```
number_of_toes = [8.5]
win_or_lose_binary = [1] # (won!!!)

input = number_of_toes[0]
true = win_or_lose_binary[0]

pred = neural_network(input,weight)

error = (pred - true) ** 2
print(error)
```

Forces the raw error to be positive by multiplying it by itself. Negative error wouldn't make sense.

③ COMPARE: Making a prediction with a higher weight and evaluating error

We want to move the weight so the error goes downward. Let's try moving the weight up and down using `weight+lr` and `weight-lr`, to see which one has the lowest error.

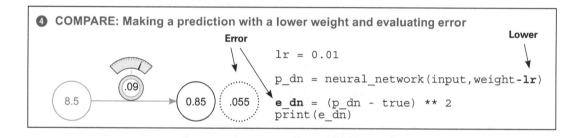

```
lr = 0.1

p_up = neural_network(input, weight+lr)

e_up = (p_up - true) ** 2
print(e_up)
```

④ COMPARE: Making a prediction with a lower weight and evaluating error

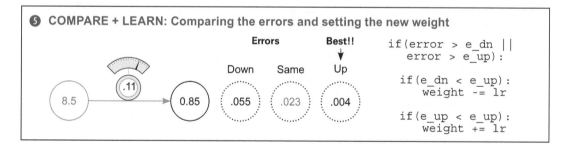

```
lr = 0.01

p_dn = neural_network(input, weight-lr)

e_dn = (p_dn - true) ** 2
print(e_dn)
```

⑤ COMPARE + LEARN: Comparing the errors and setting the new weight

```
if(error > e_dn ||
   error > e_up):

  if(e_dn < e_up):
    weight -= lr

  if(e_up < e_up):
    weight += lr
```

These last five steps are one iteration of hot and cold learning. Fortunately, this iteration got us pretty close to the correct answer all by itself (the new error is only 0.004). But under normal circumstances, we'd have to repeat this process many times to find the correct weights. Some people have to train their networks for weeks or months before they find a good enough weight configuration.

This reveals what learning in neural networks really is: a *search problem*. You're *searching* for the best possible configuration of weights so the network's error falls to 0 (and predicts perfectly). As with all other forms of search, you might not find exactly what you're looking for, and even if you do, it may take some time. Next, we'll use hot and cold learning for a slightly more difficult prediction so you can see this searching in action!

Hot and cold learning

This is perhaps the simplest form of learning.

Execute the following code in your Jupyter notebook. (New neural network modifications are in **bold**.) This code attempts to correctly predict 0.8:

```
weight = 0.5
input = 0.5
goal_prediction = 0.8

step_amount = 0.001

for iteration in range(1101):

    prediction = input * weight
    error = (prediction - goal_prediction) ** 2

    print("Error:" + str(error) + " Prediction:" + str(prediction))

    up_prediction = input * (weight + step_amount)
    up_error = (goal_prediction - up_prediction) ** 2

    down_prediction = input * (weight - step_amount)
    down_error = (goal_prediction - down_prediction) ** 2

    if(down_error < up_error):
        weight = weight - step_amount

    if(down_error > up_error):
        weight = weight + step_amount
```

How much to move the weights each iteration

Repeat learning many times so the error can keep getting smaller.

Try up!

Try down!

If down is better, go down!

If up is better, go up!

When I run this code, I see the following output:

```
Error:0.3025 Prediction:0.25
Error:0.30195025 Prediction:0.2505
    ....
Error:2.50000000033e-07 Prediction:0.7995
Error:1.07995057925e-27 Prediction:0.8
```

The last step correctly predicts 0.8!

Characteristics of hot and cold learning

It's simple.

Hot and cold learning is simple. After making a prediction, you predict two more times, once with a slightly higher weight and again with a slightly lower weight. You then move `weight` depending on which direction gave a smaller `error`. Repeating this enough times eventually reduces `error` to 0.

Why did I iterate exactly 1,101 times?

The neural network in the example reaches 0.8 after exactly that many iterations. If you go past that, it wiggles back and forth between 0.8 and just above or below 0.8, making for a less pretty error log printed at the bottom of the left page. Feel free to try it.

Problem 1: It's inefficient.

You have to predict *multiple times* to make a single `knob_weight` update. This seems very inefficient.

Problem 2: Sometimes it's impossible to predict the exact goal prediction.

With a set `step_amount`, unless the perfect `weight` is exactly n*`step_amount` away, the network will eventually overshoot by some number less than `step_amount`. When it does, it will then start alternating back and forth between each side of `goal_prediction`. Set `step_amount` to 0.2 to see this in action. If you set `step_amount` to 10, you'll really break it. When I try this, I see the following output. It never remotely comes close to 0.8!

```
Error:0.3025 Prediction:0.25
Error:19.8025 Prediction:5.25
Error:0.3025 Prediction:0.25
Error:19.8025 Prediction:5.25
Error:0.3025 Prediction:0.25
....
.... repeating infinitely...
```

The real problem is that even though you know the correct *direction* to move `weight`, you don't know the correct *amount*. Instead, you pick a fixed one at random (`step_amount`). Furthermore, this amount has *nothing* to do with `error`. Whether `error` is big or tiny, `step_amount` is the same. So, hot and cold learning is kind of a bummer. It's inefficient because you predict three times for each `weight` update, and `step_ amount` is arbitrary, which can prevent you from learning the correct `weight` value.

What if you had a way to compute both direction and amount for each `weight` without having to repeatedly make predictions?

Calculating both direction and amount from error

Let's measure the error and find the direction and amount!

Execute this code in your Jupyter notebook:

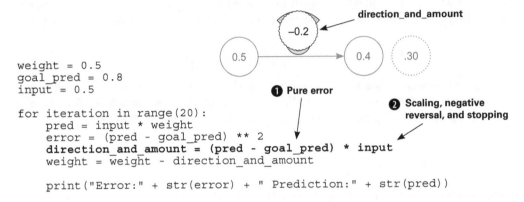

```
weight = 0.5
goal_pred = 0.8
input = 0.5

for iteration in range(20):
    pred = input * weight
    error = (pred - goal_pred) ** 2
    direction_and_amount = (pred - goal_pred) * input
    weight = weight - direction_and_amount

    print("Error:" + str(error) + " Prediction:" + str(pred))
```

What you see here is a superior form of learning known as *gradient descent*. This method allows you to (in a single line of code, shown here in **bold**) calculate both the *direction* and the *amount* you should change `weight` to reduce `error`.

What is direction_and_amount?

`direction_and_amount` represents how you want to change `weight`. The first part ❶ is what I call *pure error*, which equals (`pred - goal_pred`). (More about this shortly.) The second part ❷ is the multiplication by the `input` that performs scaling, negative reversal, and stopping, modifying the pure error so it's ready to update `weight`.

What is the pure error?

The pure error is (`pred - goal_pred`), which indicates the raw direction and amount you missed. If this is a *positive* number, you predicted too *high*, and vice versa. If this is a *big* number, you missed by a *big* amount, and so on.

What are scaling, negative reversal, and stopping?

These three attributes have the combined effect of translating the pure error into the absolute amount you want to change `weight`. They do so by addressing three major edge cases where the pure error isn't sufficient to make a good modification to `weight`.

What is stopping?

Stopping is the first (and simplest) effect on the pure error caused by multiplying it by `input`. Imagine plugging a CD player into your stereo. If you turned the volume all the way up but the CD player was off, the volume change wouldn't matter. Stopping addresses this in a neural network. If `input` is 0, then it will force `direction_and_amount` to also be 0. You don't learn (change the volume) when `input` is 0, because there's nothing to learn. Every `weight` value has the same `error`, and moving it makes no difference because `pred` is always 0.

What is negative reversal?

This is probably the most difficult and important effect. Normally (when `input` is positive), moving `weight` upward makes the prediction move upward. But if `input` is negative, then all of a sudden `weight` changes directions! When `input` is negative, moving `weight` *up* makes the prediction go *down*. It's reversed! How do you address this? Well, multiplying the pure error by `input` will *reverse the sign* of `direction_and_amount` in the event that `input` is negative. This is *negative reversal*, ensuring that `weight` moves in the correct direction even if `input` is negative.

What is scaling?

Scaling is the third effect on the pure error caused by multiplying it by `input`. Logically, if `input` is big, your `weight` update should also be big. This is more of a side effect, because it often goes out of control. Later, you'll use *alpha* to address when that happens.

When you run the previous code, you should see the following output:

```
Error:0.3025 Prediction:0.25
Error:0.17015625 Prediction:0.3875
Error:0.095712890625 Prediction:0.490625
                    . . .

Error:1.7092608064e-05 Prediction:0.79586567925
Error:9.61459203602e-06 Prediction:0.796899259437
Error:5.40820802026e-06 Prediction:0.797674444578
```

The last steps correctly approach 0.8!

In this example, you saw gradient descent in action in a bit of an oversimplified environment. Next, you'll see it in its more native environment. Some terminology will be different, but I'll code it in a way that makes it more obviously applicable to other kinds of networks (such as those with multiple inputs and outputs).

One iteration of gradient descent

This performs a weight update on a single training example (input->true) pair.

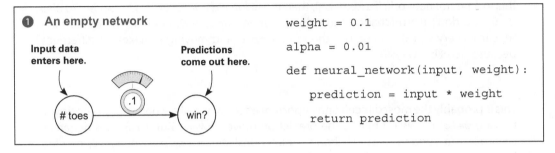

❶ An empty network

Input data enters here.   Predictions come out here.

```
weight = 0.1
alpha = 0.01
def neural_network(input, weight):
    prediction = input * weight
    return prediction
```

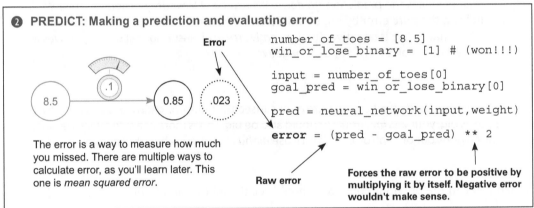

❷ PREDICT: Making a prediction and evaluating error

Error

```
number_of_toes = [8.5]
win_or_lose_binary = [1] # (won!!!)

input = number_of_toes[0]
goal_pred = win_or_lose_binary[0]

pred = neural_network(input,weight)

error = (pred - goal_pred) ** 2
```

The error is a way to measure how much you missed. There are multiple ways to calculate error, as you'll learn later. This one is *mean squared error*.

Raw error

Forces the raw error to be positive by multiplying it by itself. Negative error wouldn't make sense.

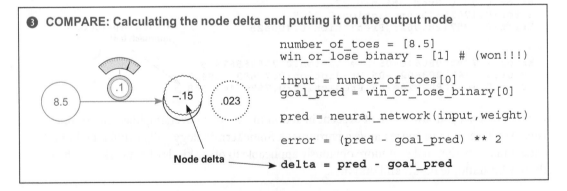

❸ COMPARE: Calculating the node delta and putting it on the output node

```
number_of_toes = [8.5]
win_or_lose_binary = [1] # (won!!!)

input = number_of_toes[0]
goal_pred = win_or_lose_binary[0]

pred = neural_network(input,weight)

error = (pred - goal_pred) ** 2

delta = pred - goal_pred
```

Node delta

`delta` is a measurement of how much this node missed. The true prediction is 1.0, and the network's prediction was 0.85, so the network was too *low* by 0.15. Thus, `delta` is *negative* 0.15.

The primary difference between gradient descent and this implementation is the new variable `delta`. It's the raw amount that the node was too high or too low. Instead of computing `direction_and_amount` directly, you first calculate how much you want the output node to be different. Only then do you compute `direction_and_amount` to change `weight` (in step 4, now renamed `weight_delta`):

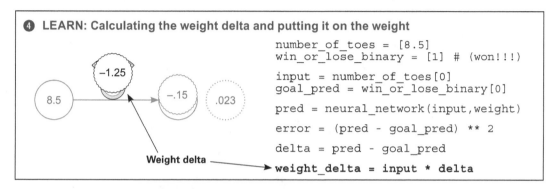

❹ LEARN: Calculating the weight delta and putting it on the weight

Weight delta

```
number_of_toes = [8.5]
win_or_lose_binary = [1] # (won!!!)

input = number_of_toes[0]
goal_pred = win_or_lose_binary[0]

pred = neural_network(input,weight)

error = (pred - goal_pred) ** 2

delta = pred - goal_pred

weight_delta = input * delta
```

`weight_delta` is a measure of how much a weight caused the network to miss. You calculate it by multiplying the weight's output node `delta` by the weight's `input`. Thus, you create each `weight_delta` by *scaling* its output node `delta` by the weight's `input`. This accounts for the three aforementioned properties of `direction_and_amount`: scaling, negative reversal, and stopping.

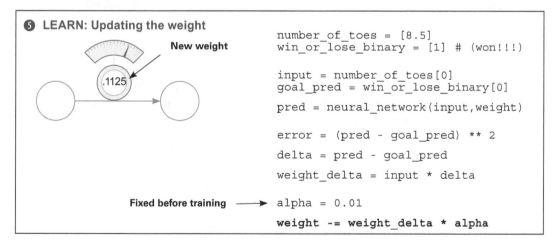

❺ LEARN: Updating the weight

New weight

```
number_of_toes = [8.5]
win_or_lose_binary = [1] # (won!!!)

input = number_of_toes[0]
goal_pred = win_or_lose_binary[0]

pred = neural_network(input,weight)

error = (pred - goal_pred) ** 2

delta = pred - goal_pred

weight_delta = input * delta
```

Fixed before training

```
alpha = 0.01

weight -= weight_delta * alpha
```

You multiply `weight_delta` by a small number `alpha` before using it to update `weight`. This lets you control how fast the network learns. If it learns too fast, it can update weights too aggressively and overshoot. (More on this later.) Note that the weight update made the same change (small increase) as hot and cold learning.

Learning is just reducing error

You can modify weight to reduce error.

Putting together the code from the previous pages, we now have the following:

```
weight, goal_pred, input = (0.0, 0.8, 0.5)


for iteration in range(4):
    pred = input * weight
    error = (pred - goal_pred) ** 2
    delta = pred - goal_pred
    weight_delta = delta * input
    weight = weight - weight_delta
    print("Error:" + str(error) + " Prediction:" + str(pred))
```

These lines
have a secret.

> ### The golden method for learning
>
> This approach adjusts each `weight` in the correct direction and by the correct amount so that `error` reduces to 0.

All you're trying to do is figure out the right direction and amount to modify `weight` so that `error` goes down. The secret lies in the `pred` and `error` calculations. Notice that you use `pred` *inside* the `error` calculation. Let's replace the `pred` variable with the code used to generate it:

```
error = ((input * weight) - goal_pred) ** 2
```

This doesn't change the value of `error` at all! It just combines the two lines of code and computes `error` directly. Remember that `input` and `goal_prediction` are fixed at 0.5 and 0.8, respectively (you set them before the network starts training). So, if you replace their variables names with the values, the secret becomes clear:

```
error = ((0.5 * weight) - 0.8) ** 2
```

The secret

For any `input` and `goal_pred`, an *exact relationship* is defined between `error` and `weight`, found by combining the `prediction` and `error` formulas. In this case:

```
error = ((0.5 * weight) - 0.8) ** 2
```

Let's say you increased `weight` by 0.5. If there's an exact relationship between `error` and `weight`, you should be able to calculate how much this also moves `error`. What if you wanted to move `error` in a specific direction? Could it be done?

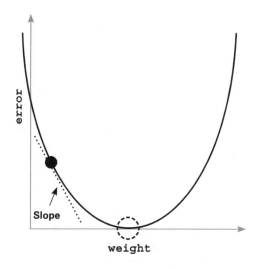

This graph represents every value of error for every weight according to the relationship in the previous formula. Notice it makes a nice bowl shape. The black dot is at the point of *both* the current `weight` and `error`. The dotted circle is where you want to be (`error == 0`).

Key takeaway

The slope points to the *bottom* of the bowl (lowest `error`) no matter where you are in the bowl. You can use this slope to help the neural network reduce the error.

Let's watch several steps of learning

Will we eventually find the bottom of the bowl?

```
weight, goal_pred, input = (0.0, 0.8, 1.1)

for iteration in range(4):
    print("-----\nWeight:" + str(weight))
    pred = input * weight
    error = (pred - goal_pred) ** 2
    delta = pred - goal_pred
    weight_delta = delta * input
    weight = weight - weight_delta
    print("Error:" + str(error) + " Prediction:" + str(pred))
    print("Delta:" + str(delta) + " Weight Delta:" + str(weight_delta))
```

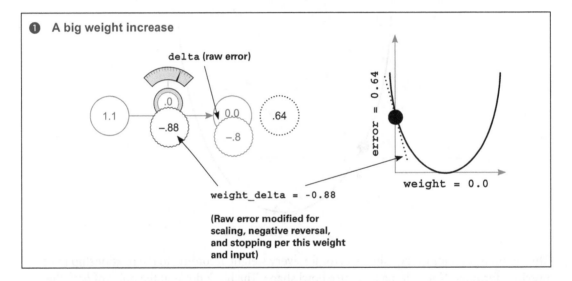

❶ A big weight increase

delta (raw error)

weight_delta = -0.88

(Raw error modified for scaling, negative reversal, and stopping per this weight and input)

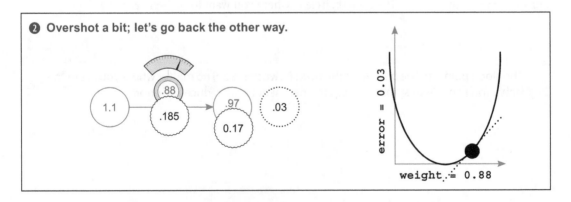

❷ Overshot a bit; let's go back the other way.

❸ Overshot again! Let's go back, but only a little.

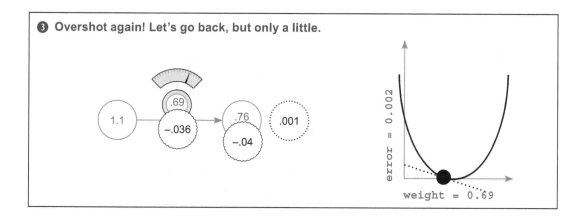

❹ OK, we're pretty much there.

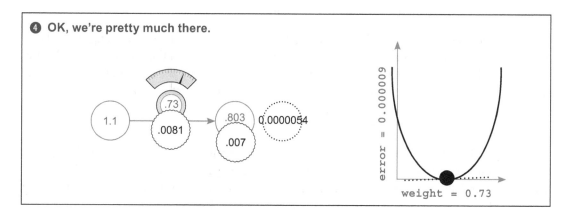

❺ Code output

```
-----
Weight:0.0
Error:0.64 Prediction:0.0
Delta:-0.8 Weight Delta:-0.88
-----
Weight:0.88
Error:0.028224 Prediction:0.968
Delta:0.168 Weight Delta:0.1848
-----
Weight:0.6952
Error:0.0012446784 Prediction:0.76472
Delta:-0.03528 Weight Delta:-0.038808
-----
Weight:0.734008
Error:5.489031744e-05 Prediction:0.8074088
Delta:0.0074088 Weight Delta:0.00814968
```

Why does this work? What is weight_delta, really?

Let's back up and talk about functions. What is a function? How do you understand one?

Consider this function:

```
def my_function(x):
    return x * 2
```

A function takes some numbers as input and gives you another number as output. As you can imagine, this means the function defines some sort of relationship between the input number(s) and the output number(s). Perhaps you can also see why the ability to learn a function is so powerful: it lets you take some numbers (say, image pixels) and convert them into other numbers (say, the probability that the image contains a cat).

Every function has what you might call *moving parts*: pieces you can tweak or change to make the output the function generates different. Consider my_function in the previous example. Ask yourself, "What's controlling the relationship between the input and the output of this function?" The answer is, the 2. Ask the same question about the following function:

```
error = ((input * weight) - goal_pred) ** 2
```

What's controlling the relationship between input and the output (error)? Plenty of things are—this function is a bit more complicated! goal_pred, input, **2, weight, and all the parentheses and algebraic operations (addition, subtraction, and so on) play a part in calculating the error. Tweaking any one of them would *change* the error. This is important to consider.

As a thought exercise, consider changing goal_pred to reduce the error. This is silly, but totally doable. In life, you might call this (setting goals to be whatever your capability is) "giving up." You're denying that you missed! That wouldn't do.

What if you changed input until error went to 0? Well, that's akin to seeing the world as you want to see it instead of as it actually is. You're changing the input data until you're predicting what you want to predict (this is loosely how *inceptionism* works).

Now consider changing the 2, or the additions, subtractions, or multiplications. This is just changing how you calculate error in the first place. The error calculation is meaningless if it doesn't actually give a good measure of how much you missed (with the right properties mentioned a few pages ago). This won't do, either.

What's left? The only variable remaining is `weight`. Adjusting it doesn't change your perception of the world, doesn't change your goal, and doesn't destroy your error measure. Changing `weight` means the function *conforms to the patterns in the data*. By forcing the rest of the function to be unchanging, you force the function to correctly model some pattern in the data. It's only allowed to modify how the network *predicts*.

To sum up: you modify specific parts of an error function until the `error` value goes to 0. This error function is calculated using a combination of variables, some of which you can change (weights) and some of which you can't (input data, output data, and the error logic):

```
weight = 0.5
goal_pred = 0.8
input = 0.5

for iteration in range(20):
    pred = input * weight
    error = (pred - goal_pred) ** 2
    direction_and_amount = (pred - goal_pred) * input
    weight = weight - direction_and_amount

    print("Error:" + str(error) + " Prediction:" + str(pred))
```

Key takeaway

You can modify *anything* in the `pred` calculation except `input`.

We'll spend the rest of this book (and many deep learning researchers will spend the rest of their lives) trying everything you can imagine on that `pred` calculation so that it can make good predictions. Learning is all about automatically changing the prediction function so that it makes good predictions—aka, so that the subsequent `error` goes down to 0.

Now that you know what you're allowed to change, how do you go about doing the changing? That's the good stuff. That's the machine learning, right? In the next section, we're going to talk about exactly that.

Tunnel vision on one concept

Concept: Learning is adjusting the weight to reduce the error to 0.

So far in this chapter, we've been hammering on the idea that learning is really just about adjusting `weight` to reduce `error` to 0. This is the secret sauce. Truth be told, knowing how to do this is all about understanding the *relationship* between `weight` and `error`. If you understand this relationship, you can know how to adjust `weight` to reduce `error`.

What do I mean by "understand the relationship"? Well, to understand the relationship between two variables is to understand *how changing one variable changes the other*. In this case, what you're really after is the *sensitivity* between these two variables. Sensitivity is another name for direction and amount. You want to know how sensitive `error` is to `weight`. You want to know the direction and the amount that `error` changes when you change `weight`. This is the goal. So far, you've seen two different methods that attempt to help you understand this relationship.

When you were wiggling `weight` (hot and cold learning) and studying its effect on `error`, you were experimentally studying the relationship between these two variables. It's like walking into a room with 15 different unlabeled light switches. You start flipping them on and off to learn about their relationship to various lights in the room. You did the same thing to study the relationship between `weight` and `error`: you wiggled `weight` up and down and watched for how it changed `error`. Once you knew the relationship, you could move `weight` in the right direction using two simple `if` statements:

```
if(down_error < up_error):
    weight = weight - step_amount

if(down_error > up_error):
    weight = weight + step_amount
```

Now, let's go back to the earlier formula that combined the `pred` and `error` logic. As mentioned, they quietly define an exact relationship between `error` and `weight`:

```
error = ((input * weight) - goal_pred) ** 2
```

This line of code, ladies and gentlemen, is the secret. This is a formula. This is the relationship between `error` and `weight`. This relationship is exact. It's computable. It's universal. It is and will always be.

Now, how can you use this formula to know how to change `weight` so that `error` moves in a particular direction? *That* is the right question. Stop. I beg you. Stop and appreciate this moment. This formula is the exact relationship between these two variables, and now you're going to figure out how to change one variable to move the other variable in a particular direction.

As it turns out, there's a method for doing this for *any* formula. You'll use it to reduce error.

A box with rods poking out of it

Picture yourself sitting in front of a cardboard box that has two circular rods sticking through two little holes. The blue rod is sticking out of the box by 2 inches, and the red rod is sticking out of the box by 4 inches. Imagine that I tell you these rods were connected, but I won't tell you in what way. You have to experiment to figure it out.

So, you take the blue rod and push it in 1 inch, and watch as, while you're pushing, the red rod also moves into the box by 2 inches. Then, you pull the blue rod back out 1 inch, and the red rod follows again, pulling out by 2 inches. What did you learn? Well, there seems to be a *relationship* between the red and blue rods. However much you move the blue rod, the red rod will move by twice as much. You might say the following is true:

```
red_length = blue_length * 2
```

As it turns out, there's a formal definition for "When I tug on this part, how much does this other part move?" It's called a *derivative*, and all it really means is "How much does rod X move when I tug on rod Y?"

In the case of the red and blue rods, the derivative for "How much does red move when I tug on blue?" is 2. Just 2. Why is it 2? That's the *multiplicative* relationship determined by the formula:

```
red_length = blue_length * 2    ← ─── Derivative
```

Notice that you always have the derivative *between two variables*. You're always looking to know how one variable moves when you change another one. If the derivative is positive, then when you change one variable, the other will move in the *same* direction. If the derivative is *negative*, then when you change one variable, the other will move in the *opposite* direction.

Consider a few examples. Because the derivative of `red_length` compared to `blue_length` is 2, both numbers move in the same direction. More specifically, red will move twice as much as blue in the same direction. If the derivative had been –1, red would move in the opposite direction by the same amount. Thus, given a function, the derivative represents the direction and the amount that one variable changes if you change the other variable. This is exactly what we were looking for.

Derivatives: Take two

Still a little unsure about them? Let's take another perspective.

I've heard people explain derivatives two ways. One way is all about understanding how one variable in a function changes when you move another variable. The other way says that a derivative is the slope at a point on a line or curve. As it turns out, if you take a function and plot it (draw it), the slope of the line you plot is the *same thing* as "how much one variable changes when you change the other." Let me show you by plotting our favorite function:

```
error = ((input * weight) - goal_pred) ** 2
```

Remember, `goal_pred` and `input` are fixed, so you can rewrite this function:

```
error = ((0.5 * weight) - 0.8) ** 2
```

Because there are only two variables left that change (all the rest of them are fixed), you can take every `weight` and compute the `error` that goes with it. Let's plot them.

As you can see, the plot looks like a big U-shaped curve. Notice that there's also a point in the middle where `error == 0`. Also notice that to the right of that point, the slope of the line is positive, and to the left of that point, the slope of the line is negative. Perhaps even more interesting, the farther away from the *goal weight* you move, the steeper the slope gets.

These are useful properties. The slope's sign gives you direction, and the slope's steepness gives you amount. You can use both of these to help find the goal `weight`.

Even now, when I look at that curve, it's easy for me to lose track of what it represents. It's similar to the hot and cold method for learning. If you tried every possible value for `weight` and plotted it out, you'd get this curve.

And what's remarkable about derivatives is that they can see past the big formula for computing error (at the beginning of this section) and see this curve. You can compute the slope (derivative) of the line for any value of `weight`. You can then use this slope (derivative) to figure out which direction reduces the error. Even better, based on the steepness, you can get at least some idea of how far away you are from the optimal point where the slope is zero (although not an exact answer, as you'll learn more about later).

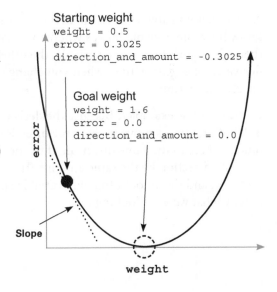

Starting weight
```
weight = 0.5
error = 0.3025
direction_and_amount = -0.3025
```

Goal weight
```
weight = 1.6
error = 0.0
direction_and_amount = 0.0
```

error

Slope

weight

What you really need to know

With derivatives, you can pick any two variables in any formula, and know how they interact.

Take a look at this *big whopper of a function*:

$$\texttt{y = (((beta * gamma) ** 2) + (epsilon + 22 - x)) ** (1/2)}$$

Here's what you need to know about derivatives. For any function (even this whopper), you can pick any two variables and understand their relationship with each other. For any function, you can pick two variables and plot them on an x-y graph as we did earlier. For any function, you can pick two variables and compute how much one changes when you change the other. Thus, for any function, you can learn how to change one variable so that you can move another variable in a direction. Sorry to harp on this point, but it's important that you know this in your bones.

Bottom line: in this book, you're going to build neural networks. A neural network is really just one thing: a bunch of weights you use to compute an error function. And for any error function (no matter how complicated), you can compute the relationship between any `weight` and the final `error` of the network. With this information, you can change each `weight` in the neural network to reduce `error` down to 0—and that's exactly what you're going to do.

What you don't really need to know

Calculus

So, it turns out that learning all the methods for taking any two variables in any function and computing their relationship takes about three semesters of college. Truth be told, if you went through all three semesters so that you could learn how to do deep learning, you'd use only a very small subset of what you learned. And really, calculus is just about memorizing and practicing every possible derivative rule for every possible function.

In this book, I'm going to do what I typically do in real life (cuz I'm lazy—I mean, efficient): look up the derivative in a reference table. All you need to know is what the derivative represents. It's the relationship between two variables in a function so you can know how much one changes when you change the other. It's just the sensitivity between two variables.

I know that was a lot of information to say, "It's the sensitivity between two variables," but it is. Note that this can include *positive sensitivity* (when variables move together), *negative sensitivity* (when they move in opposite directions), and zero sensitivity (when one stays fixed regardless of what you do to the other). For example, $y = 0 * x$. Move x, and y is always 0.

Enough about derivatives. Let's get back to gradient descent.

How to use a derivative to learn

weight_delta is your derivative.

What's the difference between `error` and
the derivative of `error` and `weight`? `error`
is a measure of how much you missed. The
derivative defines the relationship between each
weight and how much you missed. In other
words, it tells how much changing a weight
contributed to the error. So, now that you know
this, how do you use it to move the error in a
particular direction?

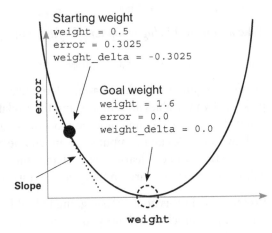

Starting weight
weight = 0.5
error = 0.3025
weight_delta = -0.3025

Goal weight
weight = 1.6
error = 0.0
weight_delta = 0.0

Slope

weight

You've learned the relationship between
two variables in a function, but how do you
exploit that relationship? As it turns out, this
is incredibly visual and intuitive. Check out
the `error` curve again. The black dot is where
`weight` starts out: (0.5). The dotted circle is where you want it to go: the goal weight. Do you see
the dotted line attached to the black dot? That's the slope, otherwise known as the derivative. It
tells you at that point in the curve how much `error` changes when you change `weight`. Notice
that it's pointed downward: it's a negative slope.

The slope of a line or curve always points in the opposite direction of the lowest point of the line or
curve. So, if you have a negative slope, you increase `weight` to find the minimum of `error`. Check it out.

So, how do you use the derivative to find the `error` minimum (lowest point in the `error` graph)?
You move the opposite direction of the slope—the opposite direction of the derivative. You can
take each `weight` value, calculate its derivative with respect to `error` (so you're comparing two
variables: `weight` and `error`), and then change `weight` in the opposite direction of that slope.
That will move you to the minimum.

Remember back to the goal again: you're trying to figure out the direction and the amount to
change the weight so the error goes down. A derivative gives you the relationship between any
two variables in a function. You use the derivative to determine the relationship between any
weight and error. You then move the weight in the opposite direction of the derivative to find the
lowest weight. Voilà! The neural network learns.

This method for learning (finding error minimums) is called *gradient descent*. This name should
seem intuitive. You move the `weight` value opposite the gradient value, which reduces `error` to
0. By *opposite*, I mean you increase the weight when you have a negative gradient, and vice versa.
It's like gravity.

Look familiar?

```
weight = 0.0
goal_pred = 0.8
input = 1.1

for iteration in range(4):
    pred = input * weight
    error = (pred - goal_pred) ** 2
    delta = pred - goal_pred
    weight_delta = delta * input
    weight = weight - weight_delta

    print("Error:" + str(error) + " Prediction:" + str(pred))
```

Derivative
(how fast the error
changes, given changes
in the weight)

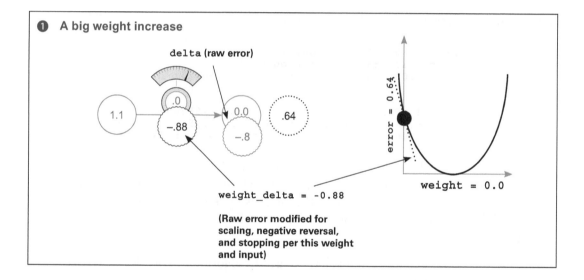

❶ **A big weight increase**

delta (raw error)

weight_delta = -0.88

(Raw error modified for
scaling, negative reversal,
and stopping per this weight
and input)

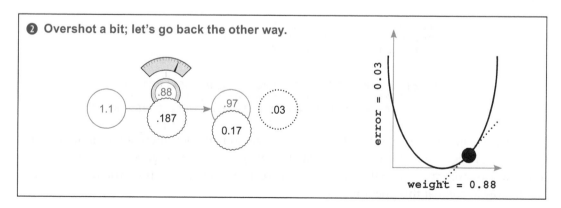

❷ **Overshot a bit; let's go back the other way.**

Breaking gradient descent

Just give me the code!

```
weight = 0.5
goal_pred = 0.8
input = 0.5

for iteration in range(20):
    pred = input * weight
    error = (pred - goal_pred) ** 2
    delta = pred - goal_pred
    weight_delta = input * delta
    weight = weight - weight_delta
    print("Error:" + str(error) + " Prediction:" + str(pred))
```

When I run this code, I see the following output:

```
Error:0.3025 Prediction:0.25
Error:0.17015625 Prediction:0.3875
Error:0.095712890625 Prediction:0.490625
                . . .

Error:1.7092608064e-05 Prediction:0.79586567925
Error:9.61459203602e-06 Prediction:0.796899259437
Error:5.40820802026e-06 Prediction:0.797674444578
```

Now that it works, let's break it. Play around with the starting `weight`, `goal_pred`, and `input` numbers. You can set them all to just about anything, and the neural network will figure out how to predict the output given the input using the weight. See if you can find some combinations the neural network can't predict. I find that trying to break something is a great way to learn about it.

Let's try setting `input` equal to 2, but still try to get the algorithm to predict 0.8. What happens? Take a look at the output:

```
Error:0.04 Prediction:1.0
Error:0.36 Prediction:0.2
Error:3.24 Prediction:2.6
                . . .

Error:6.67087267987e+14 Prediction:-25828031.8
Error:6.00378541188e+15 Prediction:77484098.6
Error:5.40340687069e+16 Prediction:-232452292.6
```

Whoa! That's not what you want. The predictions exploded! They alternate from negative to positive and negative to positive, getting farther away from the true answer at every step. In other words, every update to the weight overcorrects. In the next section, you'll learn more about how to combat this phenomenon.

Visualizing the overcorrections

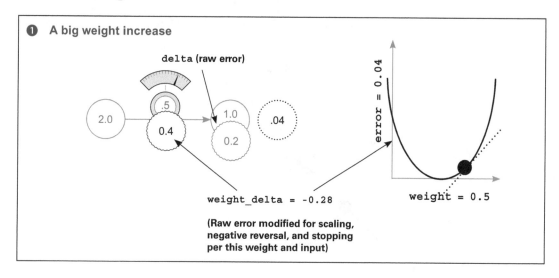

❶ A big weight increase

delta (raw error)

2.0 → .5 / 0.4 → 1.0 / 0.2 → .04

error = 0.04

weight = 0.5

weight_delta = -0.28

(Raw error modified for scaling, negative reversal, and stopping per this weight and input)

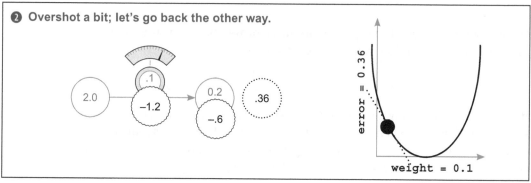

❷ Overshot a bit; let's go back the other way.

2.0 → .1 / -1.2 → 0.2 / -.6 → .36

error = 0.36

weight = 0.1

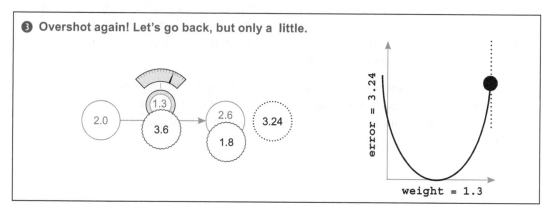

❸ Overshot again! Let's go back, but only a little.

2.0 → 1.3 / 3.6 → 2.6 / 1.8 → 3.24

error = 3.24

weight = 1.3

Divergence

Sometimes neural networks explode in value. Oops?

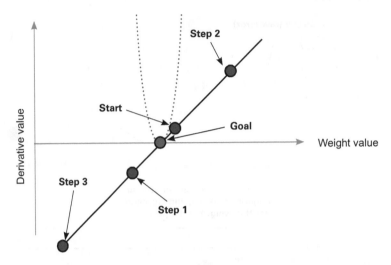

What really happened? The explosion in the error was caused by the fact that you made the input larger. Consider how you're updating the weight:

```
weight = weight - (input * (pred - goal_pred))
```

If the input is sufficiently large, this can make the weight update large even when the error is small. What happens when you have a large weight update and a small error? The network overcorrects. If the new error is even bigger, the network overcorrects even more. This causes the phenomenon you saw earlier, called *divergence*.

If you have a big input, the prediction is very sensitive to changes in the weight (because pred = input * weight). This can cause the network to overcorrect. In other words, even though the weight is still starting at 0.5, the derivative at that point is very steep. See how tight the U-shaped error curve is in the graph?

This is really intuitive. How do you predict? By multiplying the input by the weight. So, if the input is huge, small changes in the weight will cause changes in the prediction. The error is very sensitive to the weight. In other words, the derivative is really big. How do you make it smaller?

Introducing alpha

It's the simplest way to prevent overcorrecting weight updates.

What's the problem you're trying to solve? That if the input is too big, then the weight update can overcorrect. What's the symptom? That when you overcorrect, the new derivative is even larger in magnitude than when you started (although the sign will be the opposite).

Stop and consider this for a second. Look again at the graph in the previous section to understand the symptom. Step 2 is even farther away from the goal, which means the derivative is even greater in magnitude. This causes step 3 to be even farther from the goal than step 2, and the neural network continues like this, demonstrating divergence.

The symptom is this overshooting. The solution is to multiply the weight update by a fraction to make it smaller. In most cases, this involves multiplying the weight update by a single real-valued number between 0 and 1, known as *alpha*. Note: this has no effect on the core issue, which is that the input is larger. It will also reduce the weight updates for inputs that aren't too large.

Finding the appropriate alpha, even for state-of-the-art neural networks, is often done by guessing. You watch the error over time. If it starts diverging (going up), then the alpha is too high, and you decrease it. If learning is happening too slowly, then the alpha is too low, and you increase it. There are other methods than simple gradient descent that attempt to counter for this, but gradient descent is still very popular.

Alpha in code

Where does our "alpha" parameter come into play?

You just learned that alpha reduces the weight update so it doesn't overshoot. How does this affect the code? Well, you were updating the weights according to the following formula:

```
weight = weight - derivative
```

Accounting for alpha is a rather small change, as shown next. Notice that if alpha is small (say, 0.01), it will reduce the weight update considerably, thus preventing it from overshooting:

```
weight = weight - (alpha * derivative)
```

That was easy. Let's install alpha into the tiny implementation from the beginning of this chapter and run it where `input` = 2 (which previously didn't work):

```
weight = 0.5
goal_pred = 0.8
input = 2
alpha = 0.1

for iteration in range(20):
    pred = input * weight
    error = (pred - goal_pred) ** 2
    derivative = input * (pred - goal_pred)
    weight = weight - (alpha * derivative)

    print("Error:" + str(error) + " Prediction:" + str(pred))

Error:0.04 Prediction:1.0
Error:0.0144 Prediction:0.92
Error:0.005184 Prediction:0.872


    . . .


Error:1.14604719983e-09 Prediction:0.800033853319
Error:4.12576991939e-10 Prediction:0.800020311991
Error:1.48527717099e-10 Prediction:0.800012187195
```

What happens when you make alpha crazy small or big? What about making it negative?

Voilà! The tiniest neural network can now make good predictions again. How did I know to set alpha to 0.1? To be honest, I tried it, and it worked. And despite all the crazy advancements of deep learning in the past few years, most people just try several orders of magnitude of alpha (10, 1, 0.1, 0.01, 0.001, 0.0001) and then tweak it from there to see what works best. It's more art than science. There are more advanced ways to get to later, but for now, try various alphas until you get one that seems to work pretty well. Play with it.

1g

ally learn this stuff.

bit intense, but I can't stress enough the value I've found from this
can build the code from the previous section in a Jupyter notebook (or a
.py file, if you must) from memory. I know that might seem like overkill, but I (personally)
didn't have my "click" moment with neural networks until I was able to perform this task.

Why does this work? Well, for starters, the only way to know you've gleaned all the
information necessary from this chapter is to try to produce it from your head. Neural
networks have lots of small moving parts, and it's easy to miss one.

Why is this important for the rest of the book? In the following chapters, I'll be referring to
the concepts discussed in this chapter at a faster pace so that I can spend plenty of time on
the newer material. It's vitally important that when I say something like "Add your alpha
parameterization to the weight update," you immediately recognize which concepts from
this chapter I'm referring to.

All that is to say, memorizing small bits of neural network code has been hugely beneficial
for me personally, as well as for many individuals who have taken my advice on this subject
in the past.

In this chapter

- Gradient descent learning with multiple inputs

- Freezing one weight: what does it do?

- Gradient descent learning with multiple outputs

- Gradient descent learning with multiple inputs and outputs

- Visualizing weight values

- Visualizing dot products

> " You don't learn to walk by following rules. You learn by
> doing and by falling over. "
>
> —Richard Branson, http://mng.bz/oVgd

Gradient descent learning with multiple inputs

Gradient descent also works with multiple inputs.

In the preceding chapter, you learned how to use gradient descent to update a weight. In this chapter, we'll more or less reveal how the same techniques can be used to update a network that contains multiple weights. Let's start by jumping in the deep end, shall we? The following diagram shows how a network with multiple inputs can learn.

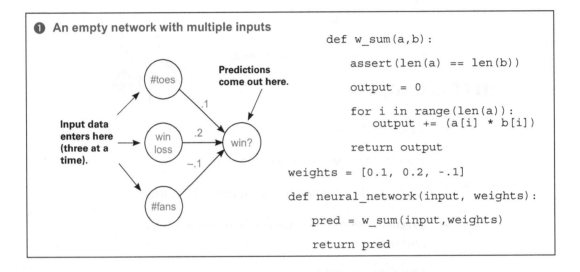

❶ An empty network with multiple inputs

Predictions come out here.

Input data enters here (three at a time).

```
def w_sum(a,b):
    assert(len(a) == len(b))
    output = 0
    for i in range(len(a)):
        output += (a[i] * b[i])
    return output

weights = [0.1, 0.2, -.1]

def neural_network(input, weights):
    pred = w_sum(input,weights)
    return pred
```

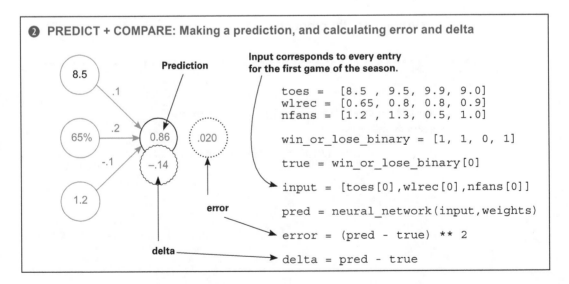

❷ PREDICT + COMPARE: Making a prediction, and calculating error and delta

Prediction

error

delta

Input corresponds to every entry for the first game of the season.

```
toes  = [8.5 , 9.5, 9.9, 9.0]
wlrec = [0.65, 0.8, 0.8, 0.9]
nfans = [1.2 , 1.3, 0.5, 1.0]

win_or_lose_binary = [1, 1, 0, 1]

true = win_or_lose_binary[0]

input = [toes[0],wlrec[0],nfans[0]]

pred = neural_network(input,weights)

error = (pred - true) ** 2

delta = pred - true
```

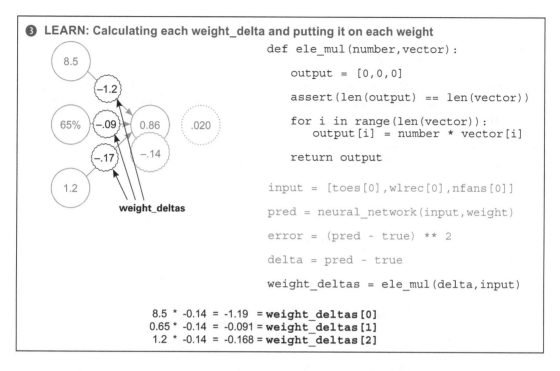

❸ LEARN: Calculating each weight_delta and putting it on each weight

```
def ele_mul(number,vector):

    output = [0,0,0]

    assert(len(output) == len(vector))

    for i in range(len(vector)):
        output[i] = number * vector[i]

    return output

input = [toes[0],wlrec[0],nfans[0]]

pred = neural_network(input,weight)

error = (pred - true) ** 2

delta = pred - true

weight_deltas = ele_mul(delta,input)
```

8.5 * -0.14 = -1.19 = **weight_deltas[0]**
0.65 * -0.14 = -0.091 = **weight_deltas[1]**
1.2 * -0.14 = -0.168 = **weight_deltas[2]**

There's nothing new in this diagram. Each `weight_delta` is calculated by taking its output `delta` and multiplying it by its `input`. In this case, because the three weights share the same output node, they also share that node's `delta`. But the weights have different weight `deltas` owing to their different `input` values. Notice further that you can reuse the `ele_mul` function from before, because you're multiplying each value in `weights` by the same value `delta`.

❹ LEARN: Updating the weights

```
input = [toes[0],wlrec[0],nfans[0]]

pred = neural_network(input,weight)
error = (pred - true) ** 2
delta = pred - true

weight_deltas = ele_mul(delta,input)

alpha = 0.01

for i in range(len(weights)):
    weights[i] -= alpha * weight_deltas[i]
print("Weights:" + str(weights))
print("Weight Deltas:" + str(weight_deltas))
```

toes   0.1119
win loss   .201   win?
        −.098
fans

0.1 - (-1.19 * 0.01) = 0.1119 = **weights[0]**
0.2 - (-.091 * 0.01) = 0.2009 = **weights[1]**
-0.1 - (-.168 * 0.01) = -0.098 = **weights[2]**

Gradient descent with multiple inputs explained

Simple to execute, and fascinating to understand.

When put side by side with the single-weight neural network, gradient descent with multiple inputs seems rather obvious in practice. But the properties involved are fascinating and worthy of discussion. First, let's take a look at them side by side.

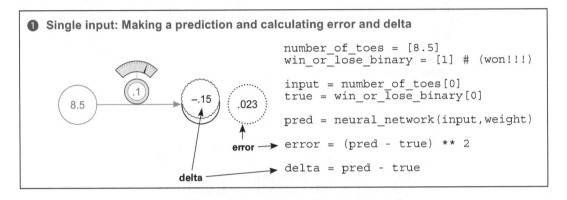

❶ Single input: Making a prediction and calculating error and delta

```
number_of_toes = [8.5]
win_or_lose_binary = [1] # (won!!!)

input = number_of_toes[0]
true = win_or_lose_binary[0]

pred = neural_network(input,weight)

error = (pred - true) ** 2

delta = pred - true
```

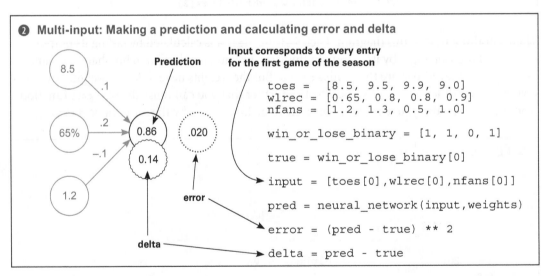

❷ Multi-input: Making a prediction and calculating error and delta

Prediction

Input corresponds to every entry
for the first game of the season

```
toes =  [8.5, 9.5, 9.9, 9.0]
wlrec = [0.65, 0.8, 0.8, 0.9]
nfans = [1.2, 1.3, 0.5, 1.0]

win_or_lose_binary = [1, 1, 0, 1]

true = win_or_lose_binary[0]

input = [toes[0],wlrec[0],nfans[0]]

pred = neural_network(input,weights)

error = (pred - true) ** 2

delta = pred - true
```

Up until the generation of `delta` on the output node, single input and multi-input gradient descent are identical (other than the prediction differences we studied in chapter 3). You make a prediction and calculate `error` and `delta` in identical ways. But the following problem remains: when you had only one `weight`, you had only one `input` (one `weight_delta` to generate). Now you have three. How do you generate three `weight_deltas`?

How do you turn a single delta (on the node) into three weight_delta values?

Remember the definition and purpose of `delta` versus `weight_delta`. `delta` is a measure of how much you want a node's value to be different. In this case, you compute it by a direct subtraction between the node's value and what you wanted the node's value to be (`pred - true`). Positive `delta` indicates the node's value was too high, and negative that it was too low.

> ### delta
>
> A measure of how much higher or lower you want a node's value to be, to predict perfectly given the current training example.

`weight_delta`, on the other hand, is an *estimate* of the direction and amount to move the weights to reduce `node_delta`, inferred by the derivative. How do you transform `delta` into a `weight_delta`? You multiply `delta` by a weight's `input`.

> ### weight_delta
>
> A derivative-based estimate of the direction and amount you should move a weight to reduce `node_delta`, accounting for scaling, negative reversal, and stopping.

Consider this from the perspective of a single weight, highlighted at right:

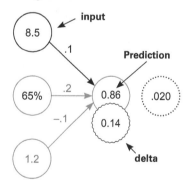

delta: Hey, `inputs`—yeah, you three. Next time, predict a little higher.

Single weight: Hmm: if my `input` was 0, then my weight wouldn't have mattered, and I wouldn't change a thing (*stopping*). If my `input` was negative, then I'd want to decrease my weight instead of increase it (*negative reversal*). But my `input` is positive and quite large, so I'm *guessing* that my personal prediction mattered a lot to the aggregated output. I'm going to move my weight up a lot to compensate (*scaling*).

The single weight increases its value.

What did those three properties/statements really say? They all (stopping, negative reversal, and scaling) made an observation of how the weight's role in `delta` was affected by its `input`. Thus, each `weight_delta` is a sort of input-modified version of `delta`.

This brings us back to the original question: how do you turn one (node) `delta` into three `weight_delta` values? Well, because each weight has a unique input and a shared `delta`, you use each respective weight's `input` multiplied by `delta` to create each respective `weight_delta`. Let's see this process in action.

In the next two figures, you can see the generation of `weight_delta` variables for the previous single-input architecture and for the new multi-input architecture. Perhaps the easiest way to see how similar they are is to read the pseudocode at the bottom of each figure. Notice that the multi-weight version multiplies `delta` (0.14) by every input to create the various `weight_deltas`. It's a simple process.

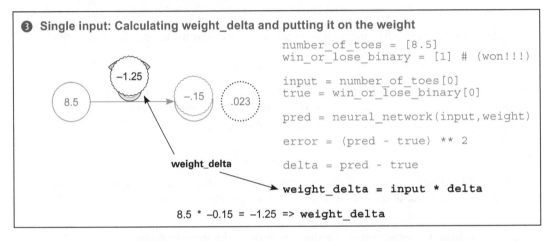

❸ **Single input: Calculating weight_delta and putting it on the weight**

```
number_of_toes = [8.5]
win_or_lose_binary = [1] # (won!!!)

input = number_of_toes[0]
true = win_or_lose_binary[0]

pred = neural_network(input,weight)

error = (pred - true) ** 2

delta = pred - true

weight_delta = input * delta
```

8.5 * −0.15 = −1.25 => **weight_delta**

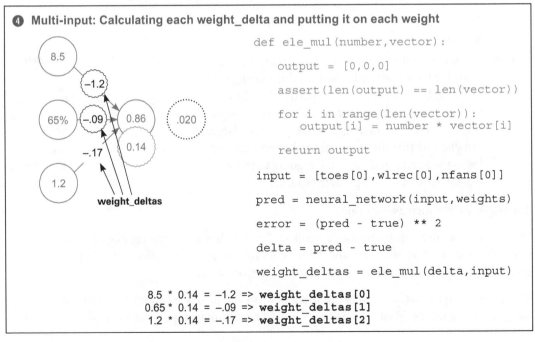

❹ **Multi-input: Calculating each weight_delta and putting it on each weight**

```
def ele_mul(number,vector):

    output = [0,0,0]

    assert(len(output) == len(vector))

    for i in range(len(vector)):
        output[i] = number * vector[i]

    return output

input = [toes[0],wlrec[0],nfans[0]]

pred = neural_network(input,weights)

error = (pred - true) ** 2

delta = pred - true

weight_deltas = ele_mul(delta,input)
```

8.5 * 0.14 = −1.2 => **weight_deltas[0]**
0.65 * 0.14 = −.09 => **weight_deltas[1]**
1.2 * 0.14 = −.17 => **weight_deltas[2]**

⑤ Updating the weight

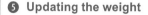
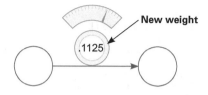

New weight

.1125

You multiply `weight_delta` by a small number, `alpha`, before using it to update the weight. This allows you to control how quickly the network learns. If it learns too quickly, it can update weights too aggressively and overshoot. Note that the weight update made the same change (small increase) as hot and cold learning.

```
number_of_toes = [8.5]
win_or_lose_binary = [1] # (won!!!)

input = number_of_toes[0]
true = win_or_lose_binary[0]

pred = neural_network(input,weight)

error = (pred - true) ** 2

delta = pred - true

weight_delta = input * delta

alpha = 0.01   ⟵——— Fixed before training

weight -= weight_delta * alpha
```

⑥ Updating the weights

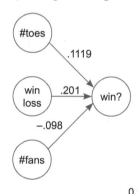

#toes

.1119

win
loss

.201

win?

−.098

#fans

```
input = [toes[0],wlrec[0],nfans[0]]

pred = neural_network(input,weights)

error = (pred - true) ** 2

delta = pred - true

weight_deltas = ele_mul(delta,input)

alpha = 0.01

for i in range(len(weights)):
    weights[i] -= alpha * weight_deltas[i]
```

0.1 − (1.19 * 0.01) = 0.1119 = **weights[0]**
0.2 − (.091 * 0.01) = 0.2009 = **weights[1]**
−0.1 − (.168 * 0.01) = −0.098 = **weights[2]**

The last step is also nearly identical to the single-input network. Once you have the `weight_delta` values, you multiply them by `alpha` and subtract them from the weights. It's literally the same process as before, repeated across multiple weights instead of a single one.

Let's watch several steps of learning

```
def neural_network(input, weights):
  out = 0
  for i in range(len(input)):
    out += (input[i] * weights[i])
  return out

def ele_mul(scalar, vector):
  out = [0,0,0]
  for i in range(len(out)):
    out[i] = vector[i] * scalar
  return out

toes  = [8.5, 9.5, 9.9, 9.0]
wlrec = [0.65, 0.8, 0.8, 0.9]
nfans = [1.2, 1.3, 0.5, 1.0]

win_or_lose_binary = [1, 1, 0, 1]
true = win_or_lose_binary[0]

alpha = 0.01
weights = [0.1, 0.2, -.1]
input = [toes[0],wlrec[0],nfans[0]]
```

```
(continued)
for iter in range(3):

  pred = neural_network(input,weights)

  error = (pred - true) ** 2
  delta = pred - true

  weight_deltas=ele_mul(delta,input)

  print("Iteration:" + str(iter+1))
  print("Pred:" + str(pred))
  print("Error:" + str(error))
  print("Delta:" + str(delta))
  print("Weights:" + str(weights))
  print("Weight_Deltas:")
  print(str(weight_deltas))
  print(
  )

for i in range(len(weights)):
  weights[i]-=alpha*weight_deltas[i]
```

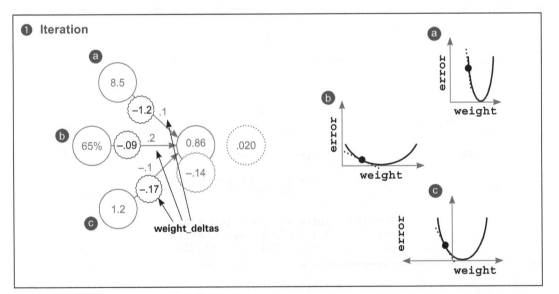

We can make three individual error/weight curves, one for each weight. As before, the slopes of these curves (the dotted lines) are reflected by the weight_delta values. Notice that **a** is steeper than the others. Why is weight_delta steeper for **a** than the others if they share the same output delta and error measure? Because **a** has an input value that's significantly higher than the others and thus, a higher derivative.

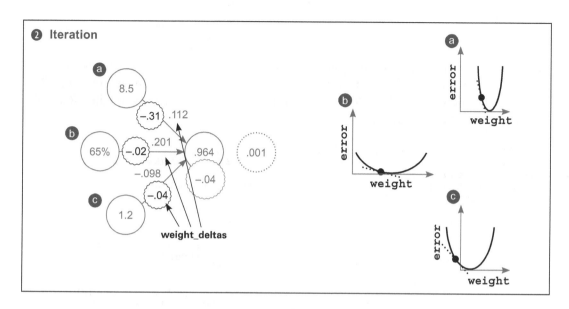

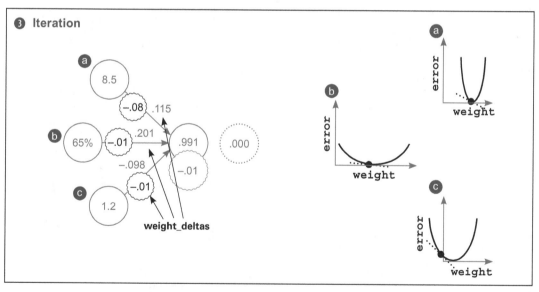

Here are a few additional takeaways. Most of the learning (weight changing) was performed on the weight with the largest input ⓐ, because the input changes the slope significantly. This isn't necessarily advantageous in all settings. A subfield called *normalization* helps encourage learning across all weights despite dataset characteristics such as this. This significant difference in slope forced me to set `alpha` lower than I wanted (0.01 instead of 0.1). Try setting `alpha` to 0.1: do you see how ⓐ causes it to diverge?

Freezing one weight: What does it do?

This experiment is a bit advanced in terms of theory, but I think it's a great exercise to understand how the weights affect each other. You're going to train again, except weight (a) won't ever be adjusted. You'll try to learn the training example using only weights (b) and (c) (`weights[1]` and `weights[2]`).

```python
def neural_network(input, weights):
    out = 0
    for i in range(len(input)):
        out += (input[i] * weights[i])
    return out

def ele_mul(scalar, vector):
    out = [0,0,0]
    for i in range(len(out)):
        out[i] = vector[i] * scalar
    return out

toes  = [8.5, 9.5, 9.9, 9.0]
wlrec = [0.65, 0.8, 0.8, 0.9]
nfans = [1.2, 1.3, 0.5, 1.0]

win_or_lose_binary = [1, 1, 0, 1]
true = win_or_lose_binary[0]

alpha = 0.3
weights = [0.1, 0.2, -.1]
input = [toes[0],wlrec[0],nfans[0]]
```

```python
(continued)
for iter in range(3):

    pred = neural_network(input,weights)

    error = (pred - true) ** 2
    delta = pred - true

    weight_deltas=ele_mul(delta,input)
    weight_deltas[0] = 0

    print("Iteration:" + str(iter+1))
    print("Pred:" + str(pred))
    print("Error:" + str(error))
    print("Delta:" + str(delta))
    print("Weights:" + str(weights))
    print("Weight_Deltas:")
    print(str(weight_deltas))
    print(
    )

    for i in range(len(weights)):
        weights[i] -=alpha*weight_deltas[i]
```

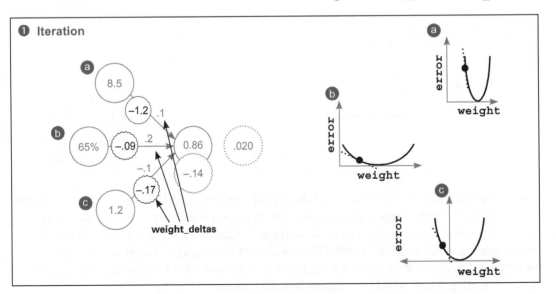

Perhaps you're surprised to see that 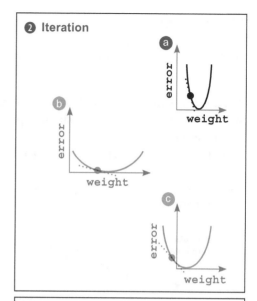ⓐ still finds the bottom of the bowl. Why is this? Well, the curves are a measure of each individual weight relative to the global error. Thus, because `error` is shared, when one weight finds the bottom of the bowl, all the weights find the bottom of the bowl.

This is an extremely important lesson. First, if you converged (reached `error` = 0) with ⓑ and ⓒ weights and then tried to train ⓐ, ⓐ wouldn't move. Why? `error` = 0, which means `weight_delta` is 0. This reveals a potentially damaging property of neural networks: ⓐ may be a powerful input with lots of predictive power, but if the network accidentally figures out how to predict accurately on the training data without it, then it will never learn to incorporate ⓐ into its prediction.

Also notice how ⓐ finds the bottom of the bowl. Instead of the black dot moving, the curve seems to move to the left. What does this mean? The black dot can move horizontally only if the weight is updated. Because the weight for ⓐ is frozen for this experiment, the dot must stay fixed. But `error` clearly goes to 0.

This tells you what the graphs really are. In truth, these are 2D slices of a four-dimensional shape. Three of the dimensions are the weight values, and the fourth dimension is the error. This shape is called the *error plane*, and, believe it or not, its curvature is determined by the training data. Why is that the case?

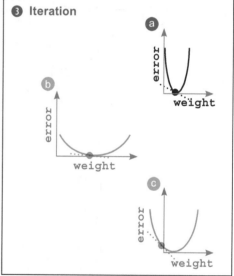

`error` is determined by the training data. Any network can have any `weight` value, but the value of `error` given any particular weight configuration is 100% determined by data. You've already seen how the steepness of the U shape is affected by the input data (on several occasions). What you're really trying to do with the neural network is find the lowest point on this big error plane, where the lowest point refers to the lowest `error`. Interesting, eh? We'll come back to this idea later, so file it away for now.

Gradient descent learning with multiple outputs

Neural networks can also make multiple predictions using only a single input.

Perhaps this will seem a bit obvious. You calculate each `delta` the same way and then multiply them all by the same, single input. This becomes each weight's `weight_delta`. At this point, I hope it's clear that a simple mechanism (stochastic gradient descent) is consistently used to perform learning across a wide variety of architectures.

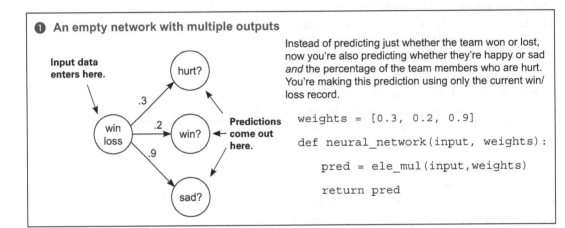

1 An empty network with multiple outputs

Input data enters here.

Instead of predicting just whether the team won or lost, now you're also predicting whether they're happy or sad *and* the percentage of the team members who are hurt. You're making this prediction using only the current win/ loss record.

```
weights = [0.3, 0.2, 0.9]

def neural_network(input, weights):

    pred = ele_mul(input,weights)

    return pred
```

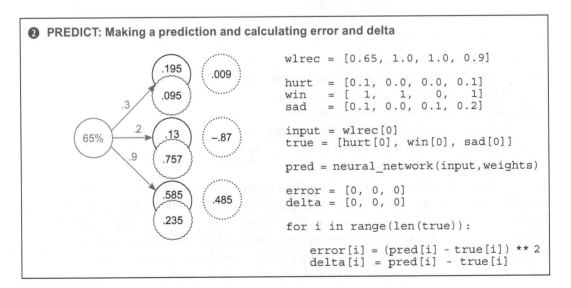

2 PREDICT: Making a prediction and calculating error and delta

```
wlrec = [0.65, 1.0, 1.0, 0.9]

hurt  = [0.1, 0.0, 0.0, 0.1]
win   = [  1,   1,   0,   1]
sad   = [0.1, 0.0, 0.1, 0.2]

input = wlrec[0]
true = [hurt[0], win[0], sad[0]]

pred = neural_network(input,weights)

error = [0, 0, 0]
delta = [0, 0, 0]

for i in range(len(true)):

        error[i] = (pred[i] - true[i]) ** 2
        delta[i] = pred[i] - true[i]
```

❸ COMPARE: Calculating each weight_delta and putting it on each weight

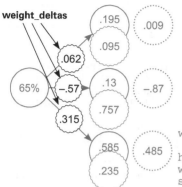

weight_deltas

```
def scalar_ele_mul(number,vector):

    output = [0,0,0]

    assert(len(output) == len(vector))

    for i in range(len(vector)):
        output[i] = number * vector[i]

    return output
```

```
wlrec = [0.65, 1.0, 1.0, 0.9]

hurt = [0.1, 0.0, 0.0, 0.1]
win  = [  1,   1,   0,   1]
sad  = [0.1, 0.0, 0.1, 0.2]
```

```
input = wlrec[0]
true = [hurt[0], win[0], sad[0]]

pred = neural_network(input,weights)

error = [0, 0, 0]
delta = [0, 0, 0]

for i in range(len(true)):

    error[i] = (pred[i] - true[i]) ** 2
    delta[i] = pred[i] - true[i]

weight_deltas = scalar_ele_mul(input,weights)
```

As before, `weight_deltas` are computed by multiplying the input node value with the output node `delta` for each weight. In this case, the `weight_deltas` share the same input node and have unique output nodes (`deltas`). Note also that you can reuse the `ele_mul` function.

❹ LEARN: Updating the weights

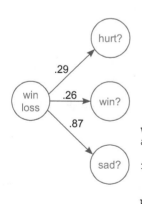

```
input = wlrec[0]
true = [hurt[0], win[0], sad[0]]
pred = neural_network(input,weights)

error = [0, 0, 0]
delta = [0, 0, 0]

for i in range(len(true)):
    error[i] = (pred[i] - true[i]) ** 2
    delta[i] = pred[i] - true[i]
weight_deltas = scalar_ele_mul(input,weights)
alpha = 0.1

for i in range(len(weights)):
    weights[i] -= (weight_deltas[i] * alpha)

print("Weights:" + str(weights))
print("Weight Deltas:" + str(weight_deltas))
```

Gradient descent with multiple inputs and outputs

Gradient descent generalizes to arbitrarily large networks.

❶ An empty network with multiple inputs and outputs

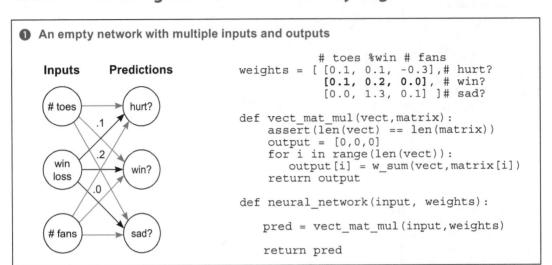

```
                           # toes %win # fans
weights = [ [0.1,  0.1, -0.3],# hurt?
            [0.1,  0.2,  0.0], # win?
            [0.0,  1.3,  0.1] ]# sad?

def vect_mat_mul(vect,matrix):
    assert(len(vect) == len(matrix))
    output = [0,0,0]
    for i in range(len(vect)):
        output[i] = w_sum(vect,matrix[i])
    return output

def neural_network(input, weights):

    pred = vect_mat_mul(input,weights)

    return pred
```

❷ PREDICT: Making a prediction and calculating error and delta

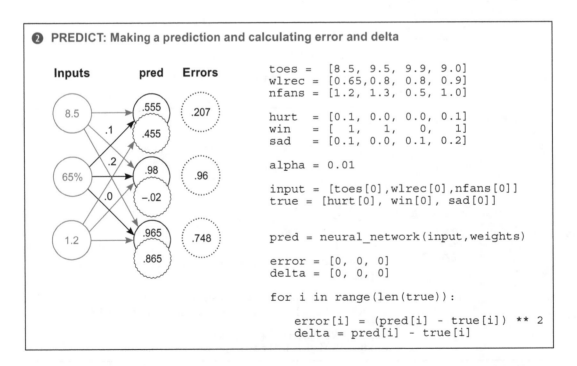

```
toes  = [8.5, 9.5, 9.9, 9.0]
wlrec = [0.65,0.8, 0.8, 0.9]
nfans = [1.2, 1.3, 0.5, 1.0]

hurt  = [0.1, 0.0, 0.0, 0.1]
win   = [  1,   1,   0,   1]
sad   = [0.1, 0.0, 0.1, 0.2]

alpha = 0.01

input = [toes[0],wlrec[0],nfans[0]]
true  = [hurt[0], win[0], sad[0]]


pred = neural_network(input,weights)

error = [0, 0, 0]
delta = [0, 0, 0]

for i in range(len(true)):

    error[i] = (pred[i] - true[i]) ** 2
    delta = pred[i] - true[i]
```

❸ COMPARE: Calculating each weight_delta and putting it on each weight

Inputs   **pred**   **Errors**

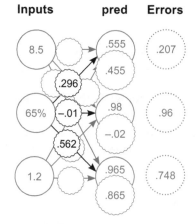

(`weight_deltas` are shown for
only one input, to save space.)

```
def outer_prod(vec_a, vec_b):

    out = zeros_matrix(len(a),len(b))

    for i in range(len(a)):
        for j in range(len(b)):
            out[i][j] = vec_a[i]*vec_b[j]

    return out

input = [toes[0],wlrec[0],nfans[0]]
true = [hurt[0], win[0], sad[0]]

pred = neural_network(input,weights)

error = [0, 0, 0]
delta = [0, 0, 0]

for i in range(len(true)):

    error[i] = (pred[i] - true[i]) ** 2
    delta = pred[i] - true[i]

weight_deltas = outer_prod(input,delta)
```

❹ LEARN: Updating the weights

Inputs   **Predictions**

toes ──→ hurt?

win loss ──→ win?

fans ──→ sad?

.09
.2
−.01

```
input = [toes[0],wlrec[0],nfans[0]]
true = [hurt[0], win[0], sad[0]]

pred = neural_network(input,weights)

error = [0, 0, 0]
delta = [0, 0, 0]

for i in range(len(true)):

    error[i] = (pred[i] - true[i]) ** 2
    delta = pred[i] - true[i]

weight_deltas = outer_prod(input,delta)

for i in range(len(weights)):
    for j in range(len(weights[0])):
        weights[i][j] -= alpha * \
                    weight_deltas[i][j]
```

What do these weights learn?

Each weight tries to reduce the error, but what do they learn in aggregate?

Congratulations! This is the part of the book where we move on to the first real-world dataset. As luck would have it, it's one with historical significance.

It's called the Modified National Institute of Standards and Technology (MNIST) dataset, and it consists of digits that high school students and employees of the US Census Bureau handwrote some years ago. The interesting bit is that these handwritten digits are black-and-white images of people's handwriting. Accompanying each digit image is the actual number they were writing (0–9). For the last few decades, people have been using this dataset to train neural networks to read human handwriting, and today, you're going to do the same.

Each image is only 784 pixels (28 × 28). Given that you have 784 pixels as input and 10 possible labels as output, you can imagine the shape of the neural network: each training example contains 784 values (one for each pixel), so the neural network must have 784 input values. Pretty simple, eh? You adjust the number of input nodes to reflect how many datapoints are in each training example. You want to predict *10 probabilities*: one for each digit. Given an input drawing, the neural network will produce these 10 probabilities, telling you which digit is most likely to be what was drawn.

How do you configure the neural network to produce 10 probabilities? In the previous section, you saw a diagram for a neural network that could take multiple inputs at a time and make multiple predictions based on that input. You should be able to modify this network to have the correct number of inputs and outputs for the new MNIST task. You'll tweak it to have 784 inputs and 10 outputs.

In the MNISTPreprocessor notebook is a script to preprocess the MNIST dataset and load the first 1,000 images and labels into two NumPy matrices called images and labels. You may be wondering, "Images are two-dimensional. How do I load the (28 × 28) pixels into a flat neural network?" For now, the answer is simple: flatten the images into a vector of 1 × 784. You'll take the first row of pixels and concatenate them with the second row, and the third row, and so on, until you have one list of pixels per image (784 pixels long).

Inputs   Predictions

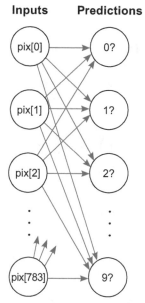

This diagram represents the new MNIST classification neural network. It most closely resembles the network you trained with multiple inputs and outputs earlier. The only difference is the number of inputs and outputs, which has increased substantially. This network has 784 inputs (one for each pixel in a 28 × 28 image) and 10 outputs (one for each possible digit in the image).

If this network could predict perfectly, it would take in an image's pixels (say, a 2, like the one in the next figure) and predict a 1.0 in the correct output position (the third one) and a 0 everywhere else. If it were able to do this correctly for all the images in the dataset, it would have no error.

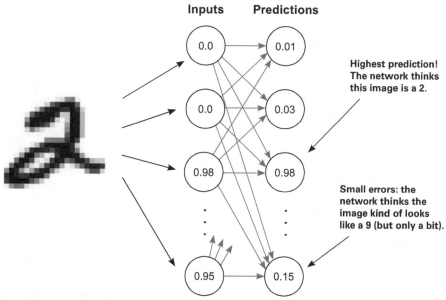

Over the course of training, the network will adjust the weights between the input and prediction nodes so that `error` falls toward 0 in training. But what does this do? What does it mean to modify a bunch of weights to learn a pattern in aggregate?

Visualizing weight values

An interesting and intuitive practice in neural network research (particularly for image classifiers) is to visualize the weights as if they were an image. If you look at this diagram, you'll see why.

Each output node has a weight coming from every pixel. For example, the 2? node has 784 input weights, each mapping the relationship between a pixel and the number 2.

What is this relationship? Well, if the weight is high, it means the model believes there's a high degree of *correlation* between that pixel and the number 2. If the number is very low (negative), then the network believes there is a very low correlation (perhaps even negative correlation) between that pixel and the number 2.

If you take the weights and print them out into an image that's the same shape as the input dataset images, you can see which pixels have the highest correlation with

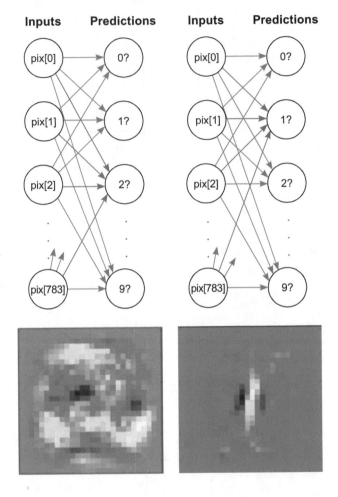

a particular output node. In our example, a very vague 2 and 1 appear in the two images, which were created using the weights for 2 and 1, respectively. The bright areas are high weights, and the dark areas are negative weights. The neutral color (red, if you're reading this in the eBook) represents 0 in the weight matrix. This illustrates that the network generally knows the shape of a 2 and of a 1.

Why does it turn out this way? This takes us back to the lesson on dot products. Let's have a quick review.

Visualizing dot products (weighted sums)

Recall how dot products work. They take two vectors, multiply them together (elementwise), and then sum over the output. Consider this example:

```
a = [ 0, 1, 0, 1]
b = [ 1, 0, 1, 0]

    [ 0, 0, 0, 0]  -> 0  <--- Score
```

First you multiply each element in a and b by each other, in this case creating a vector of 0s. The sum of this vector is also 0. Why? Because the vectors have nothing in common.

```
c = [ 0, 1, 1, 0]          b = [ 1, 0, 1, 0]
d = [.5, 0,.5, 0]          c = [ 0, 1, 1, 0]
```

But the dot products between c and d return higher scores, because there's overlap in the columns that have positive values. Performing dot products between two identical vectors tends to result in higher scores, as well. The takeaway? *A dot product is a loose measurement of similarity between two vectors.*

What does this mean for the weights and inputs? Well, if the weight vector is similar to the input vector for 2, then it will output a high score because the two vectors are similar. Inversely, if the weight vector is *not* similar to the input vector for 2, it will output a low score. You can see this in action in the following figure. Why is the top score (0.98) higher than the lower one (0.01)?

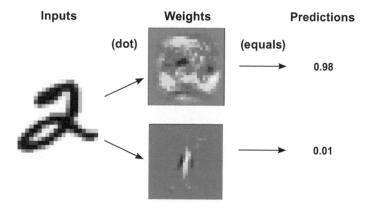

Summary

Gradient descent is a general learning algorithm.

Perhaps the most important subtext of this chapter is that gradient descent is a very flexible learning algorithm. If you combine weights in a way that allows you to calculate an error function and a `delta`, gradient descent can show you how to move the weights to reduce the error. We'll spend the rest of this book exploring different types of weight combinations and error functions for which gradient descent is useful. The next chapter is no exception.

building your first deep neural network:
introduction to backpropagation | 6

In this chapter

- The streetlight problem
- Matrices and the matrix relationship
- Full, batch, and stochastic gradient descent
- Neural networks learn correlation
- Overfitting
- Creating your own correlation
- Backpropagation: long-distance error attribution
- Linear versus nonlinear
- The secret to sometimes correlation
- Your first deep network
- Backpropagation in code: bringing it all together

> **66** O Deep Thought computer," he said, "the task we have designed **99**
> you to perform is this. We want you to tell us..." he paused,
> "The Answer."
>
> —Douglas Adams, *The Hitchhiker's Guide to the Galaxy*

The streetlight problem

This toy problem considers how a network learns entire datasets.

Consider yourself approaching a street corner in a foreign country. As you approach, you look up and realize that the street light is unfamiliar. How can you know when it's safe to cross the street?

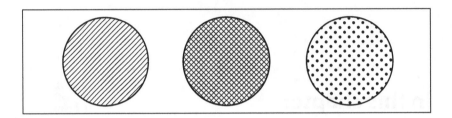

You can know when it's safe to cross the street by interpreting the streetlight. But in this case, you don't know how to interpret it. Which light combinations indicate when it's time to *walk*? Which indicate when it's time to *stop*? To solve this problem, you might sit at the street corner for a few minutes observing the correlation between each light combination and whether people around you choose to walk or stop. You take a seat and record the following pattern:

STOP

OK, nobody walked at the first light. At this point you're thinking, "Wow, this pattern could be anything. The left light or the right light could be correlated with stopping, or the central light could be correlated with walking." There's no way to know. Let's take another datapoint:

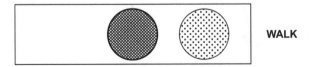

WALK

People walked, so something about this light changed the signal. The only thing you know for sure is that the far-right light doesn't seem to indicate one way or another. Perhaps it's irrelevant. Let's collect another datapoint:

Now you're getting somewhere. Only the middle light changed this time, and you got the opposite pattern. The working hypothesis is that the *middle* light indicates when people feel safe to walk. Over the next few minutes, you record the following six light patterns, noting when people walk or stop. Do you notice a pattern overall?

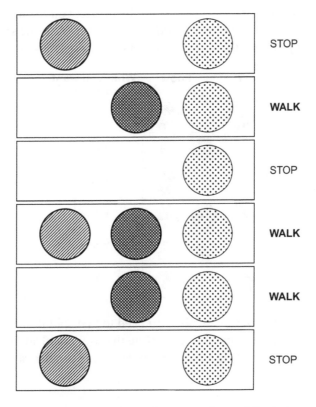

As hypothesized, there is a *perfect correlation* between the middle (crisscross) light and whether it's safe to walk. You learned this pattern by observing all the individual datapoints and *searching for correlation*. This is what you're going to train a neural network to do.

Preparing the data

Neural networks don't read streetlights.

In the previous chapters, you learned about supervised algorithms. You learned that they can take one dataset and turn it into another. More important, they can take a dataset of *what you know* and turn it into a dataset of *what you want to know.*

How do you train a supervised neural network? You present it with two datasets and ask it to learn how to transform one into the other. Think back to the streetlight problem. Can you identify two datasets? Which one do you always know? Which one do you want to know?

You do indeed have two datasets. On the one hand, you have six streetlight states. On the other hand, you have six observations of whether people walked. These are the two datasets.

You can train the neural network to convert from the dataset you *know* to the dataset that you *want to know.* In this particular real-world example, you know the state of the streetlight at any given time, and you want to know whether it's safe to cross the street.

To prepare this data for the neural network, you need to first split it into these two groups (what you know and what you want to know). Note that you could attempt to go backward if you swapped which dataset was in which group. For some problems, this works.

Matrices and the matrix relationship

Translate the streetlight into math.

Math doesn't understand streetlights. As mentioned in the previous section, you want to teach a neural network to translate a streetlight pattern into the correct stop/walk pattern. The operative word here is *pattern*. What you really want to do is mimic the pattern of the streetlight in the form of numbers. Let me show you what I mean.

Streetlights		Streetlight pattern		
	→	1	0	1
	→	0	1	1
	→	0	0	1
	→	1	1	1
	→	0	1	1
	→	1	0	1

Notice that the pattern of numbers shown here mimics the pattern from the streetlights in the form of 1s and 0s. Each light gets a column (three columns total, because there are three lights). Notice also that there are six rows representing the six different observed streetlights.

This structure of 1s and 0s is called a *matrix*. This relationship between the rows and columns is common in matrices, especially matrices of data (like the streetlights).

In data matrices, it's convention to give each *recorded example* a single *row*. It's also convention to give each *thing being recorded* a single *column*. This makes the matrix easy to read.

So, a column contains every state in which a thing was recorded. In this case, a column contains every on/off state recorded for a particular light. Each row contains the simultaneous state of every light at a particular moment in time. Again, this is common.

Good data matrices perfectly mimic the outside world.

The data matrix doesn't have to be all 1s and 0s. What if the streetlights were on dimmers and turned on and off at varying degrees of intensity? Perhaps the streetlight matrix would look more like this:

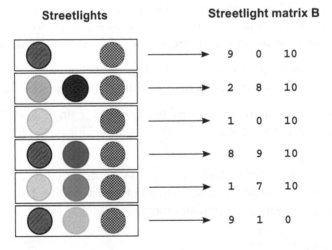

Matrix A is perfectly valid. It's mimicking the patterns that exist in the real world (streetlight), so you can ask the computer to interpret them. Would the following matrix still be valid?

Streetlights　　　　　　　**Streetlight matrix B**

9	0	10
2	8	10
1	0	10
8	9	10
1	7	10
9	1	0

Matrix (B) *is* valid. It adequately captures the relationships between various training examples (rows) and lights (columns). Note that `Matrix A * 10 == Matrix B` (`A * 10 == B`). This means these matrices are *scalar multiples* of each other.

Matrices A and B both contain the same underlying pattern.

The important takeaway is that an *infinite* number of matrices exist that perfectly reflect the streetlight patterns in the dataset. Even the one shown next is perfect.

Streetlights		**Streetlight matrix C**

⬤ ⬤	18 0 20
⬤⬤⬤	4 16 20
⬤ ⬤	2 0 20
⬤⬤⬤	16 18 20
⬤⬤⬤	2 14 20
⬤⬤⬤	18 2 0

It's important to recognize that the underlying pattern isn't the same as the matrix. It's a *property of* the matrix. In fact, it's a property of all three of these matrices (A, B, and C). The pattern is what each of these matrices is *expressing*. The pattern also existed in the streetlights.

This *input data pattern* is what you want the neural network to learn to transform into the *output data pattern*. But in order to learn the output data pattern, you also need to capture the pattern in the form of a matrix, as shown here.

Note that you could reverse the 1s and 0s, and the output matrix would still capture the underlying STOP/WALK pattern that's present in the data. You know this because regardless of whether you assign a 1 to WALK or to STOP, you can still decode the 1s and 0s into the underlying STOP/WALK pattern.

The resulting matrix is called a *lossless representation* because you can perfectly convert back and forth between your stop/walk notes and the matrix.

STOP	→	0
WALK	→	1
STOP	→	0
WALK	→	1
WALK	→	1
STOP	→	0

Creating a matrix or two in Python

Import the matrices into Python.

You've converted the streetlight pattern into a matrix (one with just 1s and 0s). Now let's create that matrix (and, more important, its underlying pattern) in Python so the neural network can read it. Python's NumPy library (introduced in chapter 3) was built just for handling matrices. Let's see it in action:

```
import numpy as np
streetlights = np.array( [ [ 1, 0, 1 ],
                           [ 0, 1, 1 ],
                           [ 0, 0, 1 ],
                           [ 1, 1, 1 ],
                           [ 0, 1, 1 ],
                           [ 1, 0, 1 ] ] )
```

If you're a regular Python user, something should be striking in this code. A matrix is just a list of lists. It's an array of arrays. What is NumPy? NumPy is really just a fancy wrapper for an array of arrays that provides special, matrix-oriented functions. Let's create a NumPy matrix for the output data, too:

```
walk _ vs _ stop = np.array( [ [ 0 ],
                               [ 1 ],
                               [ 0 ],
                               [ 1 ],
                               [ 1 ],
                               [ 0 ] ] )
```

What do you want the neural network to do? Take the `streetlights` matrix and learn to transform it into the `walk_vs_stop` matrix. More important, you want the neural network to take *any matrix containing the same underlying pattern* as `streetlights` and transform it into a matrix that contains the underlying pattern of `walk_vs_stop`. More on that later. Let's start by trying to transform `streetlights` into `walk_vs_stop` using a neural network.

Neural network

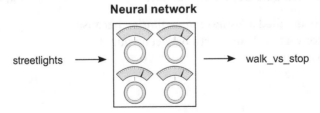

streetlights ⟶   ⟶ walk_vs_stop

Building a neural network

You've been learning about neural networks for several chapters now. You have a new dataset, and you're going to create a neural network to solve it. Following is some example code to learn the first streetlight pattern. This should look familiar:

```
import numpy as np
weights = np.array([0.5,0.48,-0.7])
alpha = 0.1

streetlights = np.array( [ [ 1, 0, 1 ],
                           [ 0, 1, 1 ],
                           [ 0, 0, 1 ],
                           [ 1, 1, 1 ],
                           [ 0, 1, 1 ],
                           [ 1, 0, 1 ] ] )

walk_vs_stop = np.array( [ 0, 1, 0, 1, 1, 0 ] )

input = streetlights[0]  ◄─────────────────── [1,0,1]
goal_prediction = walk_vs_stop[0]  ◄──────
                                          Equals 0 (stop)

for iteration in range(20):
    prediction = input.dot(weights)
    error = (goal_prediction - prediction) ** 2
    delta = prediction - goal_prediction
    weights = weights - (alpha * (input * delta))

    print("Error:" + str(error) + " Prediction:" + str(prediction))
```

This code example may bring back several nuances you learned in chapter 3. First, the use of the `dot` function was a way to perform a dot product (weighted sum) between two vectors. But not included in chapter 3 was the way NumPy matrices can perform elementwise addition and multiplication:

```
import numpy as np

a = np.array([0,1,2,1])
b = np.array([2,2,2,3])

print(a*b)
print(a+b)
print(a * 0.5)
print(a + 0.5)
```

Elementwise multiplication

Elementwise addition

Vector-scalar multiplication

Vector-scalar addition

NumPy makes these operations easy. When you put a + between two vectors, it does what you expect: it adds the two vectors together. Other than these nice NumPy operators and the new dataset, the neural network shown here is the same as the ones built previously.

Learning the whole dataset

The neural network has been learning only one streetlight. Don't we want it to learn them all?

So far in this book, you've trained neural networks that learned how to model a single training example (`input -> goal_pred` pair). But now you're trying to build a neural network that tells you whether it's safe to cross the street. You need it to know more than one streetlight. How do you do this? You train it on all the streetlights at once:

```python
import numpy as np

weights = np.array([0.5,0.48,-0.7])
alpha = 0.1

streetlights = np.array( [[ 1, 0, 1 ],
                          [ 0, 1, 1 ],
                          [ 0, 0, 1 ],
                          [ 1, 1, 1 ],
                          [ 0, 1, 1 ],
                          [ 1, 0, 1 ] ] )

walk_vs_stop = np.array( [ 0, 1, 0, 1, 1, 0 ] )

input = streetlights[0]          ◄───────────────── [1,0,1]
goal_prediction = walk_vs_stop[0]  ◄─────── Equals 0 (stop)

for iteration in range(40):
    error_for_all_lights = 0
    for row_index in range(len(walk_vs_stop)):
        input = streetlights[row_index]
        goal_prediction = walk_vs_stop[row_index]

        prediction = input.dot(weights)

        error = (goal_prediction - prediction) ** 2
        error_for_all_lights += error

        delta = prediction - goal_prediction
        weights = weights - (alpha * (input * delta))
        print("Prediction:" + str(prediction))
    print("Error:" + str(error_for_all_lights) + "\n")
```

```
Error:2.6561231104
Error:0.962870177672

...

Error:0.000614343567483
Error:0.000533736773285
```

Full, batch, and stochastic gradient descent

Stochastic gradient descent updates weights one example at a time.

As it turns out, this idea of learning one example at a time is a variant on gradient descent called *stochastic gradient descent*, and it's one of the handful of methods that can be used to learn an entire dataset.

How does stochastic gradient descent work? As you saw in the previous example, it performs a prediction and weight update for each training example separately. In other words, it takes the first streetlight, tries to predict it, calculates the `weight_delta`, and updates the weights. Then it moves on to the second streetlight, and so on. It iterates through the entire dataset many times until it can find a weight configuration that works well for all the training examples.

(Full) gradient descent updates weights one dataset at a time.

As introduced in chapter 4, another method for learning an entire dataset is gradient descent (or *average/full gradient descent*). Instead of updating the weights once for each training example, the network calculates the average `weight_delta` over the entire dataset, changing the weights only each time it computes a full average.

Batch gradient descent updates weights after n examples.

This will be covered in more detail later, but there's also a third configuration that sort of splits the difference between stochastic gradient descent and full gradient descent. Instead of updating the weights after just one example or after the entire dataset of examples, you choose a *batch size* (typically between 8 and 256) of examples, after which the weights are updated.

We'll discuss this more later in the book, but for now, recognize that the previous example created a neural network that can learn the entire streetlights dataset by training on each example, one at a time.

Neural networks learn correlation

What did the last neural network learn?

You just got done training a single-layer neural network to take a streetlight pattern and identify whether it was safe to cross the street. Let's take on the neural network's perspective for a moment. The neural network doesn't know that it was processing streetlight data. All it was trying to do was identify which input (of the three possible) correlated with the output. It correctly identified the middle light by analyzing the final weight positions of the network.

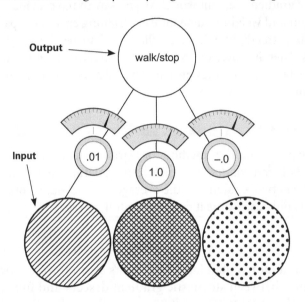

Notice that the middle weight is very near 1, whereas the far-left and far-right weights are very near 0. At a high level, all the iterative, complex processes for learning accomplished something rather simple: the network *identified correlation* between the middle input and output. The correlation is located wherever the weights were set to high numbers. Inversely, *randomness* with respect to the output was found at the far-left and far-right weights (where the weight values are very near 0).

How did the network identify correlation? Well, in the process of gradient descent, each training example asserts either *up pressure* or *down pressure* on the weights. On average, there was more up pressure for the middle weight and more down pressure for the other weights. Where does the pressure come from? Why is it different for different weights?

Up and down pressure

It comes from the data.

Each node is individually trying to correctly predict the output given the input. For the most part, each node ignores all the other nodes when attempting to do so. The only *cross communication* occurs in that all three weights must share the same error measure. The *weight update* is nothing more than taking this shared error measure and multiplying it by each respective input.

Why do you do this? A key part of why neural networks learn is *error attribution*, which means given a shared error, the network needs to figure out which weights contributed (so they can be adjusted) and which weights did *not* contribute (so they can be left alone).

Training data					Weight pressure				
1	0	1	→	0	–	0	–	→	0
0	1	1		1	0	+	+		1
0	0	1	→	0	0	0	–	→	0
1	1	1		1	+	+	+		1
0	1	1	→	1	0	+	+	→	1
1	0	1		0	–	0	–		0

Consider the first training example. Because the middle input is 0, the middle weight is *completely irrelevant* for this prediction. No matter what the weight is, it's going to be multiplied by 0 (the input). Thus, any error at that training example (regardless of whether it's too high or too low), can be *attributed* to only the far-left and right weights.

Consider the pressure of this first training example. If the network should predict 0, and two inputs are 1s, then this will cause error, which drives the weight values *toward 0*.

The Weight Pressure table helps describe the effect of each training example on each respective weight. + indicates that it has pressure toward 1, and – indicates that it has pressure toward 0. Zeros (0) indicate that there is no pressure because the input datapoint is 0, so that weight won't be changed. Notice that the far-left weight has two negatives and one positive, so on average the weight will move toward 0. The middle weight has three positives, so on average the weight will move toward 1.

Training data				Weight pressure			
1	0	1	0	–	0	–	0
0	1	1	1	0	+	+	1
0	0	1	0	0	0	–	0
1	1	1	1	+	+	+	1
0	1	1	1	0	+	+	1
1	0	1	0	–	0	–	0

Each individual weight is attempting to compensate for error. In the first training example, there's *discorrelation* between the far-right and far-left inputs and the desired output. This causes those weights to experience down pressure.

This same phenomenon occurs throughout all six training examples, rewarding correlation with pressure toward 1 and penalizing decorrelation with pressure toward 0. On average, this causes the network to find the correlation present between the middle weight and the output to be the dominant predictive force (heaviest weight in the weighted average of the input), making the network quite accurate.

> ### Bottom line
>
> The prediction is a weighted sum of the inputs. The learning algorithm rewards inputs that correlate with the output with upward pressure (toward 1) on their weight while penalizing inputs with discorrelation with downward pressure. The weighted sum of the inputs find perfect correlation between the input and the output by weighting decorrelated inputs to 0.

The mathematician in you may be cringing a little. Upward pressure and downward pressure are hardly precise mathematical expressions, and they have plenty of edge cases where this logic doesn't hold (which we'll address in a second). But you'll later find that this is an *extremely* valuable approximation, allowing you to temporarily overlook all the complexity of gradient descent and just remember that *learning rewards correlation* with larger weights (or more generally, *learning finds correlation between the two datasets*).

Edge case: Overfitting

Sometimes correlation happens accidentally.

Consider again the first example in the training data. What if the far-left weight was 0.5 and the far-right weight was −0.5? Their prediction would equal 0. The network would predict perfectly. But it hasn't remotely learned how to safely predict streetlights (those weights would fail in the real world). This phenomenon is known as *overfitting*.

> ### Deep learning's greatest weakness: Overfitting
>
> Error is shared among all the weights. If a particular configuration of weights *accidentally* creates perfect correlation between the prediction and the output dataset (such that `error == 0`) without giving the heaviest weight to the best inputs, *the neural network will stop learning*.

If it wasn't for the other training examples, this fatal flaw would cripple the neural network. What do the other training examples do? Well, let's look at the second training example. It bumps the far-right weight upward while not changing the far-left weight. This throws off the equilibrium that stopped the learning in the first example. As long as you don't train exclusively on the first example, the rest of the training examples will help the network avoid getting stuck in these edge-case configurations that exist for any one training example.

This is *very important*. Neural networks are so flexible that they can find many, many different weight configurations that will correctly predict for a subset of training data. If you trained this neural network on the first two training examples, it would likely stop learning at a point where it did *not* work well for the other training examples. In essence, it memorized the two training examples instead of finding the *correlation* that will *generalize* to any possible streetlight configuration.

If you train on only two streetlights and the network finds just these edge-case configurations, it could *fail* to tell you whether it's safe to cross the street when it sees a streetlight that wasn't in the training data.

> ### Key takeaway
>
> The greatest challenge you'll face with deep learning is convincing your neural network to *generalize* instead of just *memorize*. You'll see this again.

Edge case: Conflicting pressure

Sometimes correlation fights itself.

Consider the far-right column in the following Weight Pressure table. What do you see?

This column seems to have an equal number of upward and downward pressure moments. But the network correctly pushes this (far-right) weight down to 0, which means the downward pressure moments must be larger than the upward ones. How does this work?

	Training data				Weight pressure			
1	0	1	→	0	–	0	–	→	0
0	1	1		1	0	+	+		1
0	0	1	→	0	0	0	–	→	0
1	1	1		1	+	+	+		1
0	1	1		1	0	+	+		1
1	0	1	→	0	–	0	–	→	0

The left and middle weights have enough signal to converge on their own. The left weight falls to 0, and the middle weight moves toward 1. As the middle weight moves higher and higher, the error for positive examples continues to decrease. But as they approach their optimal positions, the decorrelation on the far-right weight becomes more apparent.

Let's consider the extreme example, where the left and middle weights are perfectly set to 0 and 1, respectively. What happens to the network? If the right weight is above 0, then the network predicts too high; and if the right weight is beneath 0, the network predicts too low.

As other nodes learn, they absorb some of the error; they absorb part of the correlation. They cause the network to predict with *moderate* correlative power, which reduces the error. The other weights then only try to adjust their weights to correctly predict what's left.

In this case, because the middle weight has consistent signal to absorb all the correlation (because of the 1:1 relationship between the middle input and the output), the error when you want to predict 1 becomes very small, but the error to predict 0 becomes large, pushing the middle weight downward.

It doesn't always work out like this.

In some ways, you kind of got lucky. If the middle node hadn't been so perfectly correlated, the network might have struggled to silence the far-right weight. Later you'll learn about *regularization*, which forces weights with conflicting pressure to move toward 0.

As a preview, regularization is advantageous because if a weight has equal pressure upward and downward, it isn't good for anything. It's not helping either direction. In essence, regularization aims to say that only weights with really strong correlation can stay on; everything else should be silenced because it's contributing noise. It's sort of like natural selection, and as a side effect it would cause the neural network to train faster (fewer iterations) because the far-right weight has this problem of both positive and negative pressure.

In this case, because the far-right node isn't definitively correlative, the network would immediately start driving it toward 0. Without regularization (as you trained it before), you won't end up learning that the far-right input is useless until after the left and middle start to figure out their patterns. More on this later.

If networks look for correlation between an input column of data and the output column, what would the neural network do with the following dataset?

Training data				
1	0	1	→	1
0	1	1	→	1
0	0	1	→	0
1	1	1	→	0

Weight pressure				
+	0	+	→	1
0	+	+	→	1
0	0	−	→	0
−	−	−	→	0

There is no correlation between any input column and the output column. Every weight has an equal amount of upward pressure and downward pressure. *This dataset is a real problem for the neural network.*

Previously, you could solve for input datapoints that had both upward and downward pressure because other nodes would start solving for either the positive or negative predictions, drawing the balanced node to favor up or down. But in this case, all the inputs are equally balanced between positive and negative pressure. What do you do?

Learning indirect correlation

If your data doesn't have correlation, create intermediate data that does!

Previously, I described a neural network as an instrument that searches for correlation between input and output *datasets*. I want to refine this just a touch. In reality, neural networks search for correlation between their input and output *layers*.

You set the values of the input layer to be individual rows of the input data, and you try to train the network so that the output layer equals the output dataset. Oddly enough, the neural network doesn't know about data. It just searches for correlation between the input and output layers.

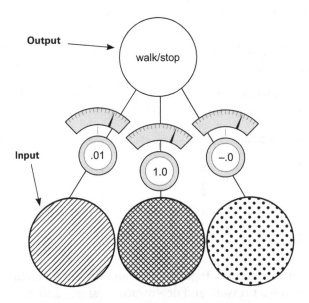

Unfortunately, this is a new streetlights dataset that has *no correlation* between the input and output. The solution is simple: use two of these networks. The first one will create an intermediate dataset that has limited correlation with the output, and the second will use that limited correlation to correctly predict the output.

> Because the input dataset doesn't correlate with the output dataset, you'll use the input dataset to create an intermediate dataset that *does* have correlation with the output. It's kind of like cheating.

Creating correlation

Here's a picture of the new neural network. You basically stack two neural networks on top of each other. The middle layer of nodes (`layer_1`) represents the *intermediate dataset*. The goal is to train this network so that even though there's no correlation between the input dataset and output dataset (`layer_0` and `layer_2`), the `layer_1` dataset that you create *using `layer_0`* will have correlation with `layer_2`.

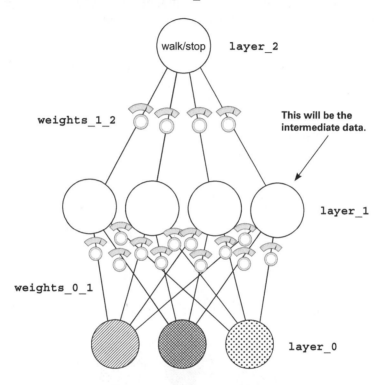

Note: this network is still just a function. It has a bunch of weights that are collected together in a particular way. Furthermore, gradient descent still works because you can calculate how much each weight contributes to the error and adjust it to reduce the error to 0. And that's exactly what you're going to do.

Stacking neural networks: A review

Chapter 3 briefly mentioned stacked neural networks. Let's review.

When you look at the following architecture, the prediction occurs exactly as you might expect when I say, "Stack neural networks." The output of the first lower network (`layer_0` to `layer_1`) is the input to the second upper neural network (`layer_1` to `layer_2`). The prediction for each of these networks is identical to what you saw before.

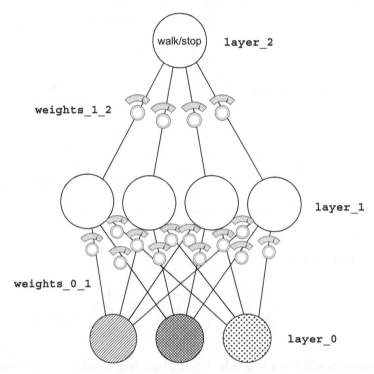

As you start to think about how this neural network learns, you already know a great deal. If you ignore the lower weights and consider their output to be the training set, the top half of the neural network (`layer_1` to `layer_2`) is just like the networks trained in the preceding chapter. You can use all the same learning logic to help them learn.

The part that you don't yet understand is how to update the weights between `layer_0` and `layer_1`. What do they use as their error measure? As you may remember from chapter 5, the cached/normalized error measure is called `delta`. In this case, you want to figure out how to know the `delta` values at `layer_1` so they can help `layer_2` make accurate predictions.

Backpropagation: Long-distance error attribution

The weighted average error

What's the prediction from `layer_1` to `layer_2`? It's a weighted average of the values at `layer_1`. If `layer_2` is too high by *x* amount, how do you know which values at `layer_1` contributed to the error? The ones with *higher weights* (`weights_1_2`) contributed more. The ones with *lower weights* from `layer_1` to `layer_2` contributed less.

Consider the extreme. Let's say the far-left weight from `layer_1` to `layer_2` was zero. How much did that node at `layer_1` cause the network's error? *Zero*.

It's so simple it's almost hilarious. The weights from `layer_1` to `layer_2` exactly describe how much each `layer_1` node contributes to the `layer_2` prediction. This means those weights also exactly describe how much each `layer_1` node contributes to the `layer_2` error.

How do you use the `delta` at `layer_2` to figure out the `delta` at `layer_1`? You multiply it by each of the respective weights for `layer_1`. It's like the prediction logic in reverse. This process of moving `delta` signal around is called *backpropagation*.

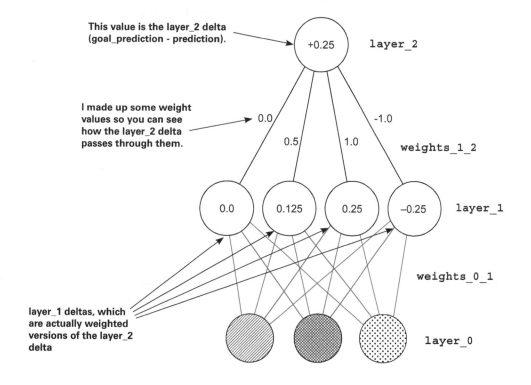

Backpropagation: Why does this work?

The weighted average delta

In the neural network from chapter 5, the `delta` variable told you the direction and amount the value of this node should change next time. All backpropagation lets you do is say, "Hey, if you want this node to be *x* amount higher, then each of these previous four nodes needs to be `x*weights_1_2` amount higher/lower, because these weights were amplifying the prediction by `weights_1_2` times."

When used in reverse, the `weights_1_2` matrix amplifies the error by the appropriate amount. It amplifies the error so you know how much each `layer_1` node should move up or down.

Once you know this, you can update each weight matrix as you did before. For each weight, multiply its output `delta` by its input `value`, and adjust the weight by that much (or you can scale it with `alpha`).

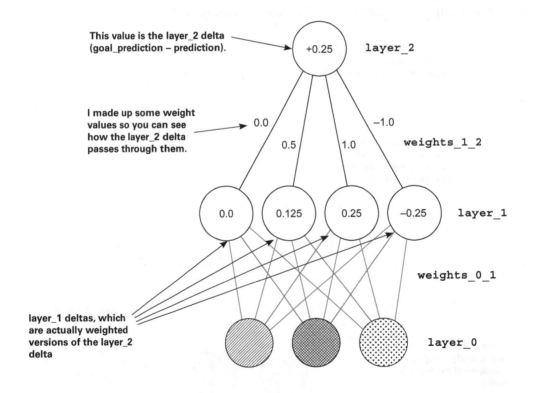

Linear vs. nonlinear

This is probably the hardest concept in the book.
Let's take it slowly.

I'm going to show you a phenomenon. As it turns out, you need one more piece to make this neural network train. Let's take it from two perspectives. The first will show why the neural network can't train without it. In other words, first I'll show you why the neural network is currently broken. Then, once you add this piece, I'll show you what it does to fix this problem. For now, check out this simple algebra:

```
1 * 10 * 2 = 100              1 * 0.25 * 0.9 = 0.225
5 * 20 = 100                  1 * 0.225 = 0.225
```

Here's the takeaway: for any two multiplications, I can accomplish the same thing using a single multiplication. As it turns out, this is bad. Check out the following:

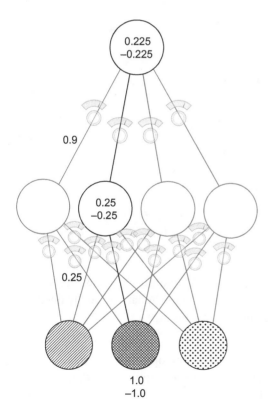

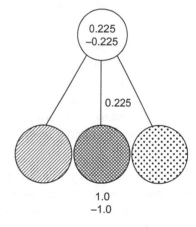

These two graphs show two training examples each, one where the input is 1.0 and another where the input is –1.0. The bottom line: *for any three-layer network you create, there's a two-layer network that has identical behavior.* Stacking two neural nets (as you know them at the moment) doesn't give you any more power. Two consecutive weighted sums is just a more expensive version of one weighted sum.

Why the neural network still doesn't work

If you trained the three-layer network as it is now, it wouldn't converge.

> **Problem:** For any two consecutive weighted sums of the input, there exists a single weighted sum with exactly identical behavior. Anything that the three-layer network can do, the two-layer network can also do.

Let's talk about the middle layer (`layer_1`) before it's fixed. Right now, each node (out of the four) has a weight coming to it from each of the inputs. Let's think about this from a correlation standpoint. Each node in the middle layer subscribes to a certain amount of correlation with each input node. If the weight from an input to the middle layer is 1.0, then it subscribes to exactly 100% of that node's movement. If that node goes up by 0.3, the middle node will follow.

If the weight connecting two nodes is 0.5, each node in the middle layer subscribes to exactly 50% of that node's movement.

The only way the middle node can escape the correlation of one particular input node is if it subscribes to additional correlation from another input node. *Nothing new* is being contributed to this neural network. Each hidden node subscribes to a little correlation from the input nodes.

The middle nodes don't get to add anything to the conversation; they don't get to have correlation of their own. They're more or less correlated to various input nodes.

layer_2

weights_1_2

layer_1

weights_0_1

layer_0

But because you *know* that in the new dataset there is no correlation between any of the inputs and the output, how can the middle layer help? It mixes up a bunch of correlation that's already useless. What you really need is for the middle layer to be able to selectively correlate with the input.

You want the middle layer to *sometimes* correlate with an input, and *sometimes not correlate*. That gives it correlation of its own. This gives the middle layer the opportunity to not just always be *x*% correlated to one input and *y*% correlated to another input. Instead, it can be *x*% correlated to one input only when it wants to be, but other times not be correlated at all. This is called *conditional correlation* or *sometimes correlation*.

The secret to sometimes correlation

Turn off the node when the value would be below 0.

This might seem too simple to work, but consider this: if a node's value dropped below 0, normally the node would still have the same correlation to the input as always. It would just happen to be negative in value. But if you turn off the node (setting it to 0) when it would be negative, then it has *zero correlation to any inputs* whenever it's negative.

What does this mean? The node can now selectively pick and choose when it wants to be correlated to something. This allows it to say something like, "Make me perfectly correlated to the left input, but only when the right input is turned off." How can it do this? Well, if the weight from the left input is 1.0 and the weight from the right input is a huge negative number, then turning on both the left and right inputs will cause the node to be 0 all the time. But if only the left input is on, the node will take on the value of the left input.

This wasn't possible before. Earlier, the middle node was either always correlated to an input or always not correlated. Now it can be conditional. Now it can speak for itself.

> **Solution:** By turning off any middle node whenever it would be negative, you allow the network to sometimes subscribe to correlation from various inputs. This is impossible for two-layer neural networks, thus adding power to three-layer nets.

The fancy term for this "if the node would be negative, set it to 0" logic is *nonlinearity*. Without this tweak, the neural network is *linear*. Without this technique, the output layer only gets to pick from the same correlation it had in the two-layer network. It's subscribing to pieces of the input layer, which means it can't solve the new streetlights dataset.

There are many kinds of nonlinearities. But the one discussed here is, in many cases, the best one to use. It's also the simplest. (It's called `relu`.)

For what it's worth, most other books and courses say that consecutive matrix multiplication is a linear transformation. I find this unintuitive. It also makes it harder to understand what nonlinearities contribute and why you choose one over the other (which we'll get to later). It says, "Without the nonlinearity, two matrix multiplications might as well be 1." My explanation, although not the most concise answer, is an intuitive explanation of why you need nonlinearities.

A quick break

That last part probably felt a little abstract, and that's totally OK.

Here's the deal. Previous chapters worked with simple algebra, so everything was ultimately grounded in fundamentally simple tools. This chapter started building on the premises you learned earlier. Previously, you learned lessons like this:

> You can compute the relationship between the error and any one of the weights so that you know how changing the weight changes the error. You can then use this to reduce the error to 0.

That was a *massive lesson*. But now we're moving past it. Because we already worked through why that works, you can take the statement at face value. The next big lesson came at the beginning of this chapter:

> Adjusting the weights to reduce the error over a series of training examples ultimately searches for correlation between the input and the output layers. If no correlation exists, then the error will never reach 0.

This is an *even bigger lesson*. It largely means you can put the previous lesson out of your mind for now. You don't need it. Now you're focused on correlation. The takeaway is that you can't constantly think about everything all at once. Take each lesson and let yourself trust it. When it's a more concise summarization (a higher abstraction) of more granular lessons, you can set aside the granular and focus on understanding the higher summarizations.

This is akin to a professional swimmer, biker, or similar athlete who requires a combined fluid knowledge of a bunch of small lessons. A baseball player who swings a bat learned thousands of little lessons to ultimately culminate in a great bat swing. But the player doesn't think of all of them when he goes to the plate. His actions are fluid—even subconscious. It's the same for studying these math concepts.

Neural networks look for correlation between input and output, and you no longer have to worry about how that happens. You just know it does. Now we're building on that idea. Let yourself relax and trust the things you've already learned.

Your first deep neural network

Here's how to make the prediction.

The following code initializes the weights and makes a forward propagation. New code is **bold**.

```python
import numpy as np

np.random.seed(1)

def relu(x):
    return (x > 0) * x

alpha = 0.2
hidden_size = 4

streetlights = np.array( [[ 1, 0, 1 ],
                          [ 0, 1, 1 ],
                          [ 0, 0, 1 ],
                          [ 1, 1, 1 ] ] )

walk_vs_stop = np.array([[ 1, 1, 0, 0]]).T

weights_0_1 = 2*np.random.random((3,hidden_size)) - 1
weights_1_2 = 2*np.random.random((hidden_size,1)) - 1

layer_0 = streetlights[0]
layer_1 = relu(np.dot(layer_0,weights_0_1))
layer_2 = np.dot(layer_1,weights_1_2)
```

This function sets all negative numbers to 0.

Two sets of weights now to connect the three layers (randomly initialized)

The output of layer_1 is sent through relu, where negative values become 0. This is the input for the next layer, layer_2.

For each piece of the code, follow along with the figure. Input data comes into `layer_0`. Via the `dot` function, the signal travels up the weights from `layer_0` to `layer_1` (performing a weighted sum at each of the four `layer_1` nodes). These weighted sums at `layer_1` are then passed through the `relu` function, which converts all negative numbers to 0. Then a final weighted sum is performed into the final node, `layer_2`.

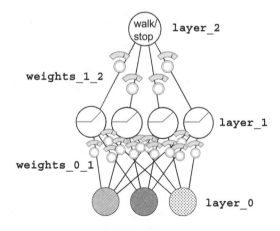

Backpropagation in code

You can learn the amount that each weight contributes to the final error.

At the end of the previous chapter, I made an assertion that it would be important to memorize the two-layer neural network code so you could quickly and easily recall it when I reference more-advanced concepts. This is when that memorization matters.

The following listing is the new learning code, and it's essential that you recognize and understand the parts addressed in the previous chapters. If you get lost, go to chapter 5, memorize the code, and then come back. It will make a big difference someday.

```python
import numpy as np

np.random.seed(1)

def relu(x):                        # Returns x if x > 0;
    return (x > 0) * x              # returns 0 otherwise

def relu2deriv(output):             # Returns 1 for input > 0;
    return output>0                 # returns 0 otherwise

alpha = 0.2
hidden_size = 4
                                    # This line computes the
weights_0_1 = 2*np.random.random((3,hidden_size)) - 1    # delta at layer_1 given
weights_1_2 = 2*np.random.random((hidden_size,1)) - 1    # the delta at layer_2
                                    # by taking the layer_2_
for iteration in range(60):                              # delta and multiplying
    layer_2_error = 0                                    # it by its connecting
    for i in range(len(streetlights)):                   # weights_1_2.
        layer_0 = streetlights[i:i+1]
        layer_1 = relu(np.dot(layer_0,weights_0_1))
        layer_2 = np.dot(layer_1,weights_1_2)

        layer_2_error += np.sum((layer_2 - walk_vs_stop[i:i+1]) ** 2)

        layer_2_delta = (walk_vs_stop[i:i+1] - layer_2)
        layer_1_delta=layer_2_delta.dot(weights_1_2.T)*relu2deriv(layer_1)

        weights_1_2 += alpha * layer_1.T.dot(layer_2_delta)
        weights_0_1 += alpha * layer_0.T.dot(layer_1_delta)

    if(iteration % 10 == 9):
        print("Error:" + str(layer_2_error))
```

Believe it or not, the only truly new code is in bold. Everything else is fundamentally the same as in previous pages. The `relu2deriv` function returns 1 when `output > 0`; otherwise, it returns 0. This is the *slope* (the *derivative*) of the `relu` function. It serves an important purpose, as you'll see in a moment.

Remember, the goal is *error attribution*. It's about figuring out how much each weight contributed to the final error. In the first (two-layer) neural network, you calculated a delta variable, which told you how much higher or lower you wanted the output prediction to be. Look at the code here. You compute the `layer_2_delta` in the same way. Nothing new. (Again, go back to chapter 5 if you've forgotten how that part works.)

Now that you know how much the final prediction should move up or down (delta), you need to figure out how much each middle (`layer_1`) node should move up or down. These are effectively *intermediate predictions*. Once you have the delta at `layer_1`, you can use the same processes as before for calculating a weight update (for each weight, multiply its input value by its output delta and increase the weight value by that much).

How do you calculate the deltas for `layer_1`? First, do the obvious: multiply the output delta by each weight attached to it. This gives a weighting of how much each weight contributed to that error. There's one more thing to factor in. If relu set the output to a `layer_1` node to be 0, then it didn't contribute to the error. When this is true, you should also set the delta of that node to 0. Multiplying each `layer_1` node by the relu2deriv function accomplishes this. relu2deriv is either 1 or 0, depending on whether the `layer_1` value is greater than 0.

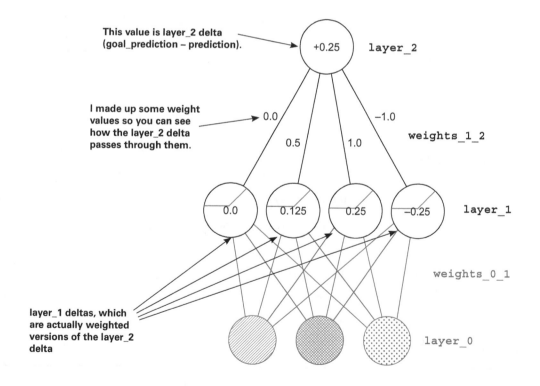

One iteration of backpropagation

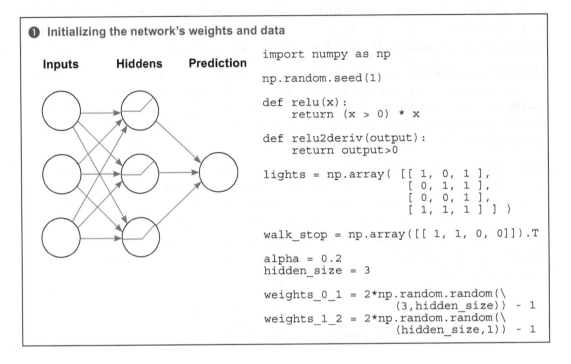

❶ **Initializing the network's weights and data**

Inputs   Hiddens   Prediction

```
import numpy as np

np.random.seed(1)

def relu(x):
    return (x > 0) * x

def relu2deriv(output):
    return output>0

lights = np.array( [[ 1, 0, 1 ],
                    [ 0, 1, 1 ],
                    [ 0, 0, 1 ],
                    [ 1, 1, 1 ] ] )

walk_stop = np.array([[ 1, 1, 0, 0]]).T

alpha = 0.2
hidden_size = 3

weights_0_1 = 2*np.random.random(\
              (3,hidden_size)) - 1
weights_1_2 = 2*np.random.random(\
              (hidden_size,1)) - 1
```

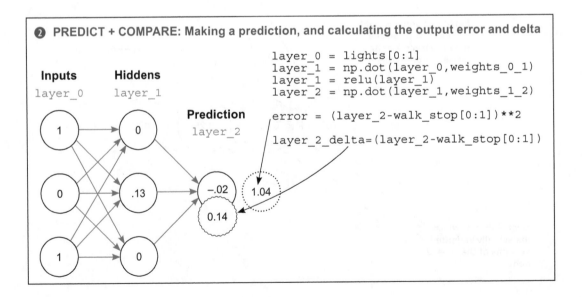

❷ **PREDICT + COMPARE: Making a prediction, and calculating the output error and delta**

Inputs   **Hiddens**
layer_0   layer_1

Prediction
layer_2

```
layer_0 = lights[0:1]
layer_1 = np.dot(layer_0,weights_0_1)
layer_1 = relu(layer_1)
layer_2 = np.dot(layer_1,weights_1_2)

error = (layer_2-walk_stop[0:1])**2

layer_2_delta=(layer_2-walk_stop[0:1])
```

Inputs: 1, 0, 1
Hiddens: 0, .13, 0
Prediction: −.02
1.04
0.14

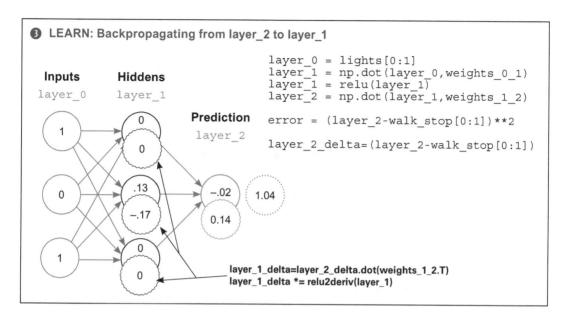

❸ **LEARN: Backpropagating from layer_2 to layer_1**

Inputs **Hiddens**
layer_0 layer_1

```
layer_0 = lights[0:1]
layer_1 = np.dot(layer_0,weights_0_1)
layer_1 = relu(layer_1)
layer_2 = np.dot(layer_1,weights_1_2)

error = (layer_2-walk_stop[0:1])**2

layer_2_delta=(layer_2-walk_stop[0:1])
```

Prediction
layer_2

```
layer_1_delta=layer_2_delta.dot(weights_1_2.T)
layer_1_delta *= relu2deriv(layer_1)
```

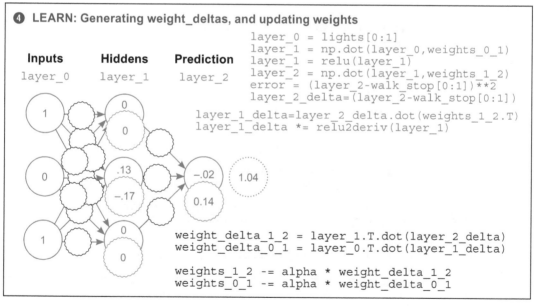

❹ **LEARN: Generating weight_deltas, and updating weights**

Inputs **Hiddens** **Prediction**
layer_0 layer_1 layer_2

```
layer_0 = lights[0:1]
layer_1 = np.dot(layer_0,weights_0_1)
layer_1 = relu(layer_1)
layer_2 = np.dot(layer_1,weights_1_2)
error = (layer_2-walk_stop[0:1])**2
layer_2_delta=(layer_2-walk_stop[0:1])

layer_1_delta=layer_2_delta.dot(weights_1_2.T)
layer_1_delta *= relu2deriv(layer_1)
```

```
weight_delta_1_2 = layer_1.T.dot(layer_2_delta)
weight_delta_0_1 = layer_0.T.dot(layer_1_delta)

weights_1_2 -= alpha * weight_delta_1_2
weights_0_1 -= alpha * weight_delta_0_1
```

As you can see, backpropagation is about calculating deltas for intermediate layers so you can perform gradient descent. To do so, you take the weighted average delta on layer_2 for layer_1 (weighted by the weights in between them). You then turn off (set to 0) nodes that weren't participating in the forward prediction, because they couldn't have contributed to the error.

Putting it all together

Here's the self-sufficient program you should be able to run (runtime output follows).

```
import numpy as np

np.random.seed(1)

def relu(x):
    return (x > 0) * x

def relu2deriv(output):
    return output>0

streetlights = np.array( [[ 1, 0, 1 ],
                          [ 0, 1, 1 ],
                          [ 0, 0, 1 ],
                          [ 1, 1, 1 ] ] )

walk_vs_stop = np.array([[ 1, 1, 0, 0]]).T

alpha = 0.2
hidden_size = 4

weights_0_1 = 2*np.random.random((3,hidden_size)) - 1
weights_1_2 = 2*np.random.random((hidden_size,1)) - 1

for iteration in range(60):
    layer_2_error = 0
    for i in range(len(streetlights)):
        layer_0 = streetlights[i:i+1]
        layer_1 = relu(np.dot(layer_0,weights_0_1))
        layer_2 = np.dot(layer_1,weights_1_2)

        layer_2_error += np.sum((layer_2 - walk_vs_stop[i:i+1]) ** 2)

        layer_2_delta = (layer_2 - walk_vs_stop[i:i+1])
        layer_1_delta=layer_2_delta.dot(weights_1_2.T)*relu2deriv(layer_1)

        weights_1_2 -= alpha * layer_1.T.dot(layer_2_delta)
        weights_0_1 -= alpha * layer_0.T.dot(layer_1_delta)

    if(iteration % 10 == 9):
        print("Error:" + str(layer_2_error))
```

Returns x if x > 0; returns 0 otherwise

Returns 1 for input > 0; returns 0 otherwise

```
Error:0.634231159844
Error:0.358384076763
Error:0.0830183113303
Error:0.0064670549571
Error:0.000329266900075
Error:1.50556226651e-05
```

Why do deep networks matter?

What's the point of creating "intermediate datasets" that have correlation?

Consider the cat picture shown here. Consider further that I had a dataset of images with cats and without cats (and I labeled them as such). If I wanted to train a neural network to take the pixel values and predict whether there's a cat in the picture, the two-layer network might have a problem.

Just as in the last streetlight dataset, no individual pixel correlates with whether there's a cat in the picture. Only different configurations of pixels correlate with whether there's a cat.

This is the essence of deep learning. Deep learning is all about creating intermediate layers (datasets) wherein each node in an intermediate layer represents the presence or absence of a different configuration of inputs.

This way, for the cat images dataset, no individual pixel has to correlate with whether there's a cat in the photo. Instead, the middle layer will attempt to identify different configurations of pixels that may or may not correlate with a cat (such as an ear, or cat eyes, or cat hair). The presence of many cat-like configurations will then give the final layer the information (correlation) it needs to correctly predict the presence or absence of a cat.

Believe it or not, you can take the three-layer network and continue to stack more and more layers. Some neural networks have hundreds of layers, each node playing its part in detecting different configurations of input data. The rest of this book will be dedicated to studying different phenomena within these layers in an effort to explore the full power of deep neural networks.

Toward that end, I must issue the same challenge I did in chapter 5: memorize the previous code. You'll need to be very familiar with each of the operations in the code in order for the following chapters to be readable. Don't progress past this point until you can build a three-layer neural network from memory!

how to picture neural networks: 7
in your head and on paper

In this chapter

- Correlation summarization

- Simplified visualization

- Seeing the network predict

- Visualizing using letters instead of pictures

- Linking variables

- The importance of visualization tools

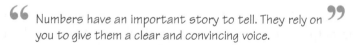

“ Numbers have an important story to tell. They rely on ” you to give them a clear and convincing voice.

—Stephen Few, IT innovator, teacher, and consultant

It's time to simplify

It's impractical to think about everything all the time. Mental tools can help.

Chapter 6 finished with a code example that was quite impressive. Just the neural network contained 35 lines of incredibly dense code. Reading through it, it's clear there's a lot going on; and that code includes over 100 pages of concepts that, when combined, can predict whether it's safe to cross the street.

I hope you're continuing to rebuild these examples from memory in each chapter. As the examples get larger, this exercise becomes less about remembering specific letters of code and more about remembering concepts and then rebuilding the code based on those concepts.

In this chapter, this construction of efficient concepts in your mind is exactly what I want to talk about. Even though it's not an architecture or experiment, it's perhaps the most important value I can give you. In this case, I want to show how I summarize all the little lessons in an efficient way in my mind so that I can do things like build new architectures, debug experiments, and use an architecture on new problems and new datasets.

Let's start by reviewing the concepts you've learned so far.

This book began with small lessons and then built layers of abstraction on top of them. We began by talking about the ideas behind machine learning in general. Then we progressed to how individual linear nodes (or *neurons*) learned, followed by horizontal groups of neurons (layers) and then vertical groups (stacks of layers). Along the way, we discussed how learning is actually just reducing error to 0, and we used calculus to discover how to change each weight in the network to help move the error in the direction of 0.

Next, we discussed how neural networks search for (and sometimes create) correlation between the input and output datasets. This last idea allowed us to overlook the previous lessons on how individual neurons behaved because it concisely summarizes the previous lessons. The sum total of the neurons, gradients, stacks of layers, and so on lead to a single idea: neural networks find and create correlation.

Holding onto this idea of correlation instead of the previous smaller ideas is important to learning deep learning. Otherwise, it would be easy to become overwhelmed with the complexity of neural networks. Let's create a name for this idea: the *correlation summarization*.

Correlation summarization

This is the key to sanely moving forward to more advanced neural networks.

Correlation summarization

Neural networks seek to find direct and indirect correlation between an input layer and an output layer, which are determined by the input and output datasets, respectively.

At the 10,000-foot level, this is what all neural networks do. Given that a neural network is really just a series of matrices connected by layers, let's zoom in slightly and consider what any particular weight matrix is doing.

Local correlation summarization

Any given set of weights optimizes to learn how to correlate its input layer with what the output layer says it should be.

When you have only two layers (input and output), the weight matrix knows what the output layer says it should be based on the output dataset. It looks for correlation between the input and output datasets because they're captured in the input and output layers. But this becomes more nuanced when you have multiple layers, remember?

Global correlation summarization

What an earlier layer says it should be can be determined by taking what a later layer says it should be and multiplying it by the weights in between them. This way, later layers can tell earlier layers what kind of signal they need, to ultimately find correlation with the output. This cross-communication is called *backpropagation*.

When global correlation teaches each layer what it should be, local correlation can optimize weights locally. When a neuron in the final layer says, "I need to be a little higher," it then proceeds to tell all the neurons in the layer immediately preceding it, "Hey, previous layer, send me higher signal." They then tell the neurons preceding them, "Hey. Send us higher signal." It's like a giant game of telephone—at the end of the game, every layer knows which of its neurons need to be higher and lower, and the local correlation summarization takes over, updating the weights accordingly.

The previously overcomplicated visualization

While simplifying the mental picture, let's simplify the visualization as well.

At this point, I expect the visualization of neural networks in your head is something like the picture shown here (because that's the one we used). The input dataset is in `layer_0`, connected by a weight matrix (a bunch of lines) to `layer_1`, and so on. This was a useful tool to learn the basics of how collections of weights and layers come together to learn a function.

But moving forward, this picture has too much detail. Given the correlation summarization, you already know you no longer need to worry about how individual weights are updated. Later layers already know how to communicate to earlier layers and tell them, "Hey, I need higher signal" or "Hey, I need lower signal." Truth be told, you don't really care about the weight values anymore, only that they're behaving as they should, properly capturing correlation in a way that generalizes.

To reflect this change, let's update the visualization on paper. We'll also do a few other things that will make sense later. As you know, the neural network is a series of weight matrices. When you're using the network, you also end up creating vectors corresponding to each layer.

In the figure, the weight matrices are the lines going from node to node, and the vectors are the strips of nodes. For example, `weights_1_2` is a matrix, `weights_0_1` is a matrix, and `layer_1` is a vector.

In later chapters, we'll arrange vectors and matrices in increasingly creative ways, so instead of all this detail showing each node connected by each weight (which gets hard to read if we have, say, 500 nodes in `layer_1`), let's instead think in general terms. Let's think of them as vectors and matrices of arbitrary size.

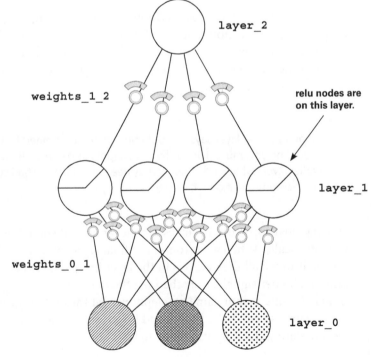

layer_2

weights_1_2

relu nodes are on this layer.

layer_1

weights_0_1

layer_0

The simplified visualization

Neural networks are like LEGO bricks, and each brick is a vector or matrix.

Moving forward, we'll build new neural network architectures in the same way people build new structures with LEGO pieces. The great thing about the correlation summarization is that all the bits and pieces that lead to it (backpropagation, gradient descent, alpha, dropout, mini-batching, and so on) don't depend on a particular configuration of the LEGOs. No matter how you piece together the series of matrices, gluing them together with layers, the neural network will try to learn the pattern in the data by modifying the weights between wherever you put the input layer and the output layer.

To reflect this, we'll build all the neural networks with the pieces shown at right. The strip is a vector, the box is a matrix, and the circles are individual weights. Note that the box can be viewed as a "vector of vectors," horizontally or vertically.

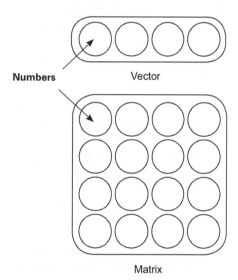

Numbers Vector

Matrix

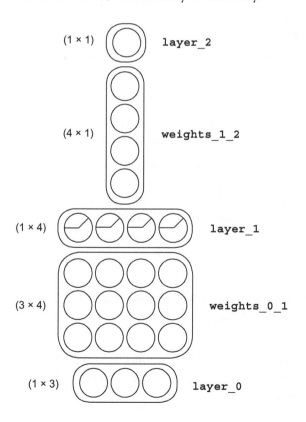

(1 × 1) layer_2

(4 × 1) weights_1_2

(1 × 4) layer_1

(3 × 4) weights_0_1

(1 × 3) layer_0

The big takeaway

The picture at left still gives you all the information you need to build a neural network. You know the shapes and sizes of all the layers and matrices. The detail from before isn't necessary when you know the correlation summarization and everything that went into it. But we aren't finished: we can simplify even further.

Simplifying even further

The dimensionality of the matrices is determined by the layers.

In the previous section, you may have noticed a pattern. Each matrix's dimensionality (number of rows and columns) has a direct relationship to the dimensionality of the layers before and after them. Thus, we can simplify the visualization even further.

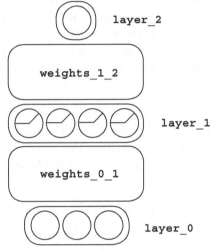

Consider the visualization shown at right. We still have all the information needed to build a neural network. We can infer that weights_0_1 is a (3 × 4) matrix because the previous layer (layer_0) has three dimensions and the next layer (layer_1) has four dimensions. Thus, in order for the matrix to be big enough to have a single weight connecting each node in layer_0 to each node in layer_1, it must be a (3 × 4) matrix.

This allows us to start thinking about the neural networks using the correlation summarization. All this neural network will to do is adjust the weights to find correlation between layer_0 and layer_2. It will do this using all the methods mentioned so far in this book. But the different configurations of weights and layers between the input and output layers have a strong impact on whether the network is successful in finding correlation (and/or how fast it finds correlation).

The particular configuration of layers and weights in a neural network is called its *architecture*, and we'll spend the majority of the rest of this book discussing the pros and cons of various architectures. As the correlation summarization reminds us, the neural network adjusts weights to find correlation between the input and output layers, sometimes even inventing correlation in the hidden layers. Different architectures *channel signal to make correlation easier to discover*.

> Good neural architectures channel signal so that correlation is easy to discover. Great architectures also filter noise to help prevent overfitting.

Much of the research into neural networks is about finding new architectures that can find correlation faster and generalize better to unseen data. We'll spend the vast majority of the rest of this book discussing new architectures.

Let's see this network predict
Let's picture data from the streetlight example flowing through the system.

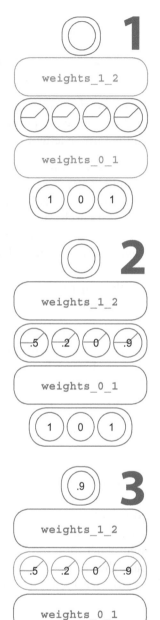

In figure 1, a single datapoint from the streetlight dataset is selected. `layer_0` is set to the correct values.

In figure 2, four different weighted sums of `layer_0` are performed. The four weighted sums are performed by `weights_0_1`. As a reminder, this process is called *vector-matrix multiplication*. These four values are deposited into the four positions of `layer_1` and passed through the `relu` function (setting negative values to 0). To be clear, the third value from the left in `layer_1` would have been negative, but the `relu` function sets it to 0.

As shown in figure 3, final step performs a weighted average of `layer_1`, again using the vector-matrix multiplication process. This yields the number 0.9, which is the network's final prediction.

> ### Review: Vector-matrix multiplication
>
> Vector-matrix multiplication performs multiple *weighted sums* of a vector. The matrix must have the same number of rows as the vector has values, so that each column in the matrix performs a unique weighted sum. Thus, if the matrix has four columns, four weighted sums will be generated. The weightings of each sum are performed depending on the values of the matrix.

Visualizing using letters instead of pictures

All these pictures and detailed explanations are actually a simple piece of algebra.

Just as we defined simpler pictures for the matrix and vector, we can perform the same visualization in the form of letters.

How do you visualize a *matrix* using math? Pick a capital letter. I try to pick one that's easy to remember, such as W for "weights." The little 0 means it's probably one of several Ws. In this case, the network has two. Perhaps surprisingly, I could have picked any capital letter. The little 0 is an extra that lets me call all my weight matrices W so I can tell them apart. It's your visualization; make it easy to remember.

How do you visualize a *vector* using math? Pick a lowercase letter. Why did I choose the letter l? Well, because I have a bunch of vectors that are layers, I thought l would be easy to remember. Why did I choose to call it l-zero? Because I have multiple layers, it seems nice to make all them ls and number them instead of having to think of new letters for every layer. There's no wrong answer here.

If that's how to visualize matrices and vectors in math, what do all the pieces in the network look like? At right, you can see a nice selection of variables pointing to their respective sections of the neural network. But defining them doesn't show how they relate. Let's combine the variables via vector-matrix multiplication.

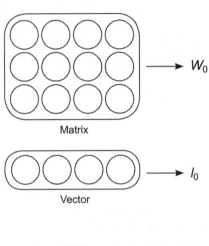

Matrix

Vector

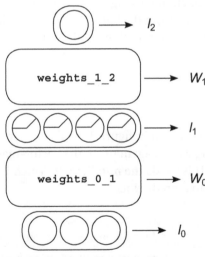

Linking the variables

The letters can be combined to indicate functions and operations.

Vector-matrix multiplication is simple. To visualize that two letters are being multiplied by each other, put them next to each other. For example:

Algebra	Translation
$l_0 W_0$	"Take the layer 0 vector and perform vector-matrix multiplication with the weight matrix 0."
$l_1 W_1$	"Take the layer 1 vector and perform vector-matrix multiplication with the weight matrix 1."

You can even throw in arbitrary functions like `relu` using notation that looks almost exactly like the Python code. This is crazy-intuitive stuff.

$l_1 = relu(l_0 W_0)$	"To create the layer 1 vector, take the layer 0 vector and perform vector-matrix multiplication with the weight matrix 0; then perform the `relu` function on the output (setting all negative numbers to 0)."
$l_2 = l_1 W_1$	"To create the layer 2 vector, take the layer 1 vector and perform vector-matrix multiplication with the weight matrix 1."

If you notice, the layer 2 algebra contains layer 1 as an input variable. This means you can represent the *entire neural network* in one expression by chaining them together.

$$l_2 = relu(l_0 W_0) W_1$$

Thus, all the logic in the forward propagation step can be contained in this one formula. Note: baked into this formula is the assumption that the vectors and matrices have the right dimensions.

Everything side by side

Let's see the visualization, algebra formula, and Python code in one place.

I don't think much dialogue is necessary on this page. Take a minute and look at each piece of forward propagation through these four different ways of seeing it. It's my hope that you'll truly grok forward propagation and understand the architecture by seeing it from different perspectives, all in one place.

```
layer_2 = relu(layer_0.dot(weights_0_1)).dot(weights_1_2)
```

$$l_2 = relu(l_0 W_0)W_1$$

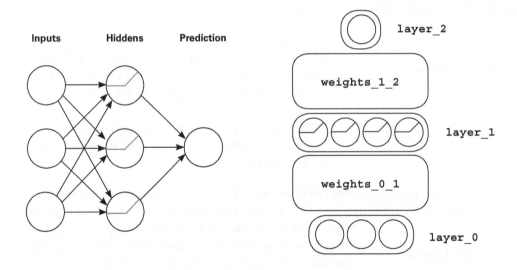

The importance of visualization tools

We're going to be studying new architectures.

In the following chapters, we'll be taking these vectors and matrices and combining them in some creative ways. My ability to describe each architecture for you is entirely dependent on our having a mutually agreed-on language for describing them. Thus, please don't move beyond this chapter until you can clearly see how forward propagation manipulates these vectors and matrices, and how these various forms of describing them are articulated.

> ### Key takeaway
>
> Good neural architectures channel signal so that correlation is easy to discover. Great architectures also filter noise to help prevent overfitting.

As mentioned previously, a neural architecture controls how signal flows through a network. How you create these architectures will affect the ways in which the network can detect correlation. You'll find that you want to create architectures that maximize the network's ability to focus on the areas where meaningful correlation exists, and minimize the network's ability to focus on the areas that contain noise.

But different datasets and domains have different characteristics. For example, image data has different kinds of signal and noise than text data. Even though neural networks can be used in many situations, different architectures will be better suited to different problems because of their ability to locate certain types of correlations. So, for the next few chapters, we'll explore how to modify neural networks to specifically find the correlation you're looking for. See you there!

learning signal and ignoring noise: introduction to regularization and batching

8

In this chapter

- Overfitting
- Dropout
- Batch gradient descent

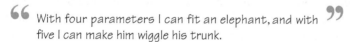

> " With four parameters I can fit an elephant, and with five I can make him wiggle his trunk. "
>
> —John von Neumann, mathematician, physicist, computer scientist, and polymath

Three-layer network on MNIST

Let's return to the MNIST dataset and attempt to classify it with the new network.

In last several chapters, you've learned that neural networks model correlation. The hidden layers (the middle one in the three-layer network) can even create intermediate correlation to help solve for a task (seemingly out of midair). How do you know the network is creating good correlation?

When we discussed stochastic gradient descent with multiple inputs, we ran an experiment where we froze one weight and then asked the network to continue training. As it was training, the dots found the bottom of the bowls, as it were. You saw the weights become adjusted to minimize the error.

When we froze the weight, the frozen weight still found the bottom of the bowl. For some reason, the bowl moved so that the frozen weight value became optimal. Furthermore, if we unfroze the weight to do some more training, it wouldn't learn. Why? Well, the error had already fallen to 0. As far as the network was concerned, there was nothing more to learn.

This begs the question, what if the input to the frozen weight was important to predicting baseball victory in the real world? What if the network had figured out a way to accurately predict the games in the training dataset (because that's what networks do: they minimize error), but it somehow forgot to include a valuable input?

Unfortunately, this phenomenon—overfitting—is extremely common in neural networks. We could say it's the archnemesis of neural networks; and the more powerful the neural network's expressive power (more layers and weights), the more prone the network is to overfit. An everlasting battle is going on in research, where people continually find tasks that need more powerful layers but then have to do lots of problem-solving to make sure the network doesn't overfit.

In this chapter, we're going to study the basics of *regularization*, which is key to combatting overfitting in neural networks. To do this, we'll start with the most powerful neural network (three-layer network with `relu` hidden layer) on the most challenging task (MNIST digit classification).

To begin, go ahead and train the network, as shown next. You should see the same results as those listed. Alas, the network learned to perfectly predict the training data. Should we celebrate?

```
import sys, numpy as np
from keras.datasets import mnist

(x_train, y_train), (x_test, y_test) = mnist.load_data()

images, labels = (x_train[0:1000].reshape(1000,28*28) \
                                              255, y_train[0:1000])
one_hot_labels = np.zeros((len(labels),10))

for i,l in enumerate(labels):
    one_hot_labels[i][l] = 1
labels = one_hot_labels

test_images = x_test.reshape(len(x_test),28*28) / 255
test_labels = np.zeros((len(y_test),10))
for i,l in enumerate(y_test):
    test_labels[i][l] = 1

np.random.seed(1)
relu = lambda x:(x>=0) * x
relu2deriv = lambda x: x>=0
alpha, iterations, hidden_size, pixels_per_image, num_labels = \
                                 (0.005, 350, 40, 784, 10)
weights_0_1 = 0.2*np.random.random((pixels_per_image,hidden_size)) - 0.1
weights_1_2 = 0.2*np.random.random((hidden_size,num_labels)) - 0.1

for j in range(iterations):
    error, correct_cnt = (0.0, 0)

    for i in range(len(images)):
        layer_0 = images[i:i+1]
        layer_1 = relu(np.dot(layer_0,weights_0_1))
        layer_2 = np.dot(layer_1,weights_1_2)
        error += np.sum((labels[i:i+1] - layer_2) ** 2)
        correct_cnt += int(np.argmax(layer_2) == \
                                          np.argmax(labels[i:i+1]))
        layer_2_delta = (labels[i:i+1] - layer_2)
        layer_1_delta = layer_2_delta.dot(weights_1_2.T)\
                                  * relu2deriv(layer_1)
        weights_1_2 += alpha * layer_1.T.dot(layer_2_delta)
        weights_0_1 += alpha * layer_0.T.dot(layer_1_delta)

    sys.stdout.write("\r"+ \
                    " I:"+str(j)+ \
                    " Error:" + str(error/float(len(images)))[0:5] +\
                    " Correct:" + str(correct_cnt/float(len(images))))
```

Returns x if x > 0;
returns 0 otherwise

Returns 1 for input > 0;
returns 0 otherwise

....
I:349 Error:0.108 Correct:1.0

Well, that was easy

The neural network perfectly learned to predict all 1,000 images.

In some ways, this is a real victory. The neural network was able to take a dataset of 1,000 images and learn to correlate each input image with the correct label.

How did it do this? It iterated through each image, made a prediction, and then updated each weight ever so slightly so the prediction was better next time. Doing this long enough on all the images eventually reached a state where the network could correctly predict on all the images.

Here's a non-obvious question: how well will the neural network do on an image it hasn't seen before? In other words, how well will it do on an image that wasn't part of the 1,000 images it was trained on? The MNIST dataset has many more images than just the 1,000 you trained on; let's try it.

In the notebook from the previous code are two variables: `test_images` and `test_labels`. If you execute the following code, it will run the neural network on these images and evaluate how well the network classifies them:

```
if(j % 10 == 0 or j == iterations-1):
  error, correct_cnt = (0.0, 0)

  for i in range(len(test_images)):

        layer_0 = test_images[i:i+1]
        layer_1 = relu(np.dot(layer_0,weights_0_1))
        layer_2 = np.dot(layer_1,weights_1_2)

        error += np.sum((test_labels[i:i+1] - layer_2) ** 2)
        correct_cnt += int(np.argmax(layer_2) == \
                                np.argmax(test_labels[i:i+1]))
  sys.stdout.write(" Test-Err:" + str(error/float(len(test_images)))[0:5] +\
            " Test-Acc:" + str(correct_cnt/float(len(test_images))))
  print()
```

```
Error:0.653 Correct:0.7073
```

The network did horribly! It predicted with an accuracy of only 70.7%. Why does it do so terribly on these new testing images when it learned to predict with 100% accuracy on the training data? How strange.

This 70.7% number is called the *test accuracy*. It's the accuracy of the neural network on data the network was *not* trained on. This number is important because it simulates how well the neural network will perform if you try to use it in the real world (which gives the network only images it hasn't seen before). This is the score that matters.

Memorization vs. generalization

Memorizing 1,000 images is easier than generalizing to all images.

Let's consider again how a neural network learns. It adjusts each weight in each matrix so the network is better able to take *specific inputs* and make a *specific prediction*. Perhaps a better question might be, "If we train it on 1,000 images, which it learns to predict perfectly, why does it work on other images at all?"

As you might expect, when the fully trained neural network is applied to a new image, it's guaranteed to work well only if the new image is *nearly identical to an image from the training data*. Why? Because the neural network learned to transform input data to output data for only *very specific input configurations*. If you give it something that doesn't look familiar, it will predict randomly.

This makes neural networks kind of pointless. What's the point of a neural network working only on the data you trained it on? You already know the correct classifications for those datapoints. Neural networks are useful only if they work on data you don't already know the answer to.

As it turns out, there's a way to combat this. Here I've printed out both the training *and testing* accuracy of the neural network *as it was training* (every 10 iterations). Notice anything interesting? You should see a clue to better networks:

```
I:0 Train-Err:0.722 Train-Acc:0.537 Test-Err:0.601 Test-Acc:0.6488
I:10 Train-Err:0.312 Train-Acc:0.901 Test-Err:0.420 Test-Acc:0.8114
I:20 Train-Err:0.260 Train-Acc:0.93 Test-Err:0.414 Test-Acc:0.8111
I:30 Train-Err:0.232 Train-Acc:0.946 Test-Err:0.417 Test-Acc:0.8066
I:40 Train-Err:0.215 Train-Acc:0.956 Test-Err:0.426 Test-Acc:0.8019
I:50 Train-Err:0.204 Train-Acc:0.966 Test-Err:0.437 Test-Acc:0.7982
I:60 Train-Err:0.194 Train-Acc:0.967 Test-Err:0.448 Test-Acc:0.7921
I:70 Train-Err:0.186 Train-Acc:0.975 Test-Err:0.458 Test-Acc:0.7864
I:80 Train-Err:0.179 Train-Acc:0.979 Test-Err:0.466 Test-Acc:0.7817
I:90 Train-Err:0.172 Train-Acc:0.981 Test-Err:0.474 Test-Acc:0.7758
I:100 Train-Err:0.166 Train-Acc:0.984 Test-Err:0.482 Test-Acc:0.7706
I:110 Train-Err:0.161 Train-Acc:0.984 Test-Err:0.489 Test-Acc:0.7686
I:120 Train-Err:0.157 Train-Acc:0.986 Test-Err:0.496 Test-Acc:0.766
I:130 Train-Err:0.153 Train-Acc:0.99 Test-Err:0.502 Test-Acc:0.7622
I:140 Train-Err:0.149 Train-Acc:0.991 Test-Err:0.508 Test-Acc:0.758
                          . . . .
I:210 Train-Err:0.127 Train-Acc:0.998 Test-Err:0.544 Test-Acc:0.7446
I:220 Train-Err:0.125 Train-Acc:0.998 Test-Err:0.552 Test-Acc:0.7416
I:230 Train-Err:0.123 Train-Acc:0.998 Test-Err:0.560 Test-Acc:0.7372
I:240 Train-Err:0.121 Train-Acc:0.998 Test-Err:0.569 Test-Acc:0.7344
I:250 Train-Err:0.120 Train-Acc:0.999 Test-Err:0.577 Test-Acc:0.7316
I:260 Train-Err:0.118 Train-Acc:0.999 Test-Err:0.585 Test-Acc:0.729
I:270 Train-Err:0.117 Train-Acc:0.999 Test-Err:0.593 Test-Acc:0.7259
I:280 Train-Err:0.115 Train-Acc:0.999 Test-Err:0.600 Test-Acc:0.723
I:290 Train-Err:0.114 Train-Acc:0.999 Test-Err:0.607 Test-Acc:0.7196
I:300 Train-Err:0.113 Train-Acc:0.999 Test-Err:0.614 Test-Acc:0.7183
I:310 Train-Err:0.112 Train-Acc:0.999 Test-Err:0.622 Test-Acc:0.7165
I:320 Train-Err:0.111 Train-Acc:0.999 Test-Err:0.629 Test-Acc:0.7133
I:330 Train-Err:0.110 Train-Acc:0.999 Test-Err:0.637 Test-Acc:0.7125
I:340 Train-Err:0.109 Train-Acc:1.0 Test-Err:0.645 Test-Acc:0.71
I:349 Train-Err:0.108 Train-Acc:1.0 Test-Err:0.653 Test-Acc:0.7073
```

Overfitting in neural networks

Neural networks can get worse if you train them too much!

For some reason, the *test* accuracy went up for the first 20 iterations and then slowly decreased as the network trained more and more (during which time the *training* accuracy was still improving). This is common in neural networks. Let me explain the phenomenon via an analogy.

Imagine you're creating a mold for a common dinner fork, but instead of using it to create other forks, you want to use it to identify whether a particular utensil is a fork. If an object fits in the mold, you'll conclude that the object is a fork, and if it doesn't, you'll conclude that it's *not* a fork.

Let's say you set out to make this mold, and you start with a wet piece of clay and a big bucket of three-pronged forks, spoons, and knives. You then press each of the forks into the same place in the mold to create an outline, which sort of looks like a mushy fork. You repeatedly place all the forks in the clay over and over, hundreds of times. When you let the clay dry, you then find that none of the spoons or knives fit into this mold, but all the forks do. Awesome! You did it. You correctly made a mold that can fit only the shape of a fork.

But what happens if someone hands you a four-pronged fork? You look at your mold and notice that there's a specific outline for three thin prongs in the clay. The four-pronged fork doesn't fit. Why not? It's still a fork.

It's because the clay wasn't molded on any four-pronged forks. It was molded only on the three-pronged variety. In this way, the clay has *overfit* to recognize only the types of forks it was "trained" to shape.

This is exactly the same phenomenon you just witnessed in the neural network. It's an even closer parallel than you might think. One way to view the weights of a neural network is as a high-dimensional shape. As you train, this shape *molds* around the shape of the data, learning to distinguish one pattern from another. Unfortunately, the images in the testing dataset were *slightly* different from the patterns in the training dataset. This caused the network to fail on many of the testing examples.

A more official definition of a neural network that overfits is a neural network that has learned the *noise* in the dataset instead of making decisions based only on the *true signal*.

Where overfitting comes from

What causes neural networks to overfit?

Let's alter this scenario a bit. Picture the fresh clay again (unmolded). What if you pushed only a single fork into it? Assuming the clay was very thick, it wouldn't have as much detail as the previous mold (which was imprinted many times). Thus, it would be only a *very general shape of a fork*. This shape might be compatible with both the three- and four-pronged varieties of fork, because it's still a fuzzy imprint.

Assuming this information, the mold got worse at the testing dataset as you imprinted more forks because it learned more-detailed information about the training dataset it was being molded to. This caused it to reject images that were even the slightest bit off from what it had repeatedly seen in the training data.

What is this *detailed information* in the images that's incompatible with the test data? In the fork analogy, it's the number of prongs on the fork. In images, it's generally referred to as *noise*. In reality, it's a bit more nuanced. Consider these two dog pictures.

Everything that makes these pictures unique beyond what captures the essence of "dog" is included in the term *noise*. In the picture on the left, the pillow and the background are both noise. In the picture on the right, the empty, middle blackness of the dog is a form of noise as well. It's really the edges that tell you it's a dog; the middle blackness doesn't tell you anything. In the picture on the left, the middle of the dog has the furry texture and color of a dog, which could help the classifier correctly identify it.

How do you get neural networks to train only on the *signal* (the essence of a dog) and ignore the noise (other stuff irrelevant to the classification)? One way is *early stopping*. It turns out a large amount of noise comes in the fine-grained detail of an image, and most of the signal (for objects) is found in the general shape and perhaps color of the image.

The simplest regularization: Early stopping

Stop training the network when it starts getting worse.

How do you get a neural network to ignore the fine-grained detail and capture only the general information present in the data (such as the general shape of a dog or of an MNIST digit)? You don't let the network train long enough to learn it.

In the fork-mold example, it takes many forks imprinted many times to create the perfect outline of a three-pronged fork. The first few imprints generally capture only the shallow outline of a fork. The same can be said for neural networks. As a result, *early stopping* is the cheapest form of regularization, and if you're in a pinch, it can be quite effective.

This brings us to the subject this chapter is all about: *regularization*. Regularization is a subfield of methods for getting a model to *generalize* to new datapoints (instead of just memorizing the training data). It's a subset of methods that help the neural network learn the signal and ignore the noise. In this case, it's a toolset at your disposal to create neural networks that have these properties.

> ### Regularization
>
> Regularization is a subset of methods used to encourage generalization in learned models, often by increasing the difficulty for a model to learn the fine-grained details of training data.

The next question might be, how do you know when to stop? The only real way to know is to run the model on data that isn't in the training dataset. This is typically done using a second test dataset called a *validation set*. In some circumstances, if you used the test set for knowing when to stop, you could *overfit to the test set*. As a general rule, you don't use it to control training. You use a validation set instead.

Industry standard regularization: Dropout

The method: Randomly turn off neurons (set them to 0) during training.

This regularization technique is as simple as it sounds. During training, you randomly set neurons in the network to 0 (and usually the deltas on the same nodes during backpropagation, but you technically don't have to). This causes the neural network to train exclusively using *random subsections* of the neural network.

Believe it or not, this regularization technique is generally accepted as the go-to, state-of-the-art regularization technique for the vast majority of networks. Its methodology is simple and inexpensive, although the intuitions behind *why* it works are a bit more complex.

> ### Why dropout works (perhaps oversimplified)
> Dropout makes a big network act like a little one by randomly training little subsections of the network at a time, and little networks don't overfit.

It turns out that the smaller a neural network is, the less it's able to overfit. Why? Well, small neural networks don't have much expressive power. They can't latch on to the more granular details (noise) that tend to be the source of overfitting. They have room to capture only the big, obvious, high-level features.

This notion of *room* or *capacity* is really important to keep in your mind. Think of it like this. Remember the clay analogy? Imagine if the clay was made of sticky rocks the size of dimes. Would that clay be able to make a good imprint of a fork? Of course not. Those stones are much like the weights. They form around the data, capturing the patterns you're interested in. If you have only a few, larger stones, they can't capture nuanced detail. Each stone instead is pushed on by large parts of the fork, more or less *averaging* the shape (ignoring fine creases and corners).

Now, imagine clay made of very fine-grained sand. It's made up of millions and millions of small stones that can fit into every nook and cranny of a fork. This is what gives big neural networks the expressive power they often use to overfit to a dataset.

How do you get the power of a large neural network with the resistance to overfitting of the small neural network? Take the big neural network and turn off nodes randomly. What happens when you take a big neural network and use only a small part of it? It behaves like a small neural network. But when you do this randomly over potentially millions of different subnetworks, the sum total of the entire network still maintains its expressive power. Neat, eh?

Why dropout works: Ensembling works

Dropout is a form of training a bunch of networks and averaging them.

Something to keep in mind: neural networks always start out randomly. Why does this matter? Well, because neural networks learn by trial and error, this ultimately means every neural network learns a little differently. It may learn equally effectively, but no two neural networks are ever exactly the same (unless they start out exactly the same for some random or intentional reason).

This has an interesting property. When you overfit two neural networks, no two neural networks overfit in exactly the same way. Overfitting occurs only until every training image can be predicted perfectly, at which point the error == 0 and the network stops learning (even if you keep iterating). But because each neural network starts by predicting randomly and then adjusting its weights to make better predictions, each network inevitably makes different mistakes, resulting in different updates. This culminates in a core concept:

> Although it's likely that large, unregularized neural networks will overfit to noise, it's unlikely they will overfit to the *same* noise.

Why don't they overfit to the same noise? Because they start randomly, and they stop training once they've learned enough noise to disambiguate between all the images in the training set. The MNIST network needs to find only a handful of random pixels that happen to correlate with the output labels, to overfit. But this is contrasted with, perhaps, an even more important concept:

> Neural networks, even though they're randomly generated, still start by learning the biggest, most broadly sweeping features before learning much about the noise.

The takeaway is this: if you train 100 neural networks (all initialized randomly), they will each tend to latch onto different noise but similar broad *signal*. Thus, when they make mistakes, they will often make *differing* mistakes. If you allowed them to vote equally, their noise would tend to cancel out, revealing only what they all learned in common: *the signal*.

Dropout in code

Here's how to use dropout in the real world.

In the MNIST classification model, let's add dropout to the hidden layer, such that 50% of the nodes are turned off (randomly) during training. You may be surprised that this is only a three-line change in the code. Following is a familiar snippet from the previous neural network logic, with the dropout mask added:

```
i = 0
layer_0 = images[i:i+1]
dropout_mask = np.random.randint(2,size=layer_1.shape)

layer_1 *= dropout_mask * 2
layer_2 = np.dot(layer_1, weights_1_2)

error += np.sum((labels[i:i+1] - layer_2) ** 2)

correct_cnt += int(np.argmax(layer_2) == \
            np.argmax(labels[i+i+1]))

layer_2_delta = (labels[i:i+1] - layer_2)
layer_1_delta = layer_2_delta.dot(weights_1_2.T)\
            * relu2deriv(layer_1)

layer_1_delta *= dropout_mask

weights_1_2 += alpha * layer_1.T.dot(layer_2_delta)
weights_0_1 += alpha * layer_0.T.dot(layer_1_delta)
```

To implement dropout on a layer (in this case, layer_1), multiply the layer_1 values by a random matrix of 1s and 0s. This has the effect of randomly turning off nodes in layer_1 by setting them to equal 0. Note that dropout_mask uses what's called a *50% Bernoulli distribution* such that 50% of the time, each value in dropout_mask is 1, and (1 – 50% = 50%) of the time, it's 0.

This is followed by something that may seem a bit peculiar. You multiply layer_1 by 2. Why do you do this? Remember that layer_2 will perform a weighted sum of layer_1. Even though it's weighted, it's still a *sum* over the values of layer_1. If you turn off half the nodes in layer_1, that sum will be cut in half. Thus, layer_2 would increase its sensitivity to layer_1, kind of like a person leaning closer to a radio when the volume is too low to better hear it. But at test time, when you no longer use dropout, the volume would be back up to normal. This throws off layer_2's ability to listen to layer_1. You need to counter this by multiplying layer_1 by (1 / the percentage of turned on nodes). In this case, that's 1/0.5, which equals 2. This way, the volume of layer_1 is the same between training and testing, despite dropout.

```
import numpy, sys
np.random.seed(1)
def relu(x):
    return (x >= 0) * x                    Returns x if x > 0;
                                           returns 0 otherwise

def relu2deriv(output):                    Returns 1
    return output >= 0                     for input > 0

alpha, iterations, hidden_size = (0.005, 300, 100)
pixels_per_image, num_labels = (784, 10)

weights_0_1 = 0.2*np.random.random((pixels_per_image,hidden_size)) - 0.1
weights_1_2 = 0.2*np.random.random((hidden_size,num_labels)) - 0.1

for j in range(iterations):
    error, correct_cnt = (0.0,0)
    for i in range(len(images)):
        layer_0 = images[i:i+1]
        layer_1 = relu(np.dot(layer_0,weights_0_1))
        dropout_mask = np.random.randint(2, size=layer_1.shape)
        layer_1 *= dropout_mask * 2
        layer_2 = np.dot(layer_1,weights_1_2)

        error += np.sum((labels[i:i+1] - layer_2) ** 2)
        correct_cnt += int(np.argmax(layer_2) == \
                                        np.argmax(labels[i:i+1]))
        layer_2_delta = (labels[i:i+1] - layer_2)
        layer_1_delta=layer_2_delta.dot(weights_1_2.T)*relu2deriv(layer_1)
        layer_1_delta *= dropout_mask

        weights_1_2 += alpha * layer_1.T.dot(layer_2_delta)
        weights_0_1 += alpha * layer_0.T.dot(layer_1_delta)

    if(j%10 == 0):
        test_error = 0.0
        test_correct_cnt = 0

        for i in range(len(test_images)):
            layer_0 = test_images[i:i+1]
            layer_1 = relu(np.dot(layer_0,weights_0_1))
            layer_2 = np.dot(layer_1, weights_1_2)

            test_error += np.sum((test_labels[i:i+1] - layer_2) ** 2)
            test_correct_cnt += int(np.argmax(layer_2) == \
                                        np.argmax(test_labels[i:i+1]))

        sys.stdout.write("\n" + \
            "I:" + str(j) + \
            " Test-Err:" + str(test_error/ float(len(test_images)))[0:5] +\
            " Test-Acc:" + str(test_correct_cnt/ float(len(test_images)))+\
            " Train-Err:" + str(error/ float(len(images)))[0:5] +\
            " Train-Acc:" + str(correct_cnt/ float(len(images))))
```

Dropout evaluated on MNIST

If you remember from before, the neural network (without dropout) previously reached a test accuracy of 81.14% before falling down to finish training at 70.73% accuracy. When you add dropout, the neural network instead behaves this way:

```
I:0 Test-Err:0.641 Test-Acc:0.6333 Train-Err:0.891 Train-Acc:0.413
I:10 Test-Err:0.458 Test-Acc:0.787 Train-Err:0.472 Train-Acc:0.764
I:20 Test-Err:0.415 Test-Acc:0.8133 Train-Err:0.430 Train-Acc:0.809
I:30 Test-Err:0.421 Test-Acc:0.8114 Train-Err:0.415 Train-Acc:0.811
I:40 Test-Err:0.419 Test-Acc:0.8112 Train-Err:0.413 Train-Acc:0.827
I:50 Test-Err:0.409 Test-Acc:0.8133 Train-Err:0.392 Train-Acc:0.836
I:60 Test-Err:0.412 Test-Acc:0.8236 Train-Err:0.402 Train-Acc:0.836
I:70 Test-Err:0.412 Test-Acc:0.8033 Train-Err:0.383 Train-Acc:0.857
I:80 Test-Err:0.410 Test-Acc:0.8054 Train-Err:0.386 Train-Acc:0.854
I:90 Test-Err:0.411 Test-Acc:0.8144 Train-Err:0.376 Train-Acc:0.868
I:100 Test-Err:0.411 Test-Acc:0.7903 Train-Err:0.369 Train-Acc:0.864
I:110 Test-Err:0.411 Test-Acc:0.8003 Train-Err:0.371 Train-Acc:0.868
I:120 Test-Err:0.402 Test-Acc:0.8046 Train-Err:0.353 Train-Acc:0.857
I:130 Test-Err:0.408 Test-Acc:0.8091 Train-Err:0.352 Train-Acc:0.867
I:140 Test-Err:0.405 Test-Acc:0.8083 Train-Err:0.355 Train-Acc:0.885
I:150 Test-Err:0.404 Test-Acc:0.8107 Train-Err:0.342 Train-Acc:0.883
I:160 Test-Err:0.399 Test-Acc:0.8146 Train-Err:0.361 Train-Acc:0.876
I:170 Test-Err:0.404 Test-Acc:0.8074 Train-Err:0.344 Train-Acc:0.889
I:180 Test-Err:0.399 Test-Acc:0.807 Train-Err:0.333 Train-Acc:0.892
I:190 Test-Err:0.407 Test-Acc:0.8066 Train-Err:0.335 Train-Acc:0.898
I:200 Test-Err:0.405 Test-Acc:0.8036 Train-Err:0.347 Train-Acc:0.893
I:210 Test-Err:0.405 Test-Acc:0.8034 Train-Err:0.336 Train-Acc:0.894
I:220 Test-Err:0.402 Test-Acc:0.8067 Train-Err:0.325 Train-Acc:0.896
I:230 Test-Err:0.404 Test-Acc:0.8091 Train-Err:0.321 Train-Acc:0.894
I:240 Test-Err:0.415 Test-Acc:0.8091 Train-Err:0.332 Train-Acc:0.898
I:250 Test-Err:0.395 Test-Acc:0.8182 Train-Err:0.320 Train-Acc:0.899
I:260 Test-Err:0.390 Test-Acc:0.8204 Train-Err:0.321 Train-Acc:0.899
I:270 Test-Err:0.382 Test-Acc:0.8194 Train-Err:0.312 Train-Acc:0.906
I:280 Test-Err:0.396 Test-Acc:0.8208 Train-Err:0.317 Train-Acc:0.9
I:290 Test-Err:0.399 Test-Acc:0.8181 Train-Err:0.301 Train-Acc:0.908
```

Not only does the network instead peak at a score of 82.36%, it also doesn't overfit nearly as badly, finishing training with a testing accuracy of 81.81%. Notice that the dropout also slows down `Training-Acc`, which previously went straight to 100% and stayed there.

This should point to what dropout really is: it's noise. It makes it more difficult for the network to train on the training data. It's like running a marathon with weights on your legs. It's harder to train, but when you take off the weights for the big race, you end up running quite a bit faster because you trained for something that was much more difficult.

Batch gradient descent

Here's a method for increasing the speed of training and the rate of convergence.

In the context of this chapter, I'd like to briefly apply a concept introduced several chapters ago: mini-batched stochastic gradient descent. I won't go into too much detail, because it's something that's largely taken for granted in neural network training. Furthermore, it's a simple concept that doesn't get more advanced even with the most state-of-the-art neural networks.

Previously we trained one training example at a time, updating the weights after each example. Now, let's train 100 training examples at a time, averaging the weight updates among all 100 examples. The training/testing output is shown next, followed by the code for the training logic.

```
I:0 Test-Err:0.815 Test-Acc:0.3832 Train-Err:1.284 Train-Acc:0.165
I:10 Test-Err:0.568 Test-Acc:0.7173 Train-Err:0.591 Train-Acc:0.672
I:20 Test-Err:0.510 Test-Acc:0.7571 Train-Err:0.532 Train-Acc:0.729
I:30 Test-Err:0.485 Test-Acc:0.7793 Train-Err:0.498 Train-Acc:0.754
I:40 Test-Err:0.468 Test-Acc:0.7877 Train-Err:0.489 Train-Acc:0.749
I:50 Test-Err:0.458 Test-Acc:0.793 Train-Err:0.468 Train-Acc:0.775
I:60 Test-Err:0.452 Test-Acc:0.7995 Train-Err:0.452 Train-Acc:0.799
I:70 Test-Err:0.446 Test-Acc:0.803 Train-Err:0.453 Train-Acc:0.792
I:80 Test-Err:0.451 Test-Acc:0.7968 Train-Err:0.457 Train-Acc:0.786
I:90 Test-Err:0.447 Test-Acc:0.795 Train-Err:0.454 Train-Acc:0.799
I:100 Test-Err:0.448 Test-Acc:0.793 Train-Err:0.447 Train-Acc:0.796
I:110 Test-Err:0.441 Test-Acc:0.7943 Train-Err:0.426 Train-Acc:0.816
I:120 Test-Err:0.442 Test-Acc:0.7966 Train-Err:0.431 Train-Acc:0.813
I:130 Test-Err:0.441 Test-Acc:0.7906 Train-Err:0.434 Train-Acc:0.816
I:140 Test-Err:0.447 Test-Acc:0.7874 Train-Err:0.437 Train-Acc:0.822
I:150 Test-Err:0.443 Test-Acc:0.7899 Train-Err:0.414 Train-Acc:0.823
I:160 Test-Err:0.438 Test-Acc:0.797 Train-Err:0.427 Train-Acc:0.811
I:170 Test-Err:0.440 Test-Acc:0.7884 Train-Err:0.418 Train-Acc:0.828
I:180 Test-Err:0.436 Test-Acc:0.7935 Train-Err:0.407 Train-Acc:0.834
I:190 Test-Err:0.434 Test-Acc:0.7935 Train-Err:0.410 Train-Acc:0.831
I:200 Test-Err:0.435 Test-Acc:0.7972 Train-Err:0.416 Train-Acc:0.829
I:210 Test-Err:0.434 Test-Acc:0.7923 Train-Err:0.409 Train-Acc:0.83
I:220 Test-Err:0.433 Test-Acc:0.8032 Train-Err:0.396 Train-Acc:0.832
I:230 Test-Err:0.431 Test-Acc:0.8036 Train-Err:0.393 Train-Acc:0.853
I:240 Test-Err:0.430 Test-Acc:0.8047 Train-Err:0.397 Train-Acc:0.844
I:250 Test-Err:0.429 Test-Acc:0.8028 Train-Err:0.386 Train-Acc:0.843
I:260 Test-Err:0.431 Test-Acc:0.8038 Train-Err:0.394 Train-Acc:0.843
I:270 Test-Err:0.428 Test-Acc:0.8014 Train-Err:0.384 Train-Acc:0.845
I:280 Test-Err:0.430 Test-Acc:0.8067 Train-Err:0.401 Train-Acc:0.846
I:290 Test-Err:0.428 Test-Acc:0.7975 Train-Err:0.383 Train-Acc:0.851
```

Notice that the training accuracy has a smoother trend than it did before. Taking an average weight update consistently creates this kind of phenomenon during training. As it turns out, individual training examples are very noisy in terms of the weight updates they generate. Thus, averaging them makes for a smoother learning process.

```
import numpy as np
np.random.seed(1)

def relu(x):
    return (x >= 0) * x          ←——————  Returns x
                                           if x > 0

def relu2deriv(output):
    return output >= 0           ←——————  Returns 1
                                           for input > 0

batch_size = 100
alpha, iterations = (0.001, 300)
pixels_per_image, num_labels, hidden_size = (784, 10, 100)

weights_0_1 = 0.2*np.random.random((pixels_per_image,hidden_size)) - 0.1
weights_1_2 = 0.2*np.random.random((hidden_size,num_labels)) - 0.1

for j in range(iterations):
    error, correct_cnt = (0.0, 0)
    for i in range(int(len(images) / batch_size)):
        batch_start, batch_end = ((i * batch_size),((i+1)*batch_size))

        layer_0 = images[batch_start:batch_end]
        layer_1 = relu(np.dot(layer_0,weights_0_1))
        dropout_mask = np.random.randint(2,size=layer_1.shape)
        layer_1 *= dropout_mask * 2
        layer_2 = np.dot(layer_1,weights_1_2)

        error += np.sum((labels[batch_start:batch_end] - layer_2) ** 2)
        for k in range(batch_size):
            correct_cnt += int(np.argmax(layer_2[k:k+1]) == \
                    np.argmax(labels[batch_start+k:batch_start+k+1]))

            layer_2_delta = (labels[batch_start:batch_end]-layer_2) \
                                                        /batch_size
            layer_1_delta = layer_2_delta.dot(weights_1_2.T) * \
                                                relu2deriv(layer_1)
            layer_1_delta *= dropout_mask

            weights_1_2 += alpha * layer_1.T.dot(layer_2_delta)
            weights_0_1 += alpha * layer_0.T.dot(layer_1_delta)

    if(j%10 == 0):
        test_error = 0.0
        test_correct_cnt = 0

        for i in range(len(test_images)):
            layer_0 = test_images[i:i+1]
            layer_1 = relu(np.dot(layer_0,weights_0_1))
            layer_2 = np.dot(layer_1, weights_1_2)
```

The first thing you'll notice when running this code is that it runs much faster. This is because each `np.dot` function is now performing 100 vector dot products at a time. CPU architectures are much faster at performing dot products batched this way.

There's more going on here, however. Notice that `alpha` is 20 times larger than before. You can increase it for a fascinating reason. Imagine you were trying to find a city using a very wobbly compass. If you looked down, got a heading, and then ran 2 miles, you'd likely be way off course. But if you looked down, took 100 headings, and then averaged them, running 2 miles would probably take you in the general right direction.

Because the example takes an average of a noisy signal (the average weight change over 100 training examples), it can take bigger steps. You'll generally see batching ranging from size 8 to as high as 256. Generally, researchers pick numbers randomly until they find a `batch_size/alpha` pair that seems to work well.

Summary

This chapter addressed two of the most widely used methods for increasing the accuracy and training speed of almost any neural architecture. In the following chapters, we'll pivot from sets of tools that are universally applicable to nearly all neural networks, to special-purpose architectures that are advantageous for modeling specific types of phenomena in data.

modeling probabilities and nonlinearities: | 9
activation functions

In this chapter

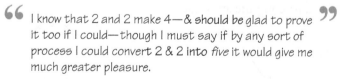

" I know that 2 and 2 make 4—& should be glad to prove it too if I could—though I must say if by any sort of process I could convert 2 & 2 into *five* it would give me much greater pleasure. "

—George Gordon Byron, letter to Annabella Milbanke, November 10, 1813

What is an activation function?

It's a function applied to the neurons in a layer during prediction.

An *activation function* is a function applied to the neurons in a layer during prediction. This should seem very familiar, because you've been using an activation function called `relu` (shown here in the three-layer neural network). The `relu` function had the effect of turning all negative numbers to 0.

Oversimplified, an activation function is any function that can take one number and return another number. But there are an infinite number of functions in the universe, and not all them are useful as activation functions.

There are several constraints on what makes a function an activation function. Using functions outside of these constraints is usually a bad idea, as you'll see.

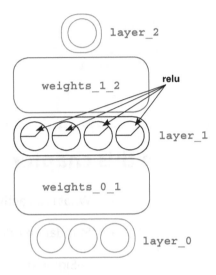

Constraint 1: The function must be continuous and infinite in domain.

The first constraint on what makes a proper activation function is that it must have an output number for *any* input. In other words, you shouldn't be able to put in a number that doesn't have an output for some reason.

A bit overkill, but see how the function on the left (four distinct lines) doesn't have y values for every x value? It's defined in only four spots. This would make for a horrible activation function. The function on the right, however, is continuous and infinite in domain. There is no input (x) for which you can't compute an output (y).

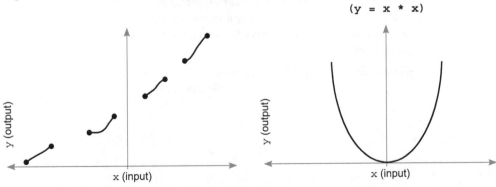

Constraint 2: Good activation functions are monotonic, never changing direction.

The second constraint is that the function is 1:1. It must never change direction. In other words, it must either be always increasing or always decreasing.

As an example, look at the following two functions. These shapes answer the question, "Given x as input, what value of y does the function describe?" The function on the left (y = x * x) isn't an ideal activation function because it isn't either always increasing or always decreasing.

How can you tell? Well, notice that there are many cases in which two values of x have a single value of y (this is true for every value except 0). The function on the right, however, is always increasing! There is no point at which two values of x have the same value of y:

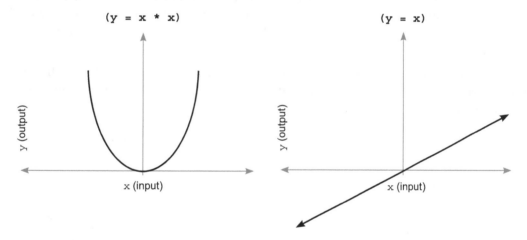

This particular constraint isn't technically a requirement. Unlike functions that have missing values (noncontinuous), you can optimize functions that aren't monotonic. But consider the implication of having multiple input values map to the same output value.

When you're learning in neural networks, you're searching for the right weight configurations to give a specific output. This problem can get a lot harder if there are multiple right answers. If there are multiple ways to get the same output, then the network has multiple possible perfect configurations.

An optimist might say, "Hey, this is great! You're more likely to find the right answer if it can be found in multiple places!" A pessimist would say, "This is terrible! Now you don't have a correct direction to go to reduce the error, because you can go in either direction and theoretically make progress."

Unfortunately, the phenomenon the pessimist identified is more important. For an advanced study of this subject, look more into convex versus non-convex optimization; many universities (and online classes) have entire courses dedicated to these kinds of questions.

Constraint 3: Good activation functions are nonlinear (they squiggle or turn).

The third constraint requires a bit of recollection back to chapter 6. Remember *sometimes correlation*? In order to create it, you had to allow the neurons to selectively correlate to input neurons such that a very negative signal from one input into a neuron could reduce how much it correlated to any input (by forcing the neuron to drop to 0, in the case of `relu`).

As it turns out, this phenomenon is facilitated by *any function that curves*. Functions that look like straight lines, on the other hand, scale the weighted average coming in. Scaling something (multiplying it by a constant like 2) doesn't affect how correlated a neuron is to its various inputs. It makes the collective correlation that's represented louder or softer. But the activation doesn't allow one weight to affect how correlated the neuron is to the other weights. What you *really* want is *selective* correlation. Given a neuron with an activation function, you want one incoming signal to be able to increase or decrease how correlated the neuron is to all the other incoming signals. All curved lines do this (to varying degrees, as you'll see).

Thus, the function shown here on the left is considered a linear function, whereas the one on the right is considered nonlinear and will usually make for a better activation function (there are exceptions, which we'll discuss later).

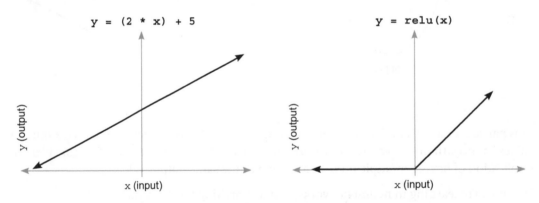

Constraint 4: Good activation functions (and their derivatives) should be efficiently computable.

This one is pretty simple. You'll be calling this function a lot (sometimes billions of times), so you don't want it to be too slow to compute. Many recent activation functions have become popular because they're so easy to compute at the expense of their expressiveness (`relu` is a great example of this).

Standard hidden-layer activation functions

Of the infinite possible functions, which ones are most commonly used?

Even with these constraints, it should be clear that an infinite (possibly transfinite?) number of functions could be used as activation functions. The last few years have seen a lot of progress in state-of-the-art activations. But there's still a relatively small list of activations that account for the vast majority of activation needs, and improvements on them have been minute in most cases.

sigmoid is the bread-and-butter activation.

sigmoid is great because it smoothly squishes the infinite amount of input to an output between 0 and 1. In many circumstances, this lets you interpret the output of any individual neuron as a probability. Thus, people use this nonlinearity both in hidden layers and output layers.

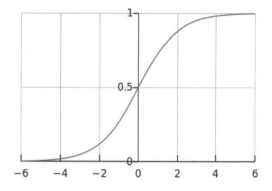

(Image: Wikipedia)

tanh is better than sigmoid for hidden layers.

Here's the cool thing about tanh. Remember modeling selective correlation? Well, sigmoid gives varying degrees of positive correlation. That's nice. tanh is the same as sigmoid except it's between –1 and 1!

This means it can also throw in some *negative correlation*. Although it isn't that useful for output layers (unless the data you're predicting goes between –1 and 1), this aspect of negative correlation is powerful for hidden layers; on many problems, tanh will outperform sigmoid in hidden layers.

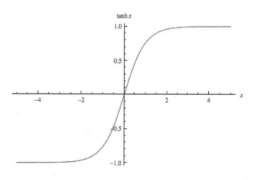

(Image: Wolfram Alpha)

Standard output layer activation functions
Choosing the best one depends on what you're trying to predict.

It turns out that what's best for hidden-layer activation functions can be quite different from what's best for output-layer activation functions, especially when it comes to classification. Broadly speaking, there are three major types of output layer.

Configuration 1: Predicting raw data values (no activation function)

This is perhaps the most straightforward but least common type of output layer. In some cases, people want to train a neural network to transform one matrix of numbers into another matrix of numbers, where the range of the output (difference between lowest and highest values) is something other than a probability. One example might be predicting the average temperature in Colorado given the temperature in the surrounding states.

The main thing to focus on here is ensuring that the output nonlinearity can predict the right answers. In this case, a `sigmoid` or `tanh` would be inappropriate because it forces every prediction to be between 0 and 1 (you want to predict any temperature, not just between 0 and 1). If I were training a network to do this prediction, I'd very likely train the network without an activation function on the output.

Configuration 2: Predicting unrelated yes/no probabilities (sigmoid)

You'll often want to make multiple binary probabilities in one neural network. We did this in the "Gradient descent with multiple inputs and outputs" section of chapter 5, predicting whether the team would win, whether there would be injuries, and the morale of the team (happy or sad) based on the input data.

As an aside, when a neural network has hidden layers, predicting multiple things at once can be beneficial. Often the network will learn something when predicting one label that will be useful to one of the other labels. For example, if the network got really good at predicting whether the team would win ballgames, the same hidden layer would likely be very useful for predicting whether the team would be happy or sad. But the network might have a harder time predicting happiness or sadness without this extra signal. This tends to vary greatly from problem to problem, but it's good to keep in mind.

In these instances, it's best to use the `sigmoid` activation function, because it models individual probabilities separately for each output node.

Configuration 3: Predicting which-one probabilities (softmax)

By far the most common use case in neural networks is predicting a single label out of many. For example, in the MNIST digit classifier, you want to predict *which* number is in the image. You know ahead of time that the image can't be more than one number. You can train this network with a `sigmoid` activation function and declare that the highest output probability is the most likely. This will work reasonably well. But it's far better to have an activation function that models the idea that "The more likely it's one label, the less likely it's any of the other labels."

Why do we like this phenomenon? Consider how weight updates are performed. Let's say the MNIST digit classifier should predict that the image is a 9. Also say that the raw weighted sums going into the final layer (before applying an activation function) are the following values:

	0	1	2	3	4	5	6	7	8	9
Raw dot product values	0.0	0.0	0.0	0.0	0.0	0.0	0.0	0.0	0.0	100

The network's raw input to the last layer predicts a 0 for every node but 9, where it predicts 100. You might call this perfect. Let's see what happens when these numbers are run through a `sigmoid` activation function:

`sigmoid`	.50	.50	.50	.50	.50	.50	.50	.50	.50	.99

Strangely, the network seems less sure now: 9 is still the highest, but the network seems to think there's a 50% chance that it could be any of the other numbers. Weird! `softmax`, on the other hand, interprets the input very differently:

`softmax`	0.0	0.0	0.0	0.0	0.0	0.0	0.0	0.0	0.0	1.0

This looks great. Not only is 9 the highest, but the network doesn't even suspect it's any of the other possible MNIST digits. This might seem like a theoretical flaw of `sigmoid`, but it can have serious consequences when you backpropagate. Consider how the mean squared error is calculated on the `sigmoid` output. In theory, the network is predicting nearly perfectly, right? Surely it won't backprop much error. Not so for `sigmoid`:

`sigmoid` MSE	.25	.25	.25	.25	.25	.25	.25	.25	.25	.00

Look at all the error! These weights are in for a massive weight update even though the network predicted perfectly. Why? For `sigmoid` to reach 0 error, it doesn't just have to predict the highest positive number for the true output; it also has to predict a 0 everywhere else. Where `softmax` asks, "Which digit seems like the best fit for this input?" `sigmoid` says, "You better believe that it's only digit 9 and doesn't have anything in common with the other MNIST digits."

The core issue: Inputs have similarity

Different numbers share characteristics. It's good to let the network believe that.

MNIST digits aren't all completely different: they have overlapping pixel values. The average 2 shares quite a bit in common with the average 3.

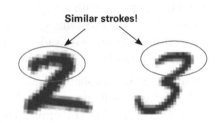

Similar strokes!

Why is this important? Well, as a general rule, similar inputs create similar outputs. When you take some numbers and multiply them by a matrix, if the starting numbers are pretty similar, the ending numbers will be pretty similar.

Consider the 2 and 3 shown here. If we forward propagate the 2 and a small amount of probability accidentally goes to the label 3, what does it mean for the network to consider this a big mistake and respond with a big weight update? It will penalize the network for recognizing a 2 by anything other than features that are exclusively related to 2s. It penalizes the network for recognizing a 2 based on, say, the top curve. Why? Because 2 and 3 share the same curve at the top of the image. Training with `sigmoid` would penalize the network for trying to predict a 2 based on this input, because by doing so it would be looking for the same input it does for 3s. Thus, when a 3 came along, the 2 label would get some probability (because part of the image looks 2ish).

What's the side effect? Most images share lots of pixels in the middle of images, so the network will start trying to focus on the edges. Consider the 2-detector node weights shown at right.

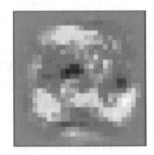

See how muddy the middle of the image is? The heaviest weights are the end points of the 2 toward the edge of the image. On one hand, these are probably the best individual indicators of a 2, but the best overall is a network that sees the entire shape for what it is. These individual indicators can be accidentally triggered by a 3 that's slightly off-center or tilted the wrong way. The network isn't learning the true essence of a 2 because it needs to learn 2 and *not* 1, *not* 3, *not* 4, and so on.

We want an output activation that won't penalize labels that are similar. Instead, we want it to pay attention to all the information that can be indicative of any potential input. It's also nice that a `softmax`'s probabilities always sum to 1. You can interpret any individual prediction as a global probability that the prediction is a particular label. `softmax` works better in both theory and practice.

softmax computation

softmax raises each input value exponentially and then divides by the layer's sum.

Let's see a softmax computation on the neural network's hypothetical output values from earlier. I'll show them here again so you can see the input to softmax:

	0	1	2	3	4	5	6	7	8	9
Raw dot product values	0.0	0.0	0.0	0.0	0.0	0.0	0.0	0.0	0.0	100

To compute a softmax on the whole layer, first raise each value exponentially. For each value x, compute e to the power of x (e is a special number ~2.71828...). The value of e^x is shown on the right.

Notice that it turns every prediction into a positive number, where negative numbers turn into very small positive numbers, and big numbers turn into very big numbers. (If you've heard of exponential growth, it was likely talking about this function or one very similar to it.)

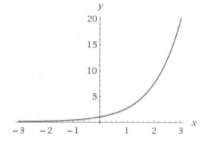

	0	1	2	3	4	5	6	7	8	9
e^x	1.0	1.0	1.0	1.0	1.0	1.0	1.0	1.0	1.0	...

2.688 * 10^43

In short, all the 0s turn to 1s (because 1 is the y intercept of e^x), and the 100 turns into a massive number (2 followed by 43 zeros). If there were any negative numbers, they turned into something between 0 and 1. The next step is to sum all the nodes in the layer and divide each value in the layer by that sum. This effectively makes every number 0 except the value for label 9.

softmax	0.0	0.0	0.0	0.0	0.0	0.0	0.0	0.0	0.0	1.0

The nice thing about softmax is that the higher the network predicts one value, the lower it predicts all the others. It increases what is called the *sharpness of attenuation*. It encourages the network to predict one output with very high probability.

To adjust how aggressively it does this, use numbers slightly higher or lower than e when exponentiating. Lower numbers will result in lower attenuation, and higher numbers will result in higher attenuation. But most people just stick with e.

Activation installation instructions

How do you add your favorite activation function to any layer?

Now that we've covered a wide variety of activation functions and explained their usefulness in hidden and output layers of neural networks, let's talk about the proper way to install one into a neural network. Fortunately, you've already seen an example of how to use a nonlinearity in your first deep neural network: you added a `relu` activation function to the hidden layer. Adding this to forward propagation was relatively straightforward. You took what `layer_1` would have been (without an activation) and applied the `relu` function to each value:

```
layer_0 = images[i:i+1]
layer_1 = relu(np.dot(layer_0,weights_0_1))
layer_2 = np.dot(layer_1,weights_1_2)
```

There's a bit of lingo here to remember. The *input to a layer* refers to the value before the nonlinearity. In this case, the input to `layer_1` is `np.dot(layer_0,weights_0_1)`. This isn't to be confused with the previous layer, `layer_0`.

Adding an activation function to a layer in forward propagation is relatively straightforward. But properly compensating for the activation function in backpropagation is a bit more nuanced.

In chapter 6, we performed an interesting operation to create the `layer_1_delta` variable. Wherever `relu` had forced a `layer_1` value to be 0, we also multiplied the `delta` by 0. The reasoning at the time was, "Because a `layer_1` value of 0 had no effect on the output prediction, it shouldn't have any impact on the weight update either. It wasn't responsible for the error." This is the extreme form of a more nuanced property. Consider the shape of the `relu` function.

The slope of `relu` for positive numbers is exactly 1. The slope of `relu` for negative numbers is exactly 0. Modifying the input to this function (by a tiny amount) will have a 1:1 effect if it was predicting positively, and will have a 0:1 effect (none) if it was predicting negatively. This slope is a measure of how much the output of `relu` will change given a change in its input.

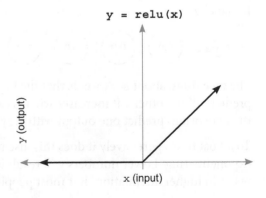

Because the purpose of `delta` at this point is to tell earlier layers "make my input higher or lower next time," this `delta` is very useful. It modifies the `delta` backpropagated from the following layer to take into account whether this node contributed to the error.

Thus, when you backpropagate, in order to generate `layer_1_delta`, multiply the backpropagated `delta` from `layer_2` (`layer_2_delta.dot(weights_1_2.T)`) by the slope of `relu` *at the point predicted in forward propagation*. For some `delta`s the slope is 1 (positive numbers), and for others it's 0 (negative numbers):

```
error += np.sum((labels[i:i+1] - layer_2) ** 2)

correct_cnt += int(np.argmax(layer_2) == \
                          np.argmax(labels[i:i+1]))

layer_2_delta = (labels[i:i+1] - layer_2)
layer_1_delta = layer_2_delta.dot(weights_1_2.T)\
                          * relu2deriv(layer_1)

weights_1_2 += alpha * layer_1.T.dot(layer_2_delta)
weights_0_1 += alpha * layer_0.T.dot(layer_1_delta)

def relu(x):
    return (x >= 0) * x              ←———————   Returns x if x > 0;
                                                returns 0 otherwise

def relu2deriv(output):
    return output >= 0              ←———————   Returns 1 for input > 0;
                                                returns 0 otherwise
```

`relu2deriv` is a special function that can take the output of `relu` and calculate the slope of `relu` at that point (it does this for all the values in the output vector). This begs the question, how do you make similar adjustments for all the other nonlinearities that aren't `relu`? Consider `relu` and `sigmoid`:

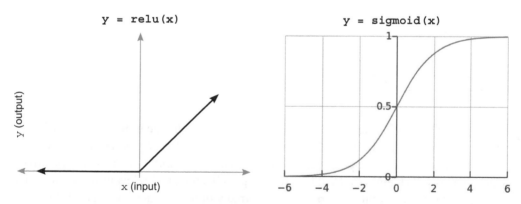

The important thing in these figures is that the slope is an indicator of how much a *tiny* change to the input affects the output. You want to modify the incoming `delta` (from the following layer) to take into account whether a weight update before this node would have any effect. Remember, the end goal is to adjust weights to reduce error. This step encourages the network to leave weights alone if adjusting them will have little to no effect. It does so by multiplying it by the slope. It's no different for `sigmoid`.

Multiplying delta by the slope

To compute layer_delta, multiply the backpropagated delta by the layer's slope.

layer_1_delta[0] represents how much higher or lower the first hidden node of layer 1 should be in order to reduce the error of the network (for a particular training example). When there's no nonlinearity, this is the weighted average delta of layer_2.

But the end goal of delta on a neuron is to inform the weights whether they should move. If moving them would have no effect, they (as a group) should be left alone. This is obvious for relu, which is either on or off. sigmoid is, perhaps, more nuanced.

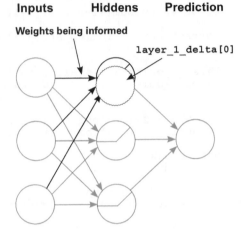

Inputs   Hiddens   Prediction

Weights being informed

layer_1_delta[0]

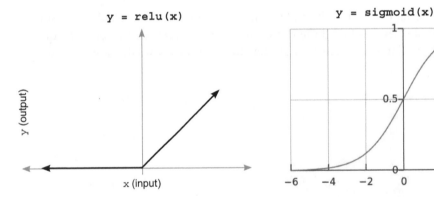

y = relu(x)

y (output)

x (input)

y = sigmoid(x)

1

0.5

0

−6   −4   −2   0   2   4   6

Consider a single sigmoid neuron. sigmoid's sensitivity to change in the input slowly increases as the input approaches 0 from either direction. But very positive and very negative inputs approach a slope of very near 0. Thus, as the input becomes very positive or very negative, small changes to the incoming weights become less relevant to the neuron's error at this training example. In broader terms, many hidden nodes are irrelevant to the accurate prediction of a 2 (perhaps they're used only for 8s). You shouldn't mess with their weights too much, because you could corrupt their usefulness elsewhere.

Inversely, this also creates a notion of *stickiness*. Weights that have previously been updated a lot in one direction (for similar training examples) confidently predict a high value or low value. These nonlinearities help make it harder for occasional erroneous training examples to corrupt intelligence that has been reinforced many times.

Converting output to slope (derivative)

Most great activations can convert their output to their slope. (Efficiency win!)

Now that you know that adding an activation to a layer changes how to compute `delta` for that layer, let's discuss how the industry does this efficiently. The new operation necessary is the computation of the derivative of whatever nonlinearity was used.

Most nonlinearities (all the popular ones) use a method of computing a derivative that will seem surprising to those of you who are familiar with calculus. Instead of computing the derivative at a certain point on its curve the normal way, most great activation functions have a means by which the *output* of the layer (at forward propagation) can be used to compute the derivative. This has become the standard practice for computing derivatives in neural networks, and it's quite handy.

Following is a small table for the functions you've seen so far, paired with their derivatives. `input` is a NumPy vector (corresponding to the input to a layer). `output` is the prediction of the layer. `deriv` is the derivative of the vector of activation derivatives corresponding to the derivative of the activation at each node. `true` is the vector of true values (typically 1 for the correct label position, 0 everywhere else).

Function	Forward prop	Backprop delta
relu	`ones_and_zeros = (input > 0)` `output = input*ones_and_zeros`	`mask = output > 0` `deriv = output * mask`
sigmoid	`output = 1/(1 + np.exp(-input))`	`deriv = output*(1-output)`
tanh	`output = np.tanh(input)`	`deriv = 1 - (output**2)`
softmax	`temp = np.exp(input)` `output /= np.sum(temp)`	`temp = (output - true)` `output = temp/len(true)`

Note that the `delta` computation for `softmax` is special because it's used only for the last layer. There's a bit more going on (theoretically) than we have time to discuss here. For now, let's install some better activation functions in the MNIST classification network.

Upgrading the MNIST network

Let's upgrade the MNIST network to reflect what you've learned.

Theoretically, the tanh function should make for a better hidden-layer activation, and softmax should make for a better output-layer activation function. When we test them, they do in fact reach a higher score. But things aren't always as simple as they seem.

I had to make a couple of adjustments in order to tune the network properly with these new activations. For tanh, I had to reduce the standard deviation of the incoming weights. Remember that you initialize the weights randomly. np.random.random creates a random matrix with numbers randomly spread between 0 and 1. By multiplying by 0.2 and subtracting by 0.1, you rescale this random range to be between –0.1 and 0.1. This worked great for relu but is less optimal for tanh. tanh likes to have a narrower random initialization, so I adjusted it to be between –0.01 and 0.01.

I also removed the error calculation, because we're not ready for that yet. Technically, softmax is best used with an error function called *cross entropy*. This network properly computes layer_2_delta for this error measure, but because we haven't analyzed why this error function is advantageous, I removed the lines to compute it.

Finally, as with almost all changes made to a neural network, I had to revisit the alpha tuning. I found that a much higher alpha was required to reach a good score within 300 iterations. And voilà! As expected, the network reached a higher testing accuracy of 87%.

```python
import numpy as np, sys
np.random.seed(1)

from keras.datasets import mnist
(x_train, y_train), (x_test, y_test) = mnist.load_data()

images, labels = (x_train[0:1000].reshape(1000,28*28)\
                                               / 255, y_train[0:1000])
one_hot_labels = np.zeros((len(labels),10))
for i,l in enumerate(labels):
    one_hot_labels[i][l] = 1
labels = one_hot_labels

test_images = x_test.reshape(len(x_test),28*28) / 255
test_labels = np.zeros((len(y_test),10))
for i,l in enumerate(y_test):
    test_labels[i][l] = 1

def tanh(x):
    return np.tanh(x)
def tanh2deriv(output):
    return 1 - (output ** 2)
def softmax(x):
    temp = np.exp(x)
    return temp / np.sum(temp, axis=1, keepdims=True)
```

```
alpha, iterations, hidden_size = (2, 300, 100)
pixels_per_image, num_labels = (784, 10)
batch_size = 100

weights_0_1 = 0.02*np.random.random((pixels_per_image,hidden_size))-0.01
weights_1_2 = 0.2*np.random.random((hidden_size,num_labels)) - 0.1

for j in range(iterations):
    correct_cnt = 0
    for i in range(int(len(images) / batch_size)):
        batch_start, batch_end=((i * batch_size),((i+1)*batch_size))
        layer_0 = images[batch_start:batch_end]
        layer_1 = tanh(np.dot(layer_0,weights_0_1))
        dropout_mask = np.random.randint(2,size=layer_1.shape)
        layer_1 *= dropout_mask * 2
        layer_2 = softmax(np.dot(layer_1,weights_1_2))

        for k in range(batch_size):
            correct_cnt += int(np.argmax(layer_2[k:k+1]) == \
                           np.argmax(labels[batch_start+k:batch_start+k+1]))
        layer_2_delta = (labels[batch_start:batch_end]-layer_2)\
                                     / (batch_size * layer_2.shape[0])
        layer_1_delta = layer_2_delta.dot(weights_1_2.T) \
                                             * tanh2deriv(layer_1)
        layer_1_delta *= dropout_mask

        weights_1_2 += alpha * layer_1.T.dot(layer_2_delta)
        weights_0_1 += alpha * layer_0.T.dot(layer_1_delta)
    test_correct_cnt = 0

    for i in range(len(test_images)):

        layer_0 = test_images[i:i+1]
        layer_1 = tanh(np.dot(layer_0,weights_0_1))
        layer_2 = np.dot(layer_1,weights_1_2)
        test_correct_cnt += int(np.argmax(layer_2) == \
                                np.argmax(test_labels[i:i+1]))
    if(j % 10 == 0):
        sys.stdout.write("\n"+ "I:" + str(j) + \
         " Test-Acc:"+str(test_correct_cnt/float(len(test_images)))+\
         " Train-Acc:" + str(correct_cnt/float(len(images))))
```

```
I:0 Test-Acc:0.394 Train-Acc:0.156      I:150 Test-Acc:0.8555 Train-Acc:0.914
I:10 Test-Acc:0.6867 Train-Acc:0.723    I:160 Test-Acc:0.8577 Train-Acc:0.925
I:20 Test-Acc:0.7025 Train-Acc:0.732    I:170 Test-Acc:0.8596 Train-Acc:0.918
I:30 Test-Acc:0.734 Train-Acc:0.763     I:180 Test-Acc:0.8619 Train-Acc:0.933
I:40 Test-Acc:0.7663 Train-Acc:0.794    I:190 Test-Acc:0.863 Train-Acc:0.933
I:50 Test-Acc:0.7913 Train-Acc:0.819    I:200 Test-Acc:0.8642 Train-Acc:0.926
I:60 Test-Acc:0.8102 Train-Acc:0.849    I:210 Test-Acc:0.8653 Train-Acc:0.931
I:70 Test-Acc:0.8228 Train-Acc:0.864    I:220 Test-Acc:0.8668 Train-Acc:0.93
I:80 Test-Acc:0.831 Train-Acc:0.867     I:230 Test-Acc:0.8672 Train-Acc:0.937
I:90 Test-Acc:0.8364 Train-Acc:0.885    I:240 Test-Acc:0.8681 Train-Acc:0.938
I:100 Test-Acc:0.8407 Train-Acc:0.88    I:250 Test-Acc:0.8687 Train-Acc:0.937
I:110 Test-Acc:0.845 Train-Acc:0.891    I:260 Test-Acc:0.8684 Train-Acc:0.945
I:120 Test-Acc:0.8481 Train-Acc:0.90    I:270 Test-Acc:0.8703 Train-Acc:0.951
I:130 Test-Acc:0.8505 Train-Acc:0.90    I:280 Test-Acc:0.8699 Train-Acc:0.949
I:140 Test-Acc:0.8526 Train-Acc:0.90    I:290 Test-Acc:0.8701 Train-Acc:0.94
```

neural learning about edges and corners: | **10**
intro to convolutional neural networks

In this chapter

- Reusing weights in multiple places

- The convolutional layer

> " The pooling operation used in convolutional neural
> networks is a big mistake, and the fact that it works
> so well is a disaster. "
>
> —Geoffrey Hinton, from "Ask Me Anything" on Reddit

Reusing weights in multiple places

If you need to detect the same feature in multiple places, use the same weights!

The greatest challenge in neural networks is that of overfitting, when a neural network memorizes a dataset instead of learning useful abstractions that generalize to unseen data. In other words, the neural network learns to predict based on noise in the dataset as opposed to relying on the fundamental signal (remember the analogy about a fork embedded in clay?).

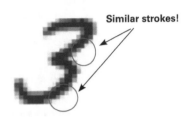
Similar strokes!

Overfitting is often caused by having more parameters than necessary to learn a specific dataset. In this case, the network has so many parameters that it can memorize every fine-grained detail in the training dataset (neural network: "Ah. I see we have image number 363 again. This was the number 2.") instead of learning high-level abstractions (neural network: "Hmm, it's got a swooping top, a swirl at the bottom left, and a tail on the right; it must be a 2."). When neural networks have lots of parameters but not very many training examples, overfitting is difficult to avoid.

We covered this topic extensively in chapter 8, when we looked at regularization as a means of countering overfitting. But regularization isn't the only technique (or even the most ideal technique) to prevent overfitting.

As I mentioned, overfitting is concerned with the ratio between the number of weights in the model and the number of datapoints it has to learn those weights. Thus, there's a better method to counter overfitting. When possible, it's preferable to use something loosely defined as *structure*.

Structure is when you selectively choose to reuse weights for multiple purposes in a neural network because we believe the same pattern needs to be detected in multiple places. As you'll see, this can significantly reduce overfitting and lead to much more accurate models, because it reduces the weight-to-data ratio.

But whereas normally removing parameters makes the model less expressive (less able to learn patterns), if you're clever in where you reuse weights, the model can be equally expressive but more robust to overfitting. Perhaps surprisingly, this technique also tends to make the model smaller (because there are fewer actual parameters to store). The most famous and widely used structure in neural networks is called a *convolution*, and when used as a layer it's called a *convolutional layer*.

The convolutional layer

Lots of very small linear layers are reused in every position, instead of a single big one.

The core idea behind a convolutional layer is that instead of having a large, dense linear layer with a connection from every input to every output, you instead have lots of very small linear layers, usually with fewer than 25 inputs and a single output, which you use in every input position. Each mini-layer is called a convolutional *kernel*, but it's really nothing more than a baby linear layer with a small number of inputs and a single output.

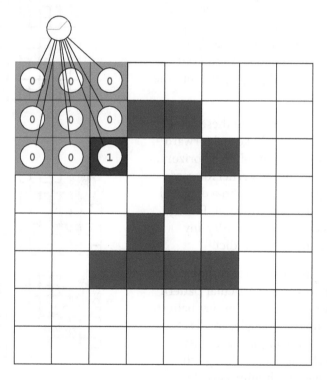

Shown here is a single 3 × 3 convolutional kernel. It will predict in its current location, move one pixel to the right, then predict again, move another pixel to the right, and so on. Once it has scanned all the way across the image, it will move down a single pixel and scan back to the left, repeating until it has made a prediction in every possible position within the image. The result will be a smaller square of kernel predictions, which are used as input to the next layer. Convolutional layers usually have many kernels.

At bottom-right are four different convolutional kernels processing the same 8 × 8 image of a 2. Each kernel results in a 6 × 6 prediction matrix. The result of the convolutional layer with four 3 × 3 kernels is four 6 × 6 prediction matrices. You can either sum these matrices elementwise (sum pooling), take the mean elementwise (mean pooling), or compute the elementwise maximum value (max pooling).

The max value of each kernel's output forms a meaningful representation and is passed to the next layer.

The last version turns out to be the most popular: for each position, look into each of the four kernel's outputs, find the max, and copy it into a final 6 × 6 matrix as pictured at upper-right of this page. This final matrix (and only this matrix) is then forward propagated into the next layers.

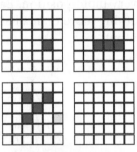

Outputs from each of the four kernels in each position

There are a few things to notice in these figures. First, the bottom-right kernel forward propagates a 1 only if it's focused on a horizontal line segment. The bottom-left kernel forward propagates a 1 only if it's focused on a diagonal line pointing upward and to the right. Finally, the bottom-right kernel didn't identify any patterns that it was trained to predict.

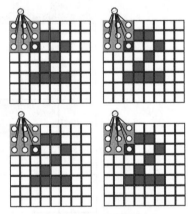

It's important to realize that this technique allows each kernel to learn a particular pattern and then search for the existence of that pattern somewhere in the image. A single, small set of weights can train over a much larger set of training examples, because even though the dataset hasn't changed, each mini-kernel is forward propagated multiple times on multiple segments of data, thus changing the ratio of weights to datapoints on which those weights are being trained. This has a powerful impact on the network, drastically reducing its ability to overfit to training data and increasing its ability to generalize.

Four convolutional kernels predicting over the same 2

A simple implementation in NumPy

Just think mini-linear layers, and you already know what you need to know.

Let's start with forward propagation. This method shows how to select a subregion in a batch of images in NumPy. Note that it selects the same subregion for the entire batch:

```
def get_image_section(layer,row_from, row_to, col_from, col_to):
    sub_section = layer[:,row_from:row_to,col_from:col_to]
    return subsection.reshape(-1,1,row_to-row_from, col_to-col_from)
```

Now, let's see how this method is used. Because it selects a subsection of a batch of input images, you need to call it multiple times (on every location within the image). Such a `for` loop looks something like this:

```
layer_0 = images[batch_start:batch_end]
layer_0 = layer_0.reshape(layer_0.shape[0],28,28)
layer_0.shape

sects = list()
for row_start in range(layer_0.shape[1]-kernel_rows):
    for col_start in range(layer_0.shape[2] - kernel_cols):
        sect = get_image_section(layer_0,
                                 row_start,
                                 row_start+kernel_rows,
                                 col_start,
                                 col_start+kernel_cols)
        sects.append(sect)

expanded_input = np.concatenate(sects,axis=1)
es = expanded_input.shape
flattened_input = expanded_input.reshape(es[0]*es[1],-1)
```

In this code, `layer_0` is a batch of images 28×28 in shape. The `for` loop iterates through every (`kernel_rows` $\times$ `kernel_cols`) subregion in the images and puts them into a list called `sects`. This list of sections is then concatenated and reshaped in a peculiar way.

Pretend (for now) that each individual subregion is its own image. Thus, if you had a batch size of 8 images, and 100 subregions per image, you'd pretend it was a batch size of 800 smaller images. Forward propagating them through a linear layer with one output neuron is the same as predicting that linear layer over every subregion in every batch (pause and make sure you get this).

If you instead forward propagate using a linear layer with n output neurons, it will generate the outputs that are the same as predicting n linear layers (kernels) in every input position of the image. You do it this way because it makes the code both simpler and faster:

```
kernels = np.random.random((kernel_rows*kernel_cols,num_kernels))
            ...
kernel_output = flattened_input.dot(kernels)
```

The following listing shows the entire NumPy implementation:

```
import numpy as np, sys
np.random.seed(1)

from keras.datasets import mnist

(x_train, y_train), (x_test, y_test) = mnist.load_data()

images, labels = (x_train[0:1000].reshape(1000,28*28) / 255,
                  y_train[0:1000])


one_hot_labels = np.zeros((len(labels),10))
for i,l in enumerate(labels):
    one_hot_labels[i][l] = 1
labels = one_hot_labels

test_images = x_test.reshape(len(x_test),28*28) / 255
test_labels = np.zeros((len(y_test),10))
for i,l in enumerate(y_test):
    test_labels[i][l] = 1

def tanh(x):
    return np.tanh(x)

def tanh2deriv(output):
    return 1 - (output ** 2)

def softmax(x):
    temp = np.exp(x)
    return temp / np.sum(temp, axis=1, keepdims=True)

alpha, iterations = (2, 300)
pixels_per_image, num_labels = (784, 10)
batch_size = 128

input_rows = 28
input_cols = 28

kernel_rows = 3
kernel_cols = 3
num_kernels = 16

hidden_size = ((input_rows - kernel_rows) *
               (input_cols - kernel_cols)) * num_kernels

kernels = 0.02*np.random.random((kernel_rows*kernel_cols,
                                 num_kernels))-0.01

weights_1_2 = 0.2*np.random.random((hidden_size,
                                    num_labels)) - 0.1

def get_image_section(layer,row_from, row_to, col_from, col_to):
    section = layer[:,row_from:row_to,col_from:col_to]
    return section.reshape(-1,1,row_to-row_from, col_to-col_from)
```

```
for j in range(iterations):
    correct_cnt = 0
    for i in range(int(len(images) / batch_size)):
        batch_start, batch_end=((i * batch_size),((i+1)*batch_size))
        layer_0 = images[batch_start:batch_end]
        layer_0 = layer_0.reshape(layer_0.shape[0],28,28)
        layer_0.shape

        sects = list()
        for row_start in range(layer_0.shape[1]-kernel_rows):
            for col_start in range(layer_0.shape[2] - kernel_cols):
                sect = get_image_section(layer_0,
                                         row_start,
                                         row_start+kernel_rows,
                                         col_start,
                                         col_start+kernel_cols)
                sects.append(sect)

        expanded_input = np.concatenate(sects,axis=1)
        es = expanded_input.shape
        flattened_input = expanded_input.reshape(es[0]*es[1],-1)

        kernel_output = flattened_input.dot(kernels)
        layer_1 = tanh(kernel_output.reshape(es[0],-1))
        dropout_mask = np.random.randint(2,size=layer_1.shape)
        layer_1 *= dropout_mask * 2
        layer_2 = softmax(np.dot(layer_1,weights_1_2))

        for k in range(batch_size):
            labelset = labels[batch_start+k:batch_start+k+1]
            _inc = int(np.argmax(layer_2[k:k+1]) ==
                              np.argmax(labelset))
            correct_cnt += _inc

        layer_2_delta = (labels[batch_start:batch_end]-layer_2)\
                         / (batch_size * layer_2.shape[0])
        layer_1_delta = layer_2_delta.dot(weights_1_2.T) * \
                         tanh2deriv(layer_1)
        layer_1_delta *= dropout_mask
        weights_1_2 += alpha * layer_1.T.dot(layer_2_delta)
        l1d_reshape = layer_1_delta.reshape(kernel_output.shape)
        k_update = flattened_input.T.dot(l1d_reshape)
        kernels -= alpha * k_update

    test_correct_cnt = 0

    for i in range(len(test_images)):

        layer_0 = test_images[i:i+1]
        layer_0 = layer_0.reshape(layer_0.shape[0],28,28)
        layer_0.shape

        sects = list()
        for row_start in range(layer_0.shape[1]-kernel_rows):
            for col_start in range(layer_0.shape[2] - kernel_cols):
                sect = get_image_section(layer_0,
                                         row_start,
                                         row_start+kernel_rows,
```

```
                                        col_start,
                                        col_start+kernel_cols)
                sects.append(sect)

        expanded_input = np.concatenate(sects,axis=1)
        es = expanded_input.shape
        flattened_input = expanded_input.reshape(es[0]*es[1],-1)

        kernel_output = flattened_input.dot(kernels)
        layer_1 = tanh(kernel_output.reshape(es[0],-1))
        layer_2 = np.dot(layer_1,weights_1_2)

        test_correct_cnt += int(np.argmax(layer_2) ==
                                np.argmax(test_labels[i:i+1]))
    if(j % 1 == 0):
        sys.stdout.write("\n"+ \
        "I:" + str(j) + \
        " Test-Acc:"+str(test_correct_cnt/float(len(test_images)))+\
        " Train-Acc:" + str(correct_cnt/float(len(images))))
```

```
        I:0 Test-Acc:0.0288 Train-Acc:0.055
        I:1 Test-Acc:0.0273 Train-Acc:0.037
        I:2 Test-Acc:0.028 Train-Acc:0.037
        I:3 Test-Acc:0.0292 Train-Acc:0.04
        I:4 Test-Acc:0.0339 Train-Acc:0.046
        I:5 Test-Acc:0.0478 Train-Acc:0.068
        I:6 Test-Acc:0.076 Train-Acc:0.083
        I:7 Test-Acc:0.1316 Train-Acc:0.096
        I:8 Test-Acc:0.2137 Train-Acc:0.127


                 . . . .

        I:297 Test-Acc:0.8774 Train-Acc:0.816
        I:298 Test-Acc:0.8774 Train-Acc:0.804
        I:299 Test-Acc:0.8774 Train-Acc:0.814
```

As you can see, swapping out the first layer from the network in chapter 9 with a convolutional layer gives another few percentage points in error reduction. The output of the convolutional layer (`kernel_output`) is itself also a series of two-dimensional images (the output of each kernel in each input position).

Most uses of convolutional layers stack multiple layers on top of each other, such that each convolutional layer treats the previous as an input image. (Feel free to do this as a personal project; it will increase accuracy further.)

Stacked convolutional layers are one of the main developments that allowed for very deep neural networks (and, by extension, the popularization of the phrase *deep learning*). It can't be overstressed that this invention was a landmark moment for the field; without it, we might still be in the previous AI winter even at the time of writing.

Summary

Reusing weights is one of the most important innovations in deep learning.

Convolutional neural networks are a more general development than you might realize. The notion of reusing weights to increase accuracy is hugely important and has an intuitive basis. Consider what you need to understand in order to detect that a cat is in an image. You first need to understand colors, then lines and edges, corners and small shapes, and eventually the combination of such lower-level features that correspond to a cat. Presumably, neural networks also need to learn about these lower-level features (like lines and edges), and the intelligence for detecting lines and edges is learned in the weights.

But if you use different weights to analyze different parts of an image, each section of weights has to independently learn what a line is. Why? Well, if one set of weights looking at one part of an image learns what a line is, there's no reason to think that another section of weights would somehow have the ability to use that information: it's in a different part of the network.

Convolutions are about taking advantage of a property of learning. Occasionally, you need to use the same idea or piece of intelligence in multiple places; and if that's the case, you should attempt to use the same weights in those locations. This brings us to one of the most important ideas in this book. If you don't learn anything else, learn this:

> ### The structure trick
>
> When a neural network needs to use the same idea in multiple places, endeavor to use the same weights in both places. This will make those weights more intelligent by giving them more samples to learn from, increasing generalization.

Many of the biggest developments in deep learning over the past five years (some before) are iterations of this idea. Convolutions, recurrent neural networks (RNNs), word embeddings, and the recently published capsule networks can all be viewed through this lens. When you know a network will need the same idea in multiple places, force it to use the same weights in those places. I fully expect that more deep learning discoveries will continue to be based on this idea, because it's challenging to discover new, higher-level abstract ideas that neural networks could use repeatedly throughout their architecture.

neural networks that understand language: king – man + woman == ? | 11

······

In this chapter

- Natural language processing (NLP)

- Supervised NLP

- Capturing word correlation in input data

- Intro to an embedding layer

- Neural architecture

- Comparing word embeddings

- Filling in the blank

- Meaning is derived from loss

- Word analogies

······

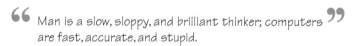

" Man is a slow, sloppy, and brilliant thinker; computers are fast, accurate, and stupid. "

—John Pfeiffer, in *Fortune*, 1961

What does it mean to understand language?

What kinds of predictions do people make about language?

Up until now, we've been using neural networks to model image data. But neural networks can be used to understand a much wider variety of datasets. Exploring new datasets also teaches us a lot about neural networks in general, because different datasets often justify different styles of neural network training according to the challenges hidden in the data.

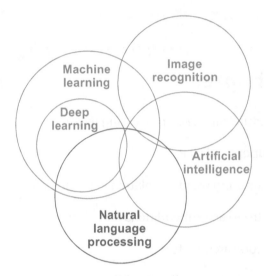

We'll begin this chapter by exploring a much older field that overlaps deep learning: *natural language processing* (NLP). This field is dedicated exclusively to the automated understanding of human language (previously not using deep learning). We'll discuss the basics of deep learning's approach to this field.

Natural language processing (NLP)

NLP is divided into a collection of tasks or challenges.

Perhaps the best way to quickly get to know NLP is to consider a few of the many challenges the NLP community seeks to solve. Here are a few types of classification problem that are common to NLP:

- Using the *characters* of a document to predict *where words start and end.*
- Using the *words* of a document to predict *where sentences start and end.*
- Using the *words in a sentence* to predict *the part of speech for each word.*
- Using *words in a sentence* to predict *where phrases start and end.*
- Using *words in a sentence* to predict *where named entity (person, place, thing) references start and end.*
- Using *sentences in a document* to predict *which pronouns refer to the same person / place / thing.*
- Using *words in a sentence* to predict the *sentiment* of a sentence.

Generally speaking, NLP tasks seek to do one of three things: label a region of text (such as part-of-speech tagging, sentiment classification, or named-entity recognition); link two or more regions of text (such as coreference, which tries to answer whether two mentions of a real-world thing are in fact referencing the same real-world thing, where the real-world thing is generally a person, place, or some other named entity); or try to fill in missing information (missing words) based on context.

Perhaps it's also apparent how machine learning and NLP are deeply intertwined. Until recently, most state-of-the-art NLP algorithms were advanced, probabilistic, non-parametric models (not deep learning). But the recent development and popularization of two major neural algorithms have swept the field of NLP: neural word embeddings and recurrent neural networks (RNNs).

In this chapter, we'll build a word-embedding algorithm and demonstrate why it increases the accuracy of NLP algorithms. In the next chapter, we'll create a recurrent neural network and demonstrate why it's so effective at predicting across sequences.

It's also worth mentioning the key role that NLP (perhaps using deep learning) plays in the advancement of artificial intelligence. AI seeks to create machines that can think and engage with the world as humans do (and beyond). NLP plays a very special role in this endeavor, because language is the bedrock of conscious logic and communication in humans. As such, methods by which machines can use and understand language form the foundation of human-like logic in machines: the foundation of thought.

Supervised NLP

Words go in, and predictions come out.

Perhaps you'll remember the following figure from chapter 2. Supervised learning is all about taking "what you know" and transforming it into "what you want to know." Up until now, "what you know" has always consisted of numbers in one way or another. But NLP uses text as input. How do you process it?

Because neural networks only map input numbers to output numbers, the first step is to convert the text into numerical form. Much as we converted the streetlight dataset, we need to convert the real-world data (in this case, text) into a *matrix* the neural network can consume. As it turns out, how we do this is extremely important!

How should we convert text to numbers? Answering that question requires some thought regarding the problem. Remember, neural networks look for correlation between their input and output layers. Thus, we want to convert text into numbers in such a way that the correlation between input and output is *most obvious* to the network. This will make for faster training and better generalization.

In order to know what input format makes input/output correlation the most obvious to the network, we need to know what the input/output dataset looks like. To explore this topic, let's take on the challenge of *topic classification*.

IMDB movie reviews dataset

You can predict whether people post positive or negative reviews.

The IMDB movie reviews dataset is a collection of review -> rating pairs that often look like the following (this is an imitation, not pulled from IMDB):

 This movie was terrible! The plot was dry, the acting unconvincing, and I spilled popcorn on my shirt."

Rating: 1 (stars)

The entire dataset consists of around 50,000 of these pairs, where the input reviews are usually a few sentences and the output ratings are between 1 and 5 stars. People consider it a *sentiment dataset* because the stars are indicative of the overall sentiment of the movie review. But it should be obvious that this sentiment dataset might be very different from other sentiment datasets, such as product reviews or hospital patient reviews.

You want to train a neural network that can use the input text to make accurate predictions of the output score. To accomplish this, you must first decide how to turn the input and output datasets into matrices. Interestingly, the output dataset is a number, which perhaps makes it an easier place to start. You'll adjust the range of stars to be between 0 and 1 instead of 1 and 5, so that you can use binary `softmax`. That's all you need to do to the output. I'll show an example on the next page.

The input data, however, is a bit trickier. To begin, let's consider the raw data. It's a list of characters. This presents a few problems: not only is the input data text instead of numbers, but it's *variable-length* text. So far, neural networks always take an input of a fixed size. You'll need to overcome this.

So, the raw input won't work. The next question to ask is, "What about this data will have correlation with the output?" Representing that property might work well. For starters, I wouldn't expect any characters (in the list of characters) to have any correlation with the sentiment. You need to think about it differently.

What about the words? Several words in this dataset would have a bit of correlation. I'd bet that *terrible* and *unconvincing* have significant negative correlation with the rating. By *negative*, I mean that as they increase in frequency in any input datapoint (any review), the rating tends to decrease.

Perhaps this property is more general! Perhaps words by themselves (even out of context) would have significant correlation with sentiment. Let's explore this further.

Capturing word correlation in input data

Bag of words: Given a review's vocabulary, predict the sentiment.

If you observe correlation between the vocabulary of an IMDB review and its rating, then you can proceed to the next step: creating an input matrix that represents the vocabulary of a movie review.

What's commonly done in this case is to create a matrix where each row (vector) corresponds to each movie review, and each column represents whether a review contains a particular word in the vocabulary. To create the vector for a review, you calculate the vocabulary of the review and then put 1 in each corresponding column for that review and 0s everywhere else. How big are these vectors? Well, if there are 2,000 words, and you need a place in each vector for each word, each vector will have 2,000 dimensions.

This form of storage, called *one-hot encoding*, is the most common format for encoding binary data (the binary presence or absence of an input datapoint among a vocabulary of possible input datapoints). If the vocabulary was only four words, the one-hot encoding might look like this:

```
import numpy as np

onehots = {}
onehots['cat'] = np.array([1,0,0,0])
onehots['the'] = np.array([0,1,0,0])
onehots['dog'] = np.array([0,0,1,0])
onehots['sat'] = np.array([0,0,0,1])

sentence = ['the','cat','sat']
x = word2hot[sentence[0]] + \
    word2hot[sentence[1]] + \
    word2hot[sentence[2]]

print("Sent Encoding:" + str(x))
```

cat (1)(0)(0)(0)

the (0)(1)(0)(0)

dog (0)(0)(1)(0)

sat (0)(0)(0)(1)

As you can see, we create a vector for each term in the vocabulary, and this allows you to use simple vector addition to create a vector representing a subset of the total vocabulary (such as a subset corresponding to the words in a sentence).

"the cat sat"

Output: Sent Encoding: [1 1 0 1]   (1)(1)(0)(1)

Note that when you create an embedding for several terms (such as "the cat sat"), you have multiple options if words occur multiple times. If the phrase was "cat cat cat," you could either sum the vector for "cat" three times (resulting in [3,0,0,0]) or just take the unique "cat" a single time (resulting in [1,0,0,0]). The latter typically works better for language.

Predicting movie reviews

With the encoding strategy and the previous network, you can predict sentiment.

Using the strategy we just identified, you can build a vector for each word in the sentiment dataset and use the previous two-layer network to predict sentiment. I'll show you the code, but I strongly recommend attempting this from memory. Open a new Jupyter notebook, load in the dataset, build your one-hot vectors, and then build a neural network to predict the rating of each movie review (positive or negative).

Here's how I would do the preprocessing step:

```python
import sys

f = open('reviews.txt')
raw_reviews = f.readlines()
f.close()

f = open('labels.txt')
raw_labels = f.readlines()
f.close()

tokens = list(map(lambda x:set(x.split(" ")),raw_reviews))

vocab = set()
for sent in tokens:
    for word in sent:
        if(len(word)>0):
            vocab.add(word)
vocab = list(vocab)

word2index = {}
for i,word in enumerate(vocab):
    word2index[word]=i

input_dataset = list()
for sent in tokens:
    sent_indices = list()
    for word in sent:
        try:
            sent_indices.append(word2index[word])
        except:
            ""
    input_dataset.append(list(set(sent_indices)))

target_dataset = list()
for label in raw_labels:
    if label == 'positive\n':
        target_dataset.append(1)
    else:
        target_dataset.append(0)
```

Intro to an embedding layer

Here's one more trick to make the network faster.

At right is the diagram from the previous neural network, which you'll now use to predict sentiment. But before that, I want to describe the layer names. The first layer is the dataset (`layer_0`). This is followed by what's called a *linear layer* (`weights_0_1`). This is followed by a `relu` layer (`layer_1`), another linear layer (`weights_1_2`), and then the output, which is the prediction layer. As it turns out, you can take a bit of a shortcut to `layer_1` by replacing the first linear layer (`weights_0_1`) with an embedding layer.

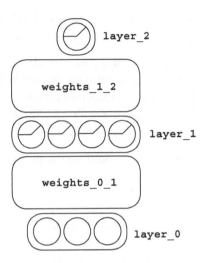

Taking a vector of 1s and 0s is mathematically equivalent to summing several rows of a matrix. Thus, it's much more efficient to select the relevant rows of `weights_0_1` and sum them as opposed to doing a big vector-matrix multiplication. Because the sentiment vocabulary is on the order of 70,000 words, most of the vector-matrix multiplication is spent multiplying 0s in the input vector by different rows of the matrix before summing them. Selecting the rows corresponding to each word in a matrix and summing them is much more efficient.

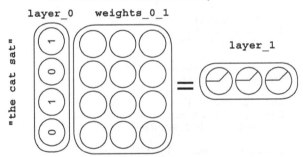

Using this process of selecting rows and performing a sum (or average) means treating the first linear layer (`weights_0_1`) as an embedding layer. Structurally, they're identical (`layer_1` is exactly the same using either method for forward propagation). The only difference is that summing a small number of rows is much faster.

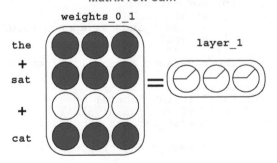

After running the previous code, run this code.

```
import numpy as np
np.random.seed(1)

def sigmoid(x):
    return 1/(1 + np.exp(-x))

alpha, iterations = (0.01, 2)
hidden_size = 100

weights_0_1 = 0.2*np.random.random((len(vocab),hidden_size)) - 0.1
weights_1_2 = 0.2*np.random.random((hidden_size,1)) - 0.1

correct,total = (0,0)
for iter in range(iterations):

    for i in range(len(input_dataset)-1000):

        x,y = (input_dataset[i],target_dataset[i])
        layer_1 = sigmoid(np.sum(weights_0_1[x],axis=0))
        layer_2 = sigmoid(np.dot(layer_1,weights_1_2))

        layer_2_delta = layer_2 - y
        layer_1_delta = layer_2_delta.dot(weights_1_2.T)

        weights_0_1[x] -= layer_1_delta * alpha
        weights_1_2 -= np.outer(layer_1,layer_2_delta) * alpha

        if(np.abs(layer_2_delta) < 0.5):
            correct += 1
        total += 1
        if(i % 10 == 9):
            progress = str(i/float(len(input_dataset)))
            sys.stdout.write('\rIter:'+str(iter)\
                             +' Progress:'+progress[2:4]\
                             +'.'+progress[4:6]\
                             +'% Training Accuracy:'\
                             + str(correct/float(total)) + '%')
    print()
correct,total = (0,0)
for i in range(len(input_dataset)-1000,len(input_dataset)):

    x = input_dataset[i]
    y = target_dataset[i]

    layer_1 = sigmoid(np.sum(weights_0_1[x],axis=0))
    layer_2 = sigmoid(np.dot(layer_1,weights_1_2))

    if(np.abs(layer_2 - y) < 0.5):
        correct += 1
    total += 1
print("Test Accuracy:" + str(correct / float(total)))
```

Trains on the first 24,000 reviews

embed + sigmoid

linear + softmax

Compares the prediction with the truth

Backpropagation

Interpreting the output

What did the neural network learn along the way?

Here's the output of the movie reviews neural network. From one perspective, this is the same correlation summarization we've already discussed:

```
Iter:0 Progress:95.99% Training Accuracy:0.832%
Iter:1 Progress:95.99% Training Accuracy:0.8663333333333333%
Test Accuracy:0.849
```

The neural network was looking for correlation between the input datapoints and the output datapoints. But those datapoints have characteristics we're familiar with (notably those of language). Furthermore, it's extremely beneficial to consider what patterns of language would be detected by the correlation summarization, and more importantly, which ones wouldn't. After all, just because the network is able to find correlation between the input and output datasets doesn't mean it understands every useful pattern of language.

Furthermore, understanding the difference between what the network (in its current configuration) is capable of learning relative to what it needs to know to properly understand language is an incredibly fruitful line of thinking. This is what researchers on the front lines of state-of-the-art research consider, and it's what we're going to consider here.

What about language did the movie reviews network learn? Let's start by considering what was presented to the network. As displayed in the diagram at top right, you presented each review's vocabulary as input and asked the network to predict one of two labels (`positive` or `negative`). Given that the correlation summarization says the network will look for correlation between the input and output datasets, at a minimum, you'd expect the network to identify words that have either a positive or negative correlation (by themselves).

This follows naturally from the correlation summarization. You present the presence or absence of a word. As such, the correlation summarization will find direct correlation between this presence/absence and each of the two labels. But this isn't the whole story.

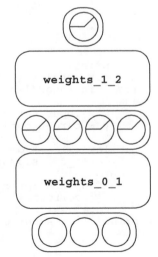

Neural architecture

How did the choice of architecture affect what the network learned?

We just discussed the first, most trivial type of information the neural network learned: direct correlation between the input and target datasets. This observation is largely the clean slate of neural intelligence. (If a network can't discover direct correlation between input and output data, something is probably broken.) The development of more-sophisticated architectures is based on the need to find more-complex patterns than direct correlation, and this network is no exception.

The minimal architecture needed to identify direct correlation is a two-layer network, where the network has a single weight matrix that connects directly from the input layer to the output layer. But we used a network that has a hidden layer. This begs the question, what does this hidden layer do?

Fundamentally, hidden layers are about grouping datapoints from a previous layer into n groups (where n is the number of neurons in the hidden layer). Each hidden neuron takes in a datapoint and answers the question, "Is this datapoint in my group?" As the hidden layer learns, it searches for useful groupings of its input. What are useful groupings?

An input datapoint grouping is useful if it does two things. First, the grouping must be useful to the prediction of an output label. If it's not useful to the output prediction, *the correlation summarization will never lead the network to find the group.* This is a hugely valuable realization. Much of neural network research is about finding training data (or some other manufactured signal for the network to artificially predict) so it finds groupings that are useful for a task (such as predicting movie review stars). We'll discuss this more in a moment.

Second, a grouping is useful if it's an actual phenomenon in the data that you care about. Bad groupings just memorize the data. Good groupings pick up on phenomena that are useful linguistically.

For example, when predicting whether a movie review is positive or negative, understanding the difference between "terrible" and "not terrible" is a powerful grouping. It would be great to have a neuron that turned *off* when it saw "awful" and turned *on* when it saw "not awful." This would be a powerful grouping for the next layer to use to make the final prediction. But because the input to the neural network is the vocabulary of a review, "it was great, not terrible" creates exactly the same `layer_1` value as "it was terrible, not great." For this reason, the network is very unlikely to create a hidden neuron that understands negation.

Testing whether a layer is the same or different based on a certain language pattern is a great first step for knowing whether an architecture is likely to find that pattern using the correlation summarization. If you can construct two examples with an identical hidden layer, one with the pattern you find interesting and one without, the network is unlikely to find that pattern.

As you just learned, a hidden layer fundamentally groups the previous layer's data. At a granular level, each neuron classifies a datapoint as either subscribing or not subscribing to its group. At a higher level, two datapoints (movie reviews) are similar if they subscribe to many of the same groups. Finally, two inputs (words) are similar if the weights linking them to various hidden neurons (a measure of each word's group affinity) are similar. Given this knowledge, in the previous neural network, what should you observe in the weights going into the hidden neurons from the words?

What should you see in the weights connecting words and hidden neurons?

Here's a hint: words that have a similar predictive power should subscribe to similar groups (hidden neuron configurations). What does this mean for the weights connecting each word to each hidden neuron?

Here's the answer. Words that correlate with similar labels (positive or negative) will have similar weights connecting them to various hidden neurons. This is because the neural network learns to bucket them into similar hidden neurons so that the final layer (`weights_1_2`) can make the correct positive or negative predictions.

You can see this phenomenon by taking a particularly positive or negative word and searching for the other words with the most similar weight values. In other words, you can take each word and see which other words have the most similar weight values connecting them to each hidden neuron (to each group).

Words that subscribe to similar groups will have similar predictive power for positive or negative labels. As such, words that subscribe to similar groups, having similar weight values, will also have similar meaning. Abstractly, in terms of neural networks, a neuron has similar meaning to other neurons in the same layer if and only if it has similar weights connecting it to the next and/or previous layers.

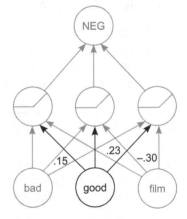

The three bold weights for "good" form the embedding for "good." They reflect how much the term "good" is a member of each group (hidden neuron). Words with similar predictive power have similar word embeddings (weight values).

Comparing word embeddings

How can you visualize weight similarity?

For each input word, you can select the list of weights proceeding out of it to the various hidden neurons by selecting the corresponding row of `weights_0_1`. Each entry in the row represents each weight proceeding from that row's word to each hidden neuron. Thus, to figure out which words are most similar to a target term, you compare each word's vector (row of the matrix) to that of the target term. The comparison of choice is called *Euclidian distance*, as shown in the following code:

```
from collections import Counter
import math

def similar(target='beautiful'):
    target_index = word2index[target]
    scores = Counter()
    for word,index in word2index.items():
        raw_difference = weights_0_1[index] - (weights_0_1[target_index])
        squared_difference = raw_difference * raw_difference
        scores[word] = -math.sqrt(sum(squared_difference))

    return scores.most_common(10)
```

This allows you to easily query for the most similar word (neuron) according to the network:

```
print(similar('beautiful'))                    print(similar('terrible'))

[('beautiful', -0.0),                          [('terrible', -0.0),
 ('atmosphere', -0.70542101298),                ('dull', -0.760788602671491),
 ('heart', -0.7339429768542354),                ('lacks', -0.76706470275372),
 ('tight', -0.7470388145765346),                ('boring', -0.7682894961694),
 ('fascinating', -0.7549291974),                ('disappointing', -0.768657),
 ('expecting', -0.759886970744),                ('annoying', -0.78786389931),
 ('beautifully', -0.7603669338),                ('poor', -0.825784172378292),
 ('awesome', -0.76647368382398),                ('horrible', -0.83154121717),
 ('masterpiece', -0.7708280057),                ('laughable', -0.8340279599),
 ('outstanding', -0.7740642167)]                ('badly', -0.84165373783678)]
```

As you might expect, the most similar term to every word is itself, followed by words with similar usefulness as the target term. Again, as you might expect, because the network has only two labels (`positive` and `negative`), the input terms are grouped according to which label they tend to predict.

This is a standard phenomenon of the correlation summarization. It seeks to create similar representations (`layer_1` values) within the network based on the label being predicted, so that it can predict the right label. In this case, the side effect is that the weights feeding into `layer_1` get grouped according to output label.

The key takeaway is a gut instinct about this phenomenon of the correlation summarization. It consistently attempts to convince the hidden layers to be similar based on which label should be predicted.

What is the meaning of a neuron?

Meaning is entirely based on the target labels being predicted.

Note that the meanings of different words didn't totally reflect how you might group them. The term most similar to "beautiful" is "atmosphere." This is a valuable lesson. For the purposes of predicting whether a movie review is positive or negative, these words have nearly identical meaning. But in the real world, their meaning is quite different (one is an adjective and another a noun, for example).

```
print(similar('beautiful'))

[('beautiful', -0.0),
 ('atmosphere', -0.70542101298),
 ('heart', -0.7339429768542354),
 ('tight', -0.7470388145765346),
 ('fascinating', -0.7549291974),
 ('expecting', -0.759886970744),
 ('beautifully', -0.7603669338),
 ('awesome', -0.76647368382398),
 ('masterpiece', -0.7708280057),
 ('outstanding', -0.7740642167)]
```

```
print(similar('terrible'))

[('terrible', -0.0),
 ('dull', -0.760788602671491),
 ('lacks', -0.76706470275372),
 ('boring', -0.7682894961694),
 ('disappointing', -0.768657),
 ('annoying', -0.78786389931),
 ('poor', -0.825784172378292),
 ('horrible', -0.83154121717),
 ('laughable', -0.8340279599),
 ('badly', -0.84165373783678)]
```

This realization is incredibly important. The meaning (of a neuron) in the network is defined based on the target labels. Everything in the neural network is contexualized based on the correlation summarization trying to correctly make predictions. Thus, even though you and I know a great deal about these words, the neural network is entirely ignorant of all information outside the task at hand.

How can you convince the network to learn more-nuanced information about neurons (in this case, word neurons)? Well, if you give it input and target data that requires a more nuanced understanding of language, it will have reason to learn more-nuanced interpretations of various terms.

What should you use the neural network to predict so that it learns more-interesting weight values for the word neurons? The task you'll use to learn more-interesting weight values for the word neurons is a glorified fill-in-the blank task. Why use this? First, there's nearly infinite training data (the internet), which means nearly infinite signal for the neural network to use to learn more-nuanced information about words. Furthermore, being able to accurately fill in the blank requires at least some notion of context about the real world.

For instance, in the following example, is it more likely that the blank is correctly filled by the word "anvil" or "wool"? Let's see if the neural network can figure it out.

Mary had a little lamb whose _____ ???? was white as snow.

Filling in the blank

Learn richer meanings for words by having a richer signal to learn.

This example uses almost exactly the same neural network as the previous one, with only a few modifications. First, instead of predicting a single label given a movie review, you'll take each (five-word) phrase, remove one word (a focus term), and attempt to train a network to figure out the identity of the word you removed using the rest of the phrase. Second, you'll use a trick called *negative sampling* to make the network train a bit faster.

Consider that in order to predict which term is missing, you need one label for each possible word. This would require several thousand labels, which would cause the network to train slowly. To overcome this, let's randomly ignore most of the labels for each forward propagation step (as in, pretend they don't exist). Although this may seem like a crude approximation, it's a technique that works well in practice. Here's the preprocessing code for this example:

```python
import sys,random,math
from collections import Counter
import numpy as np

np.random.seed(1)
random.seed(1)
f = open('reviews.txt')
raw_reviews = f.readlines()
f.close()

tokens = list(map(lambda x:(x.split(" ")),raw_reviews))
wordcnt = Counter()
for sent in tokens:
    for word in sent:
        wordcnt[word] -= 1
vocab = list(set(map(lambda x:x[0],wordcnt.most_common())))

word2index = {}
for i,word in enumerate(vocab):
    word2index[word]=i

concatenated = list()
input_dataset = list()
for sent in tokens:
    sent_indices = list()
    for word in sent:
        try:
            sent_indices.append(word2index[word])
            concatenated.append(word2index[word])
        except:
            ""
    input_dataset.append(sent_indices)
concatenated = np.array(concatenated)
random.shuffle(input_dataset)
```

```
alpha, iterations = (0.05, 2)
hidden_size,window,negative = (50,2,5)

weights_0_1 = (np.random.rand(len(vocab),hidden_size) - 0.5) * 0.2
weights_1_2 = np.random.rand(len(vocab),hidden_size)*0

layer_2_target = np.zeros(negative+1)
layer_2_target[0] = 1

def similar(target='beautiful'):
  target_index = word2index[target]

  scores = Counter()
  for word,index in word2index.items():
    raw_difference = weights_0_1[index] - (weights_0_1[target_index])
    squared_difference = raw_difference * raw_difference
    scores[word] = -math.sqrt(sum(squared_difference))
  return scores.most_common(10)

def sigmoid(x):
  return 1/(1 + np.exp(-x))

for rev_i,review in enumerate(input_dataset * iterations):
  for target_i in range(len(review)):

    target_samples = [review[target_i]]+list(concatenated\
    [(np.random.rand(negative)*len(concatenated)).astype('int').tolist()])

    left_context = review[max(0,target_i-window):target_i]
    right_context = review[target_i+1:min(len(review),target_i+window)]

    layer_1 = np.mean(weights_0_1[left_context+right_context],axis=0)
    layer_2 = sigmoid(layer_1.dot(weights_1_2[target_samples].T))
    layer_2_delta = layer_2 - layer_2_target
    layer_1_delta = layer_2_delta.dot(weights_1_2[target_samples])

    weights_0_1[left_context+right_context] -= layer_1_delta * alpha
    weights_1_2[target_samples] -= np.outer(layer_2_delta,layer_1)*alpha

  if(rev_i % 250 == 0):
    sys.stdout.write('\rProgress:'+str(rev_i/float(len(input_dataset)
      *iterations)) + "   " + str(similar('terrible')))
  sys.stdout.write('\rProgress:'+str(rev_i/float(len(input_dataset)
      *iterations)))
print(similar('terrible'))
```

Predicts only a random subset, because it's really expensive to predict every vocabulary

```
  Progress:0.99998 [('terrible', -0.0), ('horrible', -2.846300248788519),
  ('brilliant', -3.039932544396419), ('pathetic', -3.4868595532695967),
  ('superb', -3.6092947961276645), ('phenomenal', -3.660172529098085),
  ('masterful', -3.6856112636664564), ('marvelous', -3.9306620801551664),
```

Meaning is derived from loss

With this new neural network, you can subjectively see that the word embeddings cluster in a rather different way. Where before words were clustered according to their likelihood to predict a `positive` or `negative` label, now they're clustered based on their likelihood to occur within the same phrase (sometimes regardless of sentiment).

Predicting POS/NEG	Fill in the blank
`print(similar('terrible'))`	`print(similar('terrible'))`

```
[('terrible', -0.0),
 ('dull', -0.760788602671491),
 ('lacks', -0.76706470275372),
 ('boring', -0.7682894961694),
 ('disappointing', -0.768657),
 ('annoying', -0.78786389931),
 ('poor', -0.825784172378292),
 ('horrible', -0.83154121717),
 ('laughable', -0.8340279599),
 ('badly', -0.84165373783678)]
```

```
[('terrible', -0.0),
 ('horrible', -2.79600898781),
 ('brilliant', -3.3336178881),
 ('pathetic', -3.49393193646),
 ('phenomenal', -3.773268963),
 ('masterful', -3.8376122586),
 ('superb', -3.9043150978490),
 ('bad', -3.9141673639585237),
 ('marvelous', -4.0470804427),
 ('dire', -4.178749691835959)]
```

`print(similar('beautiful'))` `print(similar('beautiful'))`

```
[('beautiful', -0.0),
 ('atmosphere', -0.70542101298),
 ('heart', -0.7339429768542354),
 ('tight', -0.7470388145765346),
 ('fascinating', -0.7549291974),
 ('expecting', -0.759886970744),
 ('beautifully', -0.7603669338),
 ('awesome', -0.76647368382398),
 ('masterpiece', -0.7708280057),
 ('outstanding', -0.7740642167)]
```

```
[('beautiful', -0.0),
 ('lovely', -3.0145597243116),
 ('creepy', -3.1975363066322),
 ('fantastic', -3.2551041418),
 ('glamorous', -3.3050812101),
 ('spooky', -3.4881261617587),
 ('cute', -3.592955888181448),
 ('nightmarish', -3.60063813),
 ('heartwarming', -3.6348147),
 ('phenomenal', -3.645669007)]
```

The key takeaway is that, even though the network trained over the same dataset with a very similar architecture (three layers, cross entropy, `sigmoid` nonlinear), you can influence what the network learns within its weights by changing what you tell the network to predict. Even though it's looking at the same statistical information, you can target what it learns based on what you select as the input and target values. For the moment, let's call this process of choosing what you want the network to learn *intelligence targeting*.

Controlling the input/target values isn't the only way to perform intelligence targeting. You can also adjust how the network measures error, the size and types of layers it has, and the types of regularization to apply. In deep learning research, all of these techniques fall under the umbrella of constructing what's called a *loss function*.

Neural networks don't really learn data; they minimize the loss function.

In chapter 4, you learned that learning is about adjusting each weight in the neural network to bring the error down to 0. In this section, I'll explain the same phenomena from a different perspective, choosing the error so the neural network learns the patterns we're interested in. Remember these lessons?

The golden method for learning	The secret
Adjust each weight in the correct direction and by the correct amount so `error` reduces to 0.	For any `input` and `goal_pred`, an exact relationship is defined between `error` and `weight`, found by combining the `prediction` and `error` formulas.

$$error = ((0.5 * weight) - 0.8) ** 2$$

Perhaps you remember this formula from the one-weight neural network. In that network, you could evaluate the error by first forward propagating (`0.5 * weight`) and then comparing to the target (0.8). I encourage you not to think about this from the perspective of two different steps (forward propagation, then error evaluation), but instead to consider the entire formula (including forward prop) to be the evaluation of an error value. This context will reveal the true cause of the different word-embedding clusterings. Even though the network and datasets were similar, the error function was fundamentally different, leading to different word clusterings within each network.

Predicting POS/NEG

```
print(similar('terrible'))

[('terrible', -0.0),
 ('dull', -0.760788602671491),
 ('lacks', -0.76706470275372),
 ('boring', -0.7682894961694),
 ('disappointing', -0.768657),
 ('annoying', -0.78786389931),
 ('poor', -0.825784172378292),
 ('horrible', -0.83154121717),
 ('laughable', -0.8340279599),
 ('badly', -0.84165373783678)]
```

Fill in the blank

```
print(similar('terrible'))

[('terrible', -0.0),
 ('horrible', -2.79600898781),
 ('brilliant', -3.3336178881),
 ('pathetic', -3.49393193646),
 ('phenomenal', -3.773268963),
 ('masterful', -3.8376122586),
 ('superb', -3.9043150978490),
 ('bad', -3.9141673639585237),
 ('marvelous', -4.0470804427),
 ('dire', -4.178749691835959)]
```

The choice of loss function determines the neural network's knowledge.

The more formal term for an *error function* is a *loss function* or *objective function* (all three phrases are interchangeable). Considering learning to be all about minimizing a loss function (which includes forward propagation) gives a far broader perspective on how neural networks learn. Two neural networks can have identical starting weights, be trained over identical datasets, and ultimately learn very different patterns because you choose a different loss function. In the case of the two movie review neural networks, the loss function was different because you chose two different target values (positive or negative versus fill in the blank).

Different kinds of architectures, layers, regularization techniques, datasets, and non-linearities aren't really that different. These are the ways you can choose to construct a loss function. If the network isn't learning properly, the solution can often come from any of these possible categories.

For example, if a network is overfitting, you can augment the loss function by choosing simpler nonlinearities, smaller layer sizes, shallower architectures, larger datasets, or more-aggressive regularization techniques. All of these choices will have a fundamentally similar effect on the loss function and a similar consequence on the behavior of the network. They all interplay together, and over time you'll learn how changing one can affect the performance of another; but for now, the important takeaway is that learning is about constructing a loss function and then minimizing it.

Whenever you want a neural network to learn a pattern, everything you need to know to do so will be contained in the loss function. When you had only a single weight, this allowed the loss function to be simple, as you'll recall:

```
error = ((0.5 * weight) - 0.8) ** 2
```

But as you chain large numbers of complex layers together, the loss function will become more complicated (and that's OK). Just remember, if something is going wrong, the solution is in the loss function, which includes both the forward prediction and the raw error evaluation (such as mean squared error or cross entropy).

King – Man + Woman ~= Queen

Word analogies are an interesting consequence of the previously built network.

Before closing out this chapter, let's discuss what is, at the time of writing, still one of the most famous properties of neural word embeddings (word vectors like those we just created). The task of filling in the blank creates word embeddings with interesting phenomena known as *word analogies*, wherein you can take the vectors for different words and perform basic algebraic operations on them.

For example, if you train the previous network on a large enough corpus, you'll be able to take the vector for king, subtract from it the vector for man, add in the vector for woman, and then search for the most similar vector (other than those in the query). As it turns out, the most similar vector is often the word "queen." There are even similar phenomena in the fill-in-the-blank network trained over movie reviews.

```
def analogy(positive=['terrible','good'],negative=['bad']):

    norms = np.sum(weights_0_1 * weights_0_1,axis=1)
    norms.resize(norms.shape[0],1)

    normed_weights = weights_0_1 * norms

    query_vect = np.zeros(len(weights_0_1[0]))
    for word in positive:
        query_vect += normed_weights[word2index[word]]
    for word in negative:
        query_vect -= normed_weights[word2index[word]]

    scores = Counter()
    for word,index in word2index.items():
        raw_difference = weights_0_1[index] - query_vect
        squared_difference = raw_difference * raw_difference
        scores[word] = -math.sqrt(sum(squared_difference))

    return scores.most_common(10)[1:]
```

terrible – bad + good ~=   **elizabeth – she + he ~=**

```
analogy(['terrible','good'],['bad'])    analogy(['elizabeth','he'],['she'])

[('superb', -223.3926217861),          [('christopher', -192.7003),
 ('terrific', -223.690648739),          ('it', -193.3250398279812),
 ('decent', -223.7045545791),           ('him', -193.459063887477),
 ('fine', -223.9233021831882),          ('this', -193.59240614759),
 ('worth', -224.03031703075),           ('william', -193.63049856),
 ('perfect', -224.125194533),           ('mr', -193.6426152274126),
 ('brilliant', -224.2138041),           ('bruce', -193.6689279548),
 ('nice', -224.244182032763),           ('fred', -193.69940566948),
 ('great', -224.29115420564)]           ('there', -193.7189421836)]
```

Word analogies

Linear compression of an existing property in the data

When this property was first discovered, it created a flurry of excitement as people extrapolated many possible applications of such a technology. It's an amazing property in its own right, and it did create a veritable cottage industry around generating word embeddings of one variety or another. But the word analogy property in and of itself hasn't grown that much since then, and most of the current work in language focuses instead on recurrent architectures (which we'll get to in chapter 12).

That being said, getting a good intuition for what's going on with word embeddings as a result of a chosen loss function is extremely valuable. You've already learned that the choice of loss function can affect how words are grouped, but this word analogy phenomenon is something different. What about the new loss function causes it to happen?

If you consider a word embedding having two dimensions, it's perhaps easier to envision exactly what it means for these word analogies to work.

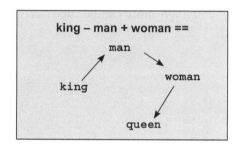

```
king  = [0.6 , 0.1]
man   = [0.5 , 0.0]
woman = [0.0 , 0.8]
queen = [0.1 , 1.0]

king - man    = [0.1 , 0.1]
queen - woman = [0.1 , 0.2]
```

The relative usefulness to the final prediction between "king"/"man" and "queen"/"woman" is similar. Why? The difference between "king" and "man" leaves a vector of `royalty`. There are a bunch of male- and female-related words in one grouping, and then there's another grouping in the royal direction.

This can be traced back to the chosen loss. When the word "king" shows up in a phrase, it changes the probability of other words showing up in a certain way. It increases the probability of words related to "man" and the probability of words related to royalty. The word "queen" appearing in a phrase increases the probability of words related to "woman" and the probability of words related to royalty (as a group). Thus, because the words have this sort of Venn diagram impact on the output probability, they end up subscribing to similar combinations of groupings.

Oversimplified, "king" subscribes to the male and the royal dimensions of the hidden layer, whereas "queen" subscribes to the female and royal dimensions of the hidden layer. Taking the vector for "king" and subtracting out some approximation of the male dimensions and adding in the female ones yields something close to "queen." The most important takeaway is that this is more about the properties of language than deep learning. Any linear compression of these co-occurrence statistics will behave similarly.

Summary

You've learned a lot about neural word embeddings and the impact of loss on learning.

In this chapter, we've unpacked the fundamental principles of using neural networks to study language. We started with an overview of the primary problems in natural language processing and then explored how neural networks model language at the word level using word embeddings. You also learned how the choice of loss function can change the kinds of properties that are captured by word embeddings. We finished with a discussion of perhaps the most magical of neural phenomena in this space: word analogies.

As with the other chapters, I encourage you to build the examples in this chapter from scratch. Although it may seem as though this chapter stands on its own, the lessons in loss-function creation and tuning are invaluable and will be extremely important as you tackle increasingly more complicated strategies in future chapters. Good luck!

neural networks that write like Shakespeare: recurrent layers for variable-length data | 12

··

In this chapter

- The challenge of arbitrary length

- The surprising power of averaged word vectors

- The limitations of bag-of-words vectors

- Using identity vectors to sum word embeddings

- Learning the transition matrices

- Learning to create useful sentence vectors

- Forward propagation in Python

- Forward propagation and backpropagation with arbitrary length

- Weight update with arbitrary length

··

 There's something magical about Recurrent Neural Networks.

—Andrej Karpathy, "The Unreasonable Effectiveness of Recurrent Neural Networks," http://mng.bz/VqPW

The challenge of arbitrary length

Let's model arbitrarily long sequences of data with neural networks!

This chapter and chapter 11 are intertwined, and I encourage you to ensure that you've mastered the concepts and techniques from chapter 11 before you dive into this one. In chapter 11, you learned about natural language processing (NLP). This included how to modify a loss function to learn a specific pattern of information within the weights of a neural network. You also developed an intuition for what a word embedding is and how it can represent shades of similarity with other word embeddings. In this chapter, we'll expand on this intuition of an embedding conveying the meaning of a single word by creating embeddings that convey the meaning of variable-length phrases and sentences.

Let's first consider this challenge. If you wanted to create a vector that held an entire sequence of symbols within its contents in the same way a word embedding stores information about a word, how would you accomplish this? We'll start with the simplest option. In theory, if you concatenated or stacked the word embeddings, you'd have a vector of sorts that held an entire sequence of symbols.

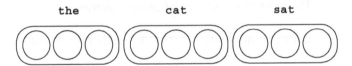

But this approach leaves something to be desired, because different sentences will have different-length vectors. This makes comparing two vectors together tricky, because one vector will stick out the side. Consider the following second sentence:

In theory, these two sentences should be very similar, and comparing their vectors should indicate a high degree of similarity. But because "the cat sat" is a shorter vector, you have to choose which part of "the cat sat still" vector to compare to. If you align left, the vectors will appear to be identical (ignoring the fact that "the cat sat still" is, in fact, a different sentence). But if you align right, then the vectors will appear to be extraordinarily different, despite the fact that three-quarters of the words are the same, in the same order. Although this naive approach shows some promise, it's far from ideal in terms of representing the meaning of a sentence in a useful way (a way that can be compared with other vectors).

Do comparisons really matter?

Why should you care about whether you can compare two sentence vectors?

The act of comparing two vectors is useful because it gives an approximation of what the neural network sees. Even though you can't read two vectors, you can tell when they're similar or different (using the function from chapter 11). If the method for generating sentence vectors doesn't reflect the similarity you observe between two sentences, then the network will also have difficulty recognizing when two sentences are similar. All it has to work with are the vectors!

As we continue to iterate and evaluate various methods for computing sentence vectors, I want you to remember why we're doing this. We're trying to take the perspective of a neural network. We're asking, "Will the correlation summarization find correlation between sentence vectors similar to this one and a desirable label, or will two nearly identical sentences instead generate wildly different vectors such that there is very little correlation between sentence vectors and the corresponding labels you're trying to predict?" We want to create sentence vectors that are useful for predicting things about the sentence, which, at a minimum, means similar sentences need to create similar vectors.

The previous way of creating the sentence vectors (concatenation) had issues because of the rather arbitrary way of aligning them, so let's explore the next-simplest approach. What if you take the vector for each word in a sentence, and average them? Well, right off the bat, you don't have to worry about alignment because each sentence vector is of the same length!

Matrix row average

Word vectors

Sentence vector

Furthermore, the sentences "the cat sat" and "the cat sat still" will have similar sentence vectors because the words going into them are similar. Even better, it's likely that "a dog walked" will be similar to "the cat sat," even though no words overlap, because the words used are also similar.

As it turns out, averaging word embeddings is a surprisingly effective way to create word embeddings. It's not perfect (as you'll see), but it does a strong job of capturing what you might perceive to be complex relationships between words. Before moving on, I think it will be extremely beneficial to take the word embeddings from chapter 11 and play around with the average strategy.

The surprising power of averaged word vectors

It's the amazingly powerful go-to tool for neural prediction.

In the previous section, I proposed the second method for creating vectors that convey the meaning of a sequence of words. This method takes the average of the vectors corresponding to the words in a sentence, and intuitively we expect these new average sentence vectors to behave in several desirable ways.

In this section, let's play with sentence vectors generated using the embeddings from the previous chapter. Break out the code from chapter 11, train the embeddings on the IMDB corpus as you did before, and let's experiment with average sentence embeddings.

At right is the same normalization performed when comparing word embeddings before. But this time, let's prenormalize all the word embeddings into a matrix called `normed_weights`. Then, create a function called `make_sent_vect` and use it to convert each review (list of words) into embeddings using the average approach. This is stored in the matrix `reviews2vectors`.

After this, you create a function that queries for the most similar reviews given an input review, by performing a dot product between the input review's vector and the vector of

```
import numpy as np
norms = np.sum(weights_0_1 * weights_0_1,axis=1)
norms.resize(norms.shape[0],1)
normed_weights = weights_0_1 * norms

def make_sent_vect(words):
  indices = list(map(lambda x:word2index[x],\
        filter(lambda x:x in word2index,words)))
  return np.mean(normed_weights[indices],axis=0)

reviews2vectors = list()
for review in tokens:                    ←——————  Tokenized reviews
  reviews2vectors.append(make_sent_vect(review))
reviews2vectors = np.array(reviews2vectors)

def most_similar_reviews(review):
  v = make_sent_vect(review)
  scores = Counter()
  for i,val in enumerate(reviews2vectors.dot(v)):
    scores[i] = val
  most_similar = list()

  for idx,score in scores.most_common(3):
    most_similar.append(raw_reviews[idx][0:40])
  return most_similar
most_similar_reviews(['boring','awful'])


    ['I am amazed at how boring this film',
     'This is truly one of the worst dep',
     'It just seemed to go on and on and.]
```

every other review in the corpus. This dot product similarity metric is the same one we briefly discussed in chapter 4 when you were learning to predict with multiple inputs.

Perhaps surprisingly, when you query for the most similar reviews to the average vector between the two words "boring" and "awful," you receive back three very negative reviews. There appears to be interesting statistical information within these vectors, such that negative and positive embeddings cluster together.

How is information stored in these embeddings?

When you average word embeddings, average shapes remain.

Considering what's going on here requires a little abstract thought. I recommend digesting this kind of information over a period of time, because it's probably a different kind of lesson than you're used to. For a moment, I'd like you to consider that a word vector can be visually observed as a *squiggly line* like this one:

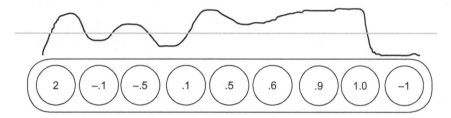

Instead of thinking of a vector as a list of numbers, think about it as a line with high and low points corresponding to high and low values at different places in the vector. If you selected several words from the corpus, they might look like this figure:

Consider the similarities between the various words. Notice that each vector's corresponding shape is unique. But "terrible" and "boring" have a certain similarity in their shape. "beautiful" and "wonderful" also have a similarity to their shape, but it's different from that of the other words. If we were to cluster these little

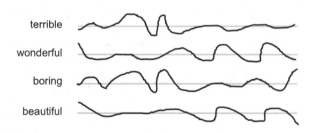

squiggles, words with similar meaning would cluster together. More important, parts of these squiggles have true meaning in and of themselves.

For example, for the negative words, there's a downward and then upward spike about 40% from the left. If I were to continue drawing lines corresponding to words, this spike would continue to be distinctive. There's nothing magical about that spike that means "negativity," and if I retrained the network, it would likely show up somewhere else. The spike indicates negativity only because all the negative words have it!

Thus, during the course of training, these shapes are molded such that different curves in different positions convey meaning (as discussed in chapter 11). When you take an average curve over the words in a sentence, the most dominant meanings of the sentence hold true, and the noise created by any particular word gets averaged away.

How does a neural network use embeddings?

Neural networks detect the curves that have correlation with a target label.

You've learned about a new way to view word embeddings as a squiggly line with distinctive properties (curves). You've also learned that these curves are developed throughout the course of training to accomplish the target objective. Words with similar meaning in one way or another will often share a distinctive bend in the curve: a combination of high-low pattern among the weights. In this section, we'll consider how the correlation summarization processes these curves as input. What does it mean for a layer to consume these curves as input?

Truth be told, a neural network consumes embeddings just as it consumed the streetlight dataset in the book's early chapters. It looks for correlation between the various bumps and curves in the hidden layer and the target label it's trying to predict. This is why words with one particular aspect of similarity share similar bumps and curves. At some point during training, a neural network starts developing unique characteristics between the shapes of different words so it can tell them apart, and grouping them (giving them similar bumps/ curves) to help make accurate predictions. But this is another way of summarizing the lessons from the end of chapter 11. We want to press further.

In this chapter, we'll consider what it means to sum these embeddings into a sentence embedding. What kinds of classifications would this summed vector be useful for? We've identified that taking an average across the word embeddings of a sentence results in a vector with an average of the characteristics of the words therein. If there are many positive words, the final embedding will look somewhat positive (with other noise from the words generally cancelling out). But note that this approach is a bit mushy: given enough words, these different wavy lines should all average together to generally be a straight line.

This brings us to the first weakness of this approach: when attempting to store arbitrarily long sequences (a sentence) of information into a fixed-length vector, if you try to store too much, eventually the sentence vector (being an average of a multitude of word vectors) will average out to a straight line (a vector of near-0s).

In short, this process of storing the information of a sentence doesn't decay nicely. If you try to store too many words into a single vector, you end up storing almost nothing. That being said, a sentence is often not that many words; and if a sentence has repeating patterns, these sentence vectors can be useful, because the sentence vector will retain the most dominant patterns present across the word vectors being summed (such as the negative spike in the previous section).

The limitations of bag-of-words vectors

Order becomes irrelevant when you average word embeddings.

The biggest issue with average embeddings is that they have no concept of order. For example, consider the two sentences "Yankees defeat Red Sox" and "Red Sox defeat Yankees." Generating sentence vectors for these two sentences using the average approach will yield identical vectors, but the sentences are conveying the exact opposite information! Furthermore, this approach ignores grammar and syntax, so "Sox Red Yankees defeat" will also yield an identical sentence embedding.

This approach of summing or averaging word embeddings to form the embedding for a phrase or sentence is classically known as a *bag-of-words* approach because, much like throwing a bunch of words into a bag, order isn't preserved. The key limitation is that you can take any sentence, scramble all the words around, and generate a sentence vector, and no matter how you scramble the words, the vector will be the same (because addition is associative: $a + b == b + a$).

The real topic of this chapter is generating sentence vectors in a way where order *does* matter. We want to create vectors such that scrambling them around changes the resulting vector. More important, the *way in which order matters* (otherwise known as *the way in which order changes the vector*) should be *learned*. In this way, the neural network's representation of order can be based around trying to solve a task in language and, by extension, hopefully capture the essence of order in language. I'm using language as an example here, but you can generalize these statements to any sequence. Language is just a particularly challenging, yet universally known, domain.

One of the most famous and successful ways of generating vectors for sequences (such as a sentence) is a *recurrent neural network* (RNN). In order to show you how it works, we'll start by coming up with a new, and seemingly wasteful, way of doing the average word embeddings using something called an *identity matrix*. An identity matrix is just an arbitrarily large, square matrix (num rows == num columns) of 0s with 1s stretching from the top-left corner to the bottom-right corner as in the examples shown here.

```
[1,0]
[0,1]
```

```
[1,0,0]
[0,1,0]
[0,0,1]
```

```
[1,0,0,0]
[0,1,0,0]
[0,0,1,0]
[0,0,0,1]
```

All three of these matrices are identity matrices, and they have one purpose: performing vector-matrix multiplication with *any* vector will return the original vector. If I multiply the vector [3,5] by the top identity matrix, the result will be [3,5].

Using identity vectors to sum word embeddings

Let's implement the same logic using a different approach.

You may think identity matrices are useless. What's the purpose of a matrix that takes a vector and outputs that same vector? In this case, we'll use it as a teaching tool to show how to set up a more complicated way of summing the word embeddings so the neural network can take order into account when generating the final sentence embedding. Let's explore another way of summing embeddings.

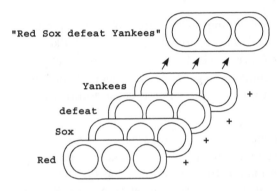

This is the standard technique for summing multiple word embeddings together to form a sentence embedding (dividing by the number of words gives the average sentence embedding). The example on the right adds a step *between* each sum: vector-matrix multiplication by an identity matrix.

The vector for "Red" is multiplied by an identity matrix, and then the output is summed with the vector for "Sox," which is then vector-matrix multiplied by the identity matrix and added to the vector for "defeat,"

and so on throughout the sentence. Note that because the vector-matrix multiplication by the identity matrix returns the same vector that goes into it, the process on the right yields *exactly the same sentence embedding* as the process at top left.

Yes, this is wasteful computation, but that's about to change. The main thing to consider here is that if the matrices used were any matrix other than the identity matrix, changing the order of the words would change the resulting embedding. Let's see this in Python.

Matrices that change absolutely nothing

Let's create sentence embeddings using identity matrices in Python.

In this section, we'll demonstrate how to play with identity matrices in Python and ultimately implement the new sentence vector technique from the previous section (proving that it produces identical sentence embeddings).

At right, we first initialize four vectors (a, b, c, and d) of length 3 as well as an identity matrix with three rows and three columns (identity matrices are always square). Notice that the identity matrix has the characteristic set of 1s running diagonally from top-left to bottom-right (which, by the way, is called the *diagonal* in linear algebra). Any square matrix with 1s along the diagonal and 0s everywhere else is an identity matrix.

```
import numpy as np

a = np.array([1,2,3])
b = np.array([0.1,0.2,0.3])
c = np.array([-1,-0.5,0])
d = np.array([0,0,0])

identity = np.eye(3)
print(identity)
```

```
[[ 1.  0.  0.]
 [ 0.  1.  0.]
 [ 0.  0.  1.]]
```

We then proceed to perform vector-matrix multiplication with each of the vectors and the identity matrix (using NumPy's dot function). As you can see, the output of this process is a new vector identical to the input vector.

```
print(a.dot(identity))
print(b.dot(identity))
print(c.dot(identity))
print(d.dot(identity))
```

Because vector-matrix multiplication by an identity matrix returns the same vector we started with, incorporating this process into the sentence embedding should seem trivial, and it is:

```
[ 1.   2.   3.]
[ 0.1  0.2  0.3]
[-1.  -0.5  0. ]
[ 0.   0.   0. ]
```

```
this = np.array([2,4,6])
movie = np.array([10,10,10])
rocks = np.array([1,1,1])

print(this + movie + rocks)
print((this.dot(identity) + movie).dot(identity) + rocks)
```

```
[13 15 17]
[ 13.  15.  17.]
```

Both ways of creating sentence embeddings generate the same vector. This is only because the identity matrix is a very special kind of matrix. But what would happen if we didn't use the identity matrix? What if, instead, we used a different matrix? In fact, the identity matrix is the *only* matrix guaranteed to return the same vector that it's vector-matrix multiplied with. No other matrix has this guarantee.

Learning the transition matrices

What if you allowed the identity matrices to change to minimize the loss?

Before we begin, let's remember the goal: generating sentence embeddings that cluster according to the meaning of the sentence, such that given a sentence, we can use the vector to find sentences with a similar meaning. More specifically, these sentence embeddings should care about the order of words.

Previously, we tried summing word embeddings. But this meant "Red Sox defeat Yankees" had an identical vector to the sentence "Yankees defeat Red Sox," despite the fact that these two sentences have opposite meanings. Instead, we want to form sentence embeddings where these two sentences generate *different* embeddings (yet still cluster in a meaningful way). The theory is that if we use the identity-matrix way of creating sentence embeddings, but used any other matrix other than the identity matrix, the sentence embeddings would be different depending on the order.

Now the obvious question: what matrix to use instead of the identity matrix. There are an infinite number of choices. But in deep learning, the standard answer to this kind of question is, "You'll learn the matrix just like you learn any other matrix in a neural network!" OK, so you'll just learn this matrix. How?

Whenever you want to train a neural network to learn something, you always need a task for it to learn. In this case, that task should require it to generate interesting sentence embeddings by learning both useful word vectors and useful modifications to the identity matrices. What task should you use?

What you know → Supervised learning → What you want to know

The goal was similar when you wanted to generate useful word embeddings (fill in the blank). Let's try to accomplish a very similar task: training a neural network to take a list of words and attempt to predict the next word.

["This", "movie", "was"] → Neural network → ["great"]

Learning to create useful sentence vectors

Create the sentence vector, make a prediction, and modify the sentence vector via its parts.

In this next experiment, I don't want you to think about the network like previous neural networks. Instead, think about creating a sentence embedding, using it to predict the next word, and then modifying the respective parts that formed the sentence embedding to make this prediction more accurate. Because you're predicting the next word, the sentence embedding will be made from the parts of the sentence you've seen so far. The neural network will look something like the figure.

It's composed of two steps: create the sentence embedding, and then use that embedding to predict which word comes next. The input to this network is the text "Red Sox defeat," and the word to be predicted is "Yankees."

I've written *Identity matrix* in the boxes between the word vectors. This matrix will only *start* as an identity matrix. During training, you'll backpropagate gradients into these matrices and update them to help the network make better predictions (just as for the rest of the weights in the network).

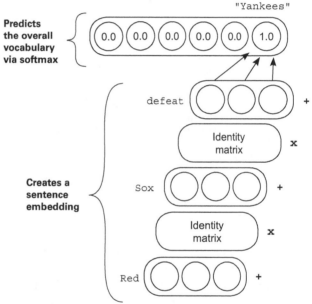

This way, the network will *learn how to incorporate more information than just a sum of word embeddings*. By allowing the (initially, identity) matrices to change (and become *not* identity matrices), you let the neural network learn how to create embeddings where the order in which the words are presented changes the sentence embedding. But this change isn't arbitrary. The network will learn how to incorporate the order of words in a way that's *useful for the task of predicting the next word*.

You'll also constrain the *transition matrices* (the matrices that are originally identity matrices) to all be the same matrix. In other words, the matrix from "Red" -> "Sox" will be reused to transition from "Sox" -> "defeat." Whatever logic the network learns in one transition will be reused in the next, and only logic that's useful at every predictive step will be allowed to be learned in the network.

Forward propagation in Python

Let's take this idea and see how to perform a simple forward propagation.

Now that you have the conceptual idea of what you're trying to build, let's check out a toy version in Python. First, let's set up the weights (I'm using a limited vocab of nine words):

```python
import numpy as np

def softmax(x_):
    x = np.atleast_2d(x_)
    temp = np.exp(x)
    return temp / np.sum(temp, axis=1, keepdims=True)

word_vects = {}
word_vects['yankees'] = np.array([[0.,0.,0.]])
word_vects['bears'] = np.array([[0.,0.,0.]])
word_vects['braves'] = np.array([[0.,0.,0.]])
word_vects['red'] = np.array([[0.,0.,0.]])
word_vects['sox'] = np.array([[0.,0.,0.]])
word_vects['lose'] = np.array([[0.,0.,0.]])
word_vects['defeat'] = np.array([[0.,0.,0.]])
word_vects['beat'] = np.array([[0.,0.,0.]])
word_vects['tie'] = np.array([[0.,0.,0.]])

sent2output = np.random.rand(3,len(word_vects))

identity = np.eye(3)
```

Word embeddings

Sentence embedding to output classification weights

Transition weights

This code creates three sets of weights. It creates a Python dictionary of word embeddings, the identity matrix (transition matrix), and a classification layer. This classification layer `sent2output` is a weight matrix to predict the next word given a sentence vector of length 3. With these tools, forward propagation is trivial. Here's how forward propagation works with the sentence "red sox defeat" -> "yankees":

```python
layer_0 = word_vects['red']
layer_1 = layer_0.dot(identity) + word_vects['sox']
layer_2 = layer_1.dot(identity) + word_vects['defeat']

pred = softmax(layer_2.dot(sent2output))
print(pred)
```

Creates a sentence embedding

Predicts over all vocabulary

```
[[ 0.11111111   0.11111111   0.11111111   0.11111111   0.11111111   0.11111111
   0.11111111   0.11111111   0.11111111]]
```

How do you backpropagate into this?

It might seem trickier, but they're the same steps you already learned.

You just saw how to perform forward prediction for this network. At first, it might not be clear how backpropagation can be performed. But it's simple. Perhaps this is what you see:

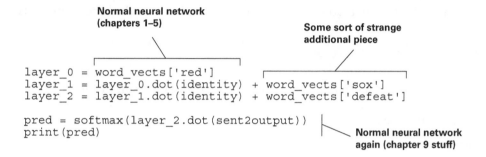

Based on previous chapters, you should feel comfortable with computing a loss and backpropagating until you get to the gradients at `layer_2`, called `layer_2_delta`. At this point, you might be wondering, "Which direction do I backprop in?" Gradients could go back to `layer_1` by going backward through the `identity` matrix multiplication, or they could go into `word_vects['defeat']`.

When you add two vectors together during forward propagation, you backpropagate the same gradient into *both* sides of the addition. When you generate `layer_2_delta`, you'll backpropagate it twice: once across the identity matrix to create `layer_1_delta`, and again to `word_vects['defeat']`:

```
y = np.array([1,0,0,0,0,0,0,0,0])                           Targets the one-hot
                                                            vector for "yankees"
pred_delta = pred - y
layer_2_delta = pred_delta.dot(sent2output.T)               Can ignore the "1"
defeat_delta = layer_2_delta * 1                            as in chapter 11
layer_1_delta = layer_2_delta.dot(identity.T)
sox_delta = layer_1_delta * 1                               Again, can
layer_0_delta = layer_1_delta.dot(identity.T)               ignore the "1"
alpha = 0.01
word_vects['red'] -= layer_0_delta * alpha
word_vects['sox'] -= sox_delta * alpha
word_vects['defeat'] -= defeat_delta * alpha
identity -= np.outer(layer_0,layer_1_delta) * alpha
identity -= np.outer(layer_1,layer_2_delta) * alpha
sent2output -= np.outer(layer_2,pred_delta) * alpha
```

Let's train it!

You have all the tools; let's train the network on a toy corpus.

So that you can get an intuition for what's going on, let's first train the new network on a toy task called the Babi dataset. This dataset is a synthetically generated question-answer corpus to teach machines how to answer simple questions about an environment. You aren't using it for QA (yet), but the simplicity of the task will help you better see the impact made by learning the identity matrix. First, download the Babi dataset. Here are the bash commands:

```
wget http://www.thespermwhale.com/jaseweston/babi/tasks_1-20_v1-1.tar.gz
tar -xvf tasks_1-20_v1-1.tar.gz
```

With some simple Python, you can open and clean a small dataset to train the network:

```
import sys,random,math
from collections import Counter
import numpy as np

f = open('tasksv11/en/qa1_single-supporting-fact_train.txt','r')
raw = f.readlines()
f.close()

tokens = list()
for line in raw[0:1000]:
    tokens.append(line.lower().replace("\n","").split(" ")[1:])

print(tokens[0:3])

[['Mary', 'moved', 'to', 'the', 'bathroom'],
 ['John', 'went', 'to', 'the', 'hallway'],
 ['Where', 'is', 'Mary', 'bathroom'],
```

As you can see, this dataset contains a variety of simple statements and questions (with punctuation removed). Each question is followed by the correct answer. When used in the context of QA, a neural network reads the statements in order and answers questions (either correctly or incorrectly) based on information in the recently read statements.

For now, you'll train the network to attempt to finish each sentence when given one or more starting words. Along the way, you'll see the importance of allowing the recurrent matrix (previously the identity matrix) to learn.

Setting things up

Before you can create matrices, you need to learn how many parameters you have.

As with the word embedding neural network, you first need to create a few useful counts, lists, and utility functions to use during the predict, compare, learn process. These utility functions and objects are shown here and should look familiar:

```
vocab = set()                          def words2indices(sentence):
for sent in tokens:                        idx = list()
    for word in sent:                      for word in sentence:
        vocab.add(word)                        idx.append(word2index[word])
vocab = list(vocab)                        return idx

word2index = {}                        def softmax(x):
for i,word in enumerate(vocab):            e_x = np.exp(x - np.max(x))
    word2index[word]=i                     return e_x / e_x.sum(axis=0)
```

At left, you create a simple list of the vocabulary words as well as a lookup dictionary allowing you to go back and forth between a word's text and its index. You'll use its index in the vocabulary list to pick which row and column of the embedding and prediction matrices correspond to which word. At right is a utility function for converting a list of words to a list of indices, as well as the function for softmax, which you'll use to predict the next word.

The following code initializes the random seed (to get consistent results) and then sets the embedding size to 10. You create a matrix of word embeddings, recurrent embeddings, and an initial start embedding. This is the embedding modeling an empty phrase, which is key to the network modeling how sentences tend to start. Finally, there's a decoder weight matrix (just like from embeddings) and a one_hot utility matrix:

```
np.random.seed(1)                                     Word embeddings
embed_size = 10

embed = (np.random.rand(len(vocab),embed_size) - 0.5) * 0.1

recurrent = np.eye(embed_size)                         Embedding ->
                                                       embedding (initially
start = np.zeros(embed_size)                            the identity matrix)

decoder = (np.random.rand(embed_size, len(vocab)) - 0.5) * 0.1

one_hot = np.eye(len(vocab))

Sentence embedding for          One-hot lookups            Embedding ->
an empty sentence               (for the loss function)    output weights
```

Forward propagation with arbitrary length

You'll forward propagate using the same logic described earlier.

The following code contains the logic to forward propagate and predict the next word. Note that although the construction might feel unfamiliar, it follows the same procedure as before for summing embeddings while using the identity matrix. Here, the identity matrix is replaced with a matrix called `recurrent`, which is initialized to be all 0s (and will be learned through training).

Furthermore, instead of predicting only at the last word, you make a prediction (`layer['pred']`) at every timestep, based on the embedding generated by the previous words. This is more efficient than doing a new forward propagation from the beginning of the phrase each time you want to predict a new term.

```
def predict(sent):

    layers = list()
    layer = {}
    layer['hidden'] = start
    layers.append(layer)                          Forward
                                                  propagates
    loss = 0
                                                                    Tries to
    preds = list()                                                  predict the
    for target_i in range(len(sent)):                               next term

        layer = {}

        layer['pred'] = softmax(layers[-1]['hidden'].dot(decoder))

        loss += -np.log(layer['pred'][sent[target_i]])

        layer['hidden'] = layers[-1]['hidden'].dot(recurrent) +\
                                           embed[sent[target_i]]
        layers.append(layer)
    return layers, loss
                                                        Generates the
                                                        next hidden state
```

There's nothing particularly new about this bit of code relative to what you've learned in the past, but there's a particular piece I want to make sure you're familiar with before we move forward. The list called `layers` is a new way to forward propagate.

Notice that you end up doing more forward propagations if the length of `sent` is larger. As a result, you can't use static layer variables as before. This time, you need to keep appending new layers to the list based on the required number. Be sure you're comfortable with what's going on in each part of this list, because if it's unfamiliar to you in the forward propagation pass, it will be very difficult to know what's going on during the backpropagation and weight update steps.

Backpropagation with arbitrary length

You'll backpropagate using the same logic described earlier.

As described with the "Red Sox defeat Yankees" example, let's implement backpropagation over arbitrary-length sequences, assuming you have access to the forward propagation objects returned from the function in the previous section. The most important object is the `layers` list, which has two vectors (`layer['state']` and `layer['previous->hidden']`).

In order to backpropagate, you'll take the output gradient and add a new object to each list called `layer['state_delta']`, which will represent the gradient at that layer. This corresponds to variables like `sox_delta`, `layer_0_delta`, and `defeat_delta` from the "Red Sox defeat Yankees" example. You're building the same logic in a way that it can consume the variable-length sequences from the forward propagation logic.

```
for iter in range(30000):              ◄────── Forward
    alpha = 0.001
    sent = words2indices(tokens[iter%len(tokens)][1:])
    layers,loss = predict(sent)

    for layer_idx in reversed(range(len(layers))):  ◄──── Backpropagates
        layer = layers[layer_idx]
        target = sent[layer_idx-1]                   If not the
                                                     first layer
        if(layer_idx > 0):  ◄──────────────
            layer['output_delta'] = layer['pred'] - one_hot[target]
            new_hidden_delta = layer['output_delta']\
                                            .dot(decoder.transpose())
If the last layer,
don't pull from a ──────►  if(layer_idx == len(layers)-1):
later one, because             layer['hidden_delta'] = new_hidden_delta
it doesn't exist           else:
                               layer['hidden_delta'] = new_hidden_delta + \
                               layers[layer_idx+1]['hidden_delta']\
                                            .dot(recurrent.transpose())
        else: # if the first layer
            layer['hidden_delta'] = layers[layer_idx+1]['hidden_delta']\
                                        .dot(recurrent.transpose())
```

Before moving on to the next section, be sure you can read this code and explain it to a friend (or at least to yourself). There are no new concepts in this code, but its construction can make it seem a bit foreign at first. Spend some time linking what's written in this code back to each line of the "Red Sox defeat Yankees" example, and you should be ready for the next section and updating the weights using the gradients you backpropagated.

Weight update with arbitrary length

You'll update weights using the same logic described earlier.

As with the forward and backprop logic, this weight update logic isn't new. But I'm presenting it after having explained it so you can focus on the engineering complexity, having (hopefully) already grokked (ha!) the theory complexity.

```
for iter in range(30000):                    ◄────────  Forward
    alpha = 0.001
    sent = words2indices(tokens[iter%len(tokens)][1:])

    layers,loss = predict(sent)

    for layer_idx in reversed(range(len(layers))):   ◄────  Backpropagates
        layer = layers[layer_idx]
        target = sent[layer_idx-1]

        if(layer_idx > 0):
            layer['output_delta'] = layer['pred'] - one_hot[target]
            new_hidden_delta = layer['output_delta']\
                                        .dot(decoder.transpose())

            if(layer_idx == len(layers)-1):   ◄──────────  If the last layer,
                layer['hidden_delta'] = new_hidden_delta    don't pull from a
            else:                                           later one, because
                layer['hidden_delta'] = new_hidden_delta + \  it doesn't exist
                layers[layer_idx+1]['hidden_delta']\
                                    .dot(recurrent.transpose())
        else:
            layer['hidden_delta'] = layers[layer_idx+1]['hidden_delta']\
                                    .dot(recurrent.transpose())
```
Updates
weights
```
    start -= layers[0]['hidden_delta'] * alpha / float(len(sent))
    for layer_idx,layer in enumerate(layers[1:]):

        decoder -= np.outer(layers[layer_idx]['hidden'],\
                        layer['output_delta']) * alpha / float(len(sent))

        embed_idx = sent[layer_idx]
        embed[embed_idx] -= layers[layer_idx]['hidden_delta'] * \
                                    alpha / float(len(sent))
        recurrent -= np.outer(layers[layer_idx]['hidden'],\
                        layer['hidden_delta']) * alpha / float(len(sent))

    if(iter % 1000 == 0):
        print("Perplexity:" + str(np.exp(loss/len(sent))))
```

Execution and output analysis
You'll update weights using the same logic described earlier.

Now the moment of truth: what happens when you run it? Well, when I run this code, I get a relatively steady downtrend in a metric called *perplexity*. Technically, perplexity is the probability of the correct label (word), passed through a log function, negated, and exponentiated ($e\wedge x$).

But what it represents theoretically is the difference between two probability distributions. In this case, the perfect probability distribution would be 100% probability allocated to the correct term and 0% everywhere else.

Perplexity is high when two probability distributions don't match, and it's low (approaching 1) when they do match. Thus, a decreasing perplexity, like all loss functions used with stochastic gradient descent, is a good thing! It means the network is learning to predict probabilities that match the data.

```
Perplexity:82.09227500075585
Perplexity:81.87615610433569
Perplexity:81.53705034457951
                ....
Perplexity:4.132556753967558
Perplexity:4.071667181580819
Perplexity:4.0167814473718435
```

But this hardly tells you what's going on in the weights. Perplexity has faced some criticism over the years (particularly in the language-modeling community) for being overused as a metric. Let's look a little more closely at the predictions:

```
sent_index = 4

l,_ = predict(words2indices(tokens[sent_index]))

print(tokens[sent_index])

for i,each_layer in enumerate(l[1:-1]):
    input = tokens[sent_index][i]
    true = tokens[sent_index][i+1]
    pred = vocab[each_layer['pred'].argmax()]
    print("Prev Input:" + input + (' ' * (12 - len(input))) +\
          "True:" + true + (" " * (15 - len(true))) + "Pred:" + pred)
```

This code takes a sentence and predicts the word the model thinks is most likely. This is useful because it gives a sense for the kinds of characteristics the model takes on. What kinds of things does it get right? What kinds of mistakes does it make? You'll see in the next section.

Looking at predictions can help you understand what's going on.

You can look at the output predictions of the neural network as it trains to learn not only what kinds of patterns it picks up, but also the order in which it learns them. After 100 training steps, the output looks like this:

```
['sandra', 'moved', 'to', 'the', 'garden.']
Prev Input:sandra        True:moved        Pred:is
Prev Input:moved         True:to           Pred:kitchen
Prev Input:to            True:the          Pred:bedroom
Prev Input:the           True:garden.      Pred:office
```

Neural networks tend to start off random. In this case, the neural network is likely only biased toward whatever words it started with in its first random state. Let's keep training:

```
['sandra', 'moved', 'to', 'the', 'garden.']
Prev Input:sandra        True:moved        Pred:the
Prev Input:moved         True:to           Pred:the
Prev Input:to            True:the          Pred:the
Prev Input:the           True:garden.      Pred:the
```

After 10,000 training steps, the neural network picks out the most common word ("the") and predicts it at every timestep. This is an extremely common error in recurrent neural networks. It takes lots of training to learn finer-grained detail in a highly skewed dataset.

```
['sandra', 'moved', 'to', 'the', 'garden.']
Prev Input:sandra        True:moved        Pred:is
Prev Input:moved         True:to           Pred:to
Prev Input:to            True:the          Pred:the
Prev Input:the           True:garden.      Pred:bedroom.
```

These mistakes are really interesting. After seeing only the word "sandra," the network predicts "is," which, although not exactly the same as "moved," isn't a bad guess. It picked the wrong verb. Next, notice that the words "to" and "the" were correct, which isn't as surprising because these are some of the more common words in the dataset, and presumably the network has been trained to predict the phrase "to the" after the verb "moved" many times. The final mistake is also compelling, mistaking "bedroom" for the word "garden."

It's important to note that there's almost no way this neural network could learn this task perfectly. After all, if I gave you the words "sandra moved to the," could you tell me the correct next word? More context is needed to solve this task, but the fact that it's unsolvable, in my opinion, creates educational analysis for the ways in which it fails.

Summary

Recurrent neural networks predict over arbitrary-length sequences.

In this chapter, you learned how to create vector representations for arbitrary-length sequences. The last exercise trained a linear recurrent neural network to predict the next term given a previous phrase of terms. To do this, it needed to learn how to create embeddings that accurately represented variable-length strings of terms into a fixed-size vector.

This last sentence should drive home a question: how does a neural network fit a variable amount of information into a fixed-size box? The truth is, sentence vectors don't encode everything in the sentence. The name of the game in recurrent neural networks is not just what these vectors remember, but also what they forget. In the case of predicting the next word, most RNNs learn that only the last couple of words are really necessary,[*] and they learn to forget (aka, not make unique patterns in their vectors for) words further back in the history.

But note that there are no nonlinearities in the generation of these representations. What kinds of limitations do you think that could create? In the next chapter, we'll explore this question and more using nonlinearities and gates to form a neural network called a *long short-term memory network* (LSTM). But first, make sure you can sit down and (from memory) code a working linear RNN that converges. The dynamics and control flow of these networks can be a bit daunting, and the complexity is about to jump by quite a bit. Before moving on, become comfortable with what you've learned in this chapter.

And with that, let's dive into LSTMs!

---

* See, for example, "Frustratingly Short Attention Spans in Neural Language Modeling" by Michał Daniluk et al. (paper presented at ICLR 2017), https://arxiv.org/abs/1702.04521.

introducing automatic optimization: | **13**
let's build a deep learning framework

In this chapter

> Whether we are based on carbon or on silicon makes
> no fundamental difference; we should each be treated
> with appropriate respect.
>
> —Arthur C. Clarke, *2010: Odyssey Two* (1982)

What is a deep learning framework?

Good tools reduce errors, speed development, and increase runtime performance.

If you've been reading about deep learning for long, you've probably come across one of the major frameworks such as PyTorch, TensorFlow, Theano (recently deprecated), Keras, Lasagne, or DyNet. Framework development has been extremely rapid over the past few years, and, despite all frameworks being free, open source software, there's a light spirit of competition and comradery around each framework.

Thus far, I've avoided the topic of frameworks because, first and foremost, it's extremely important for you to know what's going on under the hood of these frameworks by implementing algorithms yourself (from scratch in NumPy). But now we're going to transition into using a framework, because the networks you'll be training next—long short-term memory networks (LSTMs)—are very complex, and NumPy code describing their implementation is difficult to read, use, or debug (gradients are flying everywhere).

It's exactly this code complexity that deep learning frameworks were created to mitigate. Especially if you wish to train a neural network on a GPU (giving 10–100× faster training), a deep learning framework can significantly reduce code complexity (reducing errors and increasing development speed) while also increasing runtime performance. For these reasons, their use is nearly universal within the research community, and a thorough understanding of a deep learning framework will be essential on your journey toward becoming a user or researcher of deep learning.

But we won't jump into any deep learning frameworks you've heard of, because that would stifle your ability to learn about what complex models (such as LSTMs) are doing under the hood. Instead, you'll build a light deep learning framework according to the latest trends in framework development. This way, you'll have no doubt about what frameworks do when using them for complex architectures. Furthermore, building a small framework yourself should provide a smooth transition to using actual deep learning frameworks, because you'll already be familiar with the API and the functionality underneath it. I found this exercise beneficial myself, and the lessons learned in building my own framework are especially useful when attempting to debug a troublesome model.

How does a framework simplify your code? Abstractly, it eliminates the need to write code that you'd repeat multiple times. Concretely, the most beneficial pieces of a deep learning framework are its support for automatic backpropagation and automatic optimization. These features let you specify only the forward propagation code of a model, with the framework taking care of backpropagation and weight updates automatically. Most frameworks even make the forward propagation code easier by providing high-level interfaces to common layers and loss functions.

Introduction to tensors

Tensors are an abstract form of vectors and matrices.

Up to this point, we've been working exclusively with vectors and matrices as the basic data structures for deep learning. Recall that a matrix is a list of vectors, and a vector is a list of scalars (single numbers). A *tensor* is the abstract version of this form of nested lists of numbers. A vector is a one-dimensional tensor. A matrix is a two-dimensional tensor, and higher dimensions are referred to as *n*-dimensional tensors. Thus, the beginning of a new deep learning framework is the construction of this basic type, which we'll call `Tensor`:

```python
import numpy as np

class Tensor (object):

    def __init__(self, data):
        self.data = np.array(data)

    def __add__(self, other):
        return Tensor(self.data + other.data)

    def __repr__(self):
        return str(self.data.__repr__())

    def __str__(self):
        return str(self.data.__str__())

x = Tensor([1,2,3,4,5])
print(x)
```

```
[1 2 3 4 5]
```

```python
y = x + x
print(y)
```

```
[ 2  4  6  8 10]
```

This is the first version of this basic data structure. Note that it stores all the numerical information in a NumPy array (`self.data`), and it supports one tensor operation (addition). Adding more operations is relatively simple: create more functions on the tensor class with the appropriate functionality.

Introduction to automatic gradient computation (autograd)

Previously, you performed backpropagation by hand. Let's make it automatic!

In chapter 4, you learned about derivatives. Since then, you've been computing derivatives by hand for each neural network you train. Recall that this is done by moving backward through the neural network: first compute the gradient at the output of the network, then use that result to compute the derivative at the next-to-last component, and so on until all weights in the architecture have correct gradients. This logic for computing gradients can also be added to the tensor object. Let me show you what I mean. New code is in **bold**:

```
import numpy as np

class Tensor (object):

    def __init__(self, data, creators=None, creation_op=None):
        self.data = np.array(data)
        self.creation_op = creation_op
        self.creators = creators
        self.grad = None

    def backward(self, grad):
        self.grad = grad

        if(self.creation_op == "add"):
            self.creators[0].backward(grad)
            self.creators[1].backward(grad)

    def __add__(self, other):
        return Tensor(self.data + other.data,
                      creators=[self,other],
                      creation_op="add")

    def __repr__(self):
        return str(self.data.__repr__())

    def __str__(self):
        return str(self.data.__str__())

x = Tensor([1,2,3,4,5])
y = Tensor([2,2,2,2,2])

z = x + y
z.backward(Tensor(np.array([1,1,1,1,1])))
```

This method introduces two new concepts. First, each tensor gets two new attributes. creators is a list containing any tensors used in the creation of the current tensor (which defaults to None). Thus, when the two tensors x and y are added together, z has two creators, x and y. creation_op is a related feature that stores the instructions creators used in the creation process. Thus, performing z = x + y creates a *computation graph* with three nodes (x, y, and z) and two edges (z -> x and z -> y). Each edge is labeled by the creation_op add. This graph allows you to recursively backpropagate gradients.

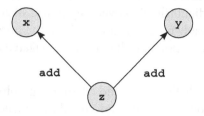

The first new concept in this implementation is the automatic creation of this graph whenever you perform math operations. If you took z and performed further operations, the graph would continue with whatever resulting new variables pointed back to z.

The second new concept introduced in this version of Tensor is the ability to use this graph to compute gradients. When you call z .backward(), it sends the correct gradient for x and y given the function that was applied to create z (add). Looking at the graph, you place a vector of gradients (np.array([1,1,1,1,1])) on z, and then they're applied to their parents. As you learned in chapter 4, backpropagating through addition means also applying addition when backpropagating. In this case, because there's only one gradient to add into x or y, you copy the gradient from z onto x and y:

```
print(x.grad)
print(y.grad)
print(z.creators)
print(z.creation_op)


[1 1 1 1 1]
[1 1 1 1 1]
[array([1, 2, 3, 4, 5]), array([2, 2, 2, 2, 2])]
add
```

Perhaps the most elegant part of this form of autograd is that it works recursively as well, because each vector calls .backward() on all of its self.creators:

```
a = Tensor([1,2,3,4,5])
b = Tensor([2,2,2,2,2])
c = Tensor([5,4,3,2,1])
d = Tensor([-1,-2,-3,-4,-5])
e = a + b
f = c + d
g = e + f
g.backward(Tensor(np.array([1,1,1,1,1])))
print(a.grad)
```

Output

```
[1 1 1 1 1]
```

A quick checkpoint

Everything in Tensor is another form of lessons already learned.

Before moving on, I want to first acknowledge that even if it feels like a bit of a stretch or a heavy lift to think about gradients flowing over a graphical structure, this is nothing new compared to what you've already been working with. In the previous chapter on RNNs, you forward propagated in one direction and then back propagated across a (virtual graph) of activations.

You just didn't explicitly encode the nodes and edges in a graphical data structure. Instead, you had a list of layers (dictionaries) and hand-coded the correct order of forward and backpropagation operations. Now you're building a nice interface so you don't have to write as much code. This interface lets you backpropagate recursively instead of having to handwrite complicated backprop code.

This chapter is only somewhat theoretical. It's mostly about commonly used engineering practices for learning deep neural networks. In particular, this notion of a graph that gets built during forward propagation is called a *dynamic computation graph* because it's built on the fly during forward prop. This is the type of autograd present in newer deep learning frameworks such as DyNet and PyTorch. Older frameworks such as Theano and TensorFlow have what's called a *static computation graph*, which is specified before forward propagation even begins.

In general, dynamic computation graphs are easier to write/experiment with, and static computation graphs have faster runtimes because of some fancy logic under the hood. But note that dynamic and static frameworks have lately been moving toward the middle, allowing dynamic graphs to compile to static ones (for faster runtimes) or allowing static graphs to be built dynamically (for easier experimentation). In the long run, you're likely to end up with both. The primary difference is whether forward propagation is happening during graph construction or after the graph is already defined. In this book, we'll stick with dynamic.

The main point of this chapter is to help prepare you for deep learning in the real world, where 10% (or less) of your time will be spent thinking up a new idea and 90% of your time will be spent figuring out how to get a deep learning framework to play nicely. Debugging these frameworks can be extremely difficult at times, because most bugs don't raise an error and print out a stack trace. Most bugs lie hidden within the code, keeping the network from training as it should (even if it appears to be training somewhat).

All that is to say, really dive into this chapter. You'll be glad you did when it's 2:00 a.m. and you're chasing down an optimization bug that's keeping you from getting that juicy state-of-the-art score.

Tensors that are used multiple times

The basic autograd has a rather pesky bug. Let's squish it!

The current version of `Tensor` supports backpropagating into a variable only once. But sometimes, during forward propagation, you'll use the same tensor multiple times (the weights of a neural network), and thus multiple parts of the graph will backpropagate gradients into the same tensor. But the code will currently compute the incorrect gradient when backpropagating into a variable that was used multiple times (is the parent of multiple children). Here's what I mean:

```
a = Tensor([1,2,3,4,5])
b = Tensor([2,2,2,2,2])
c = Tensor([5,4,3,2,1])

d = a + b
e = b + c
f = d + e
f.backward(Tensor(np.array([1,1,1,1,1])))

print(b.grad.data == np.array([2,2,2,2,2]))


array([False, False, False, False, False])
```

In this example, the b variable is used twice in the process of creating f. Thus, its gradient should be the sum of two derivatives: [2,2,2,2,2]. Shown here is the resulting graph created by this chain of operations. Notice there are now two pointers pointing into b: so, it should be the sum of the gradient coming from both e and d.

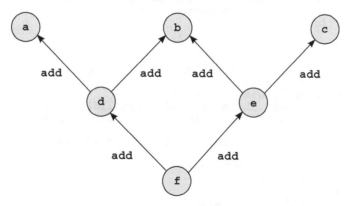

But the current implementation of `Tensor` merely overwrites each derivative with the previous. First, d applies its gradient, and then it gets overwritten with the gradient from e. We need to change the way gradients are written.

Upgrading autograd to support multiuse tensors

Add one new function, and update three old ones.

This update to the Tensor object adds two new features. First, gradients can be accumulated so that when a variable is used more than once, it receives gradients from all children:

```python
import numpy as np
class Tensor (object):

    def __init__(self,data,
                 autograd=False,
                 creators=None,
                 creation_op=None,
                 id=None):

        self.data = np.array(data)
        self.creators = creators
        self.creation_op = creation_op
        self.grad = None
        self.autograd = autograd
        self.children = {}
        if(id is None):
            id = np.random.randint(0,100000)
        self.id = id

        if(creators is not None):
            for c in creators:
                if(self.id not in c.children):
                    c.children[self.id] = 1
                else:
                    c.children[self.id] += 1

    def all_children_grads_accounted_for(self):
        for id,cnt in self.children.items():
            if(cnt != 0):
                return False
        return True

    def backward(self,grad=None, grad_origin=None):
        if(self.autograd):
            if(grad_origin is not None):
                if(self.children[grad_origin.id] == 0):
                    raise Exception("cannot backprop more than once")
                else:
                    self.children[grad_origin.id] -= 1

            if(self.grad is None):
                self.grad = grad
            else:
                self.grad += grad

            if(self.creators is not None and
               (self.all_children_grads_accounted_for() or
                grad_origin is None)):
```

Keeps track of how many children a tensor has

Checks whether a tensor has received the correct number of gradients from each child

Checks to make sure you can backpropagate or whether you're waiting for a gradient, in which case decrement the counter

Accumulates gradients from several children

```
            if(self.creation_op == "add"):
                self.creators[0].backward(self.grad, self)
                self.creators[1].backward(self.grad, self)

    def __add__(self, other):
        if(self.autograd and other.autograd):
            return Tensor(self.data + other.data,
                          autograd=True,
                          creators=[self,other],
                          creation_op="add")
        return Tensor(self.data + other.data)

    def __repr__(self):
        return str(self.data.__repr__())

    def __str__(self):
        return str(self.data.__str__())

a = Tensor([1,2,3,4,5], autograd=True)
b = Tensor([2,2,2,2,2], autograd=True)
c = Tensor([5,4,3,2,1], autograd=True)

d = a + b
e = b + c
f = d + e

f.backward(Tensor(np.array([1,1,1,1,1])))

print(b.grad.data == np.array([2,2,2,2,2]))
```

Begins actual backpropagation

```
[ True  True  True  True  True]
```

Additionally, you create a `self.children` counter that counts the number of gradients received from each child during backpropagation. This way, you also prevent a variable from accidentally backpropagating from the same child twice (which throws an exception).

The second added feature is a new function with the rather verbose name `all_children_grads_accounted_for()`. The purpose of this function is to compute whether a tensor has received gradients from all of its children in the graph. Normally, whenever `.backward()` is called on an intermediate variable in a graph, it immediately calls `.backward()` on its parents. But because some variables receive their gradient value from multiple parents, each variable needs to wait to call `.backward()` on its parents until it has the final gradient locally.

As mentioned previously, none of these concepts are new from a deep learning theory perspective; these are the kinds of engineering challenges that deep learning frameworks seek to face. More important, they're the kinds of challenges you'll face when debugging neural networks in a standard framework. Before moving on, take a moment to play around and get familiar with this code. Try deleting different parts and seeing how it breaks in various ways. Try calling `.backprop()` twice.

How does addition backpropagation work?

Let's study the abstraction to learn how to add support for more functions.

At this point, the framework has reached an exciting place! You can now add support for arbitrary operations by adding the function to the `Tensor` class and adding its derivative to the `.backward()` method. For addition, there's the following method:

```
def __add__(self, other):
    if(self.autograd and other.autograd):
        return Tensor(self.data + other.data,
                      autograd=True,
                      creators=[self,other],
                      creation_op="add")
    return Tensor(self.data + other.data)
```

And for backpropagation through the addition function, there's the following gradient propagation within the `.backward()` method:

```
if(self.creation_op == "add"):
    self.creators[0].backward(self.grad, self)
    self.creators[1].backward(self.grad, self)
```

Notice that addition isn't handled anywhere else in the class. The generic backpropagation logic is abstracted away so everything necessary for addition is defined in these two places. Note further that backpropagation logic calls `.backward()` two times, once for each variable that participated in the addition. Thus, the default setting in the backpropagation logic is to always backpropagate into every variable in the graph. But occasionally, backpropagation is skipped if the variable has autograd turned off (`self.autograd == False`). This check is performed in the `.backward()` method:

```
def backward(self,grad=None, grad_origin=None):
    if(self.autograd):

        if(grad_origin is not None):
            if(self.children[grad_origin.id] == 0):
                raise Exception("cannot backprop more than once")

        ...
```

Even though the backpropagation logic for addition backpropagates the gradient into all the variables that contributed to it, the backpropagation won't run unless `.autograd` is set to `True` for that variable (for `self.creators[0]` or `self.creators[1]`, respectively). Also notice in the first line of `__add__()` that the tensor created (which is later the tensor `running.backward()`) has `self.autograd == True` only if `self.autograd == other.autograd == True`.

Adding support for negation

Let's modify the support for addition to support negation.

Now that addition is working, you should be able to copy and paste the addition code, create a few modifications, and add autograd support for negation. Let's try it. Modifications from the __add__ function are in bold:

```
def __neg__(self):
    if(self.autograd):
        return Tensor(self.data * -1,
                      autograd=True,
                      creators=[self],
                      creation_op="neg")
    return Tensor(self.data * -1)
```

Nearly everything is identical. You don't accept any parameters so the parameter "other" has been removed in several places. Let's take a look at the backprop logic you should add to .backward(). Modifications from the __add__ function backpropagation logic are in bold:

```
if(self.creation_op == "neg"):
    self.creators[0].backward(self.grad.__neg__())
```

Because the __neg__ function has only one creator, you end up calling .backward() only once. (If you're wondering how you know the correct gradients to backpropagate, revisit chapters 4, 5, and 6.) You can now test out the new code:

```
a = Tensor([1,2,3,4,5], autograd=True)
b = Tensor([2,2,2,2,2], autograd=True)
c = Tensor([5,4,3,2,1], autograd=True)

d = a + (-b)
e = (-b) + c
f = d + e

f.backward(Tensor(np.array([1,1,1,1,1])))

print(b.grad.data == np.array([-2,-2,-2,-2,-2]))
```

```
[ True  True  True  True  True]
```

When you forward propagate using -b instead of b, the gradients that are backpropagated have a flipped sign as well. Furthermore, you don't have to change anything about the general backpropagation system to make this work. You can create new functions as you need them. Let's add some more!

Adding support for additional functions
Subtraction, multiplication, sum, expand, transpose, and matrix multiplication

Using the same ideas you learned for addition and negation, let's add the forward and backpropagation logic for several additional functions:

```python
def __sub__(self, other):
    if(self.autograd and other.autograd):
        return Tensor(self.data - other.data,
                      autograd=True,
                      creators=[self,other],
                      creation_op="sub")
    return Tensor(self.data - other.data)

def __mul__(self, other):
    if(self.autograd and other.autograd):
        return Tensor(self.data * other.data,
                      autograd=True,
                      creators=[self,other],
                      creation_op="mul")
    return Tensor(self.data * other.data)

def sum(self, dim):
    if(self.autograd):
        return Tensor(self.data.sum(dim),
                      autograd=True,
                      creators=[self],
                      creation_op="sum_"+str(dim))
    return Tensor(self.data.sum(dim))

def expand(self, dim,copies):

    trans_cmd = list(range(0,len(self.data.shape)))
    trans_cmd.insert(dim,len(self.data.shape))
    new_shape = list(self.data.shape) + [copies]
    new_data = self.data.repeat(copies).reshape(new_shape)
    new_data = new_data.transpose(trans_cmd)

    if(self.autograd):
        return Tensor(new_data,
                      autograd=True,
                      creators=[self],
                      creation_op="expand_"+str(dim))
    return Tensor(new_data)

def transpose(self):
    if(self.autograd):
        return Tensor(self.data.transpose(),
                      autograd=True,
                      creators=[self],
                      creation_op="transpose")

    return Tensor(self.data.transpose())
```

```
def mm(self, x):
    if(self.autograd):
        return Tensor(self.data.dot(x.data),
                      autograd=True,
                      creators=[self,x],
                      creation_op="mm")
    return Tensor(self.data.dot(x.data))
```

We've previously discussed the derivatives for all these functions, although sum and expand might seem foreign because they have new names. sum performs addition across a dimension of the tensor; in other words, say you have a 2 × 3 matrix called x:

$$x = Tensor(np.array([[1,2,3],$$
$$[4,5,6]]))$$

The .sum(dim) function sums across a dimension. x.sum(0) will result in a 1 × 3 matrix (a length 3 vector), whereas x.sum(1) will result in a 2 × 1 matrix (a length 2 vector):

    x.sum(0) ⟶ array([5, 7, 9])   x.sum(1) ⟶ array([6, 15])

You use expand to backpropagate through a .sum(). It's a function that copies data along a dimension. Given the same matrix x, copying along the first dimension gives two copies of the tensor:

```
                                            array([[[1, 2, 3],
                                                    [4, 5, 6]],

                                                   [[1, 2, 3],
                                                    [4, 5, 6]],

    x.expand(dim=0, copies=4)  ⟶
                                                   [[1, 2, 3],
                                                    [4, 5, 6]],

                                                   [[1, 2, 3],
                                                    [4, 5, 6]]])
```

To be clear, whereas .sum() removes a dimension (2 × 3 -> just 2 or 3), expand adds a dimension. The 2 × 3 matrix becomes 4 × 2 × 3. You can think of this as a list of four tensors, each of which is 2 × 3. But if you expand to the last dimension, it copies along the last dimension, so each entry in the original tensor becomes a list of entries instead:

```
                                            array([[[1, 1, 1, 1],
                                                    [2, 2, 2, 2],
                                                    [3, 3, 3, 3]],

    x.expand(dim=2, copies=4)  ⟶
                                                   [[4, 4, 4, 4],
                                                    [5, 5, 5, 5],
                                                    [6, 6, 6, 6]]])
```

Thus, when you perform .sum(dim=1) on a tensor with four entries in that dimension, you need to perform .expand(dim=1, copies=4) to the gradient when you backpropagate it.

You can now add the corresponding backpropagation logic to the `.backward()` method:

```
if(self.creation_op == "sub"):
    new = Tensor(self.grad.data)
    self.creators[0].backward(new, self)
    new = Tensor(self.grad.__neg__().data)
    self.creators[1].backward(, self)

if(self.creation_op == "mul"):
    new = self.grad * self.creators[1]
    self.creators[0].backward(new , self)
    new = self.grad * self.creators[0]
    self.creators[1].backward(new, self)

if(self.creation_op == "mm"):
    act = self.creators[0]
    weights = self.creators[1]
    new = self.grad.mm(weights.transpose())
    act.backward(new)
    new = self.grad.transpose().mm(act).transpose()
    weights.backward(new)

if(self.creation_op == "transpose"):
    self.creators[0].backward(self.grad.transpose())

if("sum" in self.creation_op):
    dim = int(self.creation_op.split("_")[1])
    ds = self.creators[0].data.shape[dim]
    self.creators[0].backward(self.grad.expand(dim,ds))

if("expand" in self.creation_op):
    dim = int(self.creation_op.split("_")[1])
    self.creators[0].backward(self.grad.sum(dim))
```

Usually an activation

Usually a weight matrix

If you're unsure about this functionality, the best thing to do is to look back at how you were doing backpropagation in chapter 6. That chapter has figures showing each step of backpropagation, part of which I've shown again here.

The gradients start at the end of the network. You then move the error signal *backward through the network* by calling functions that correspond to the functions used to move activations *forward through the network*. If the last operation was a matrix multiplication (and it was), you backpropagate by performing matrix multiplication (dot) on the transposed matrix.

In the following image, this happens at the line `layer_1_delta=layer_2_delta.dot (weights_1_2.T)`. In the previous code, it happens in `if(self.creation_op == "mm")` (highlighted in bold). You're doing the exact same operations as before (in reverse order of forward propagation), but the code is better organized.

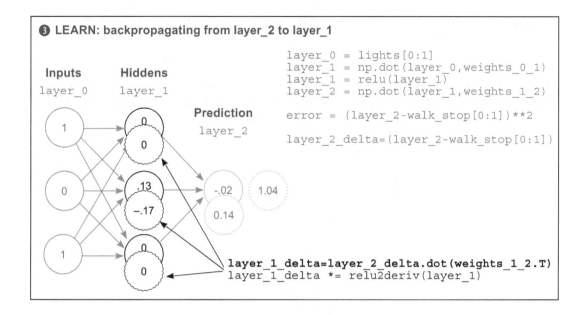

❸ LEARN: backpropagating from layer_2 to layer_1

Inputs
layer_0

Hiddens
layer_1

Prediction
layer_2

```
layer_0 = lights[0:1]
layer_1 = np.dot(layer_0,weights_0_1)
layer_1 = relu(layer_1)
layer_2 = np.dot(layer_1,weights_1_2)

error = (layer_2-walk_stop[0:1])**2

layer_2_delta=(layer_2-walk_stop[0:1])
```

Inputs: 1, 0, 1
Hiddens: 0, 0, .13, −.17, 0, 0
Prediction: −.02, 0.14, 1.04

```
layer_1_delta=layer_2_delta.dot(weights_1_2.T)
layer_1_delta *= relu2deriv(layer_1)
```

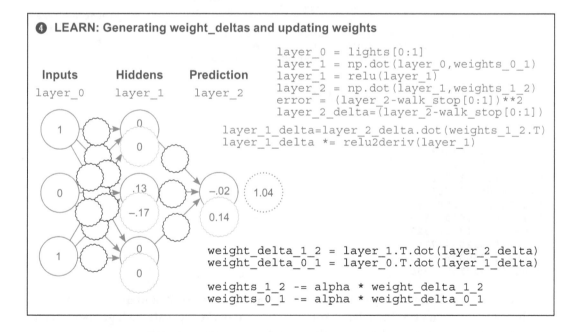

❹ LEARN: Generating weight_deltas and updating weights

Inputs
layer_0

Hiddens
layer_1

Prediction
layer_2

```
layer_0 = lights[0:1]
layer_1 = np.dot(layer_0,weights_0_1)
layer_1 = relu(layer_1)
layer_2 = np.dot(layer_1,weights_1_2)
error = (layer_2-walk_stop[0:1])**2
layer_2_delta=(layer_2-walk_stop[0:1])

layer_1_delta=layer_2_delta.dot(weights_1_2.T)
layer_1_delta *= relu2deriv(layer_1)
```

Inputs: 1, 0, 1
Hiddens: 0, 0, .13, −.17, 0, 0
Prediction: −.02, 0.14, 1.04

```
weight_delta_1_2 = layer_1.T.dot(layer_2_delta)
weight_delta_0_1 = layer_0.T.dot(layer_1_delta)

weights_1_2 -= alpha * weight_delta_1_2
weights_0_1 -= alpha * weight_delta_0_1
```

Using autograd to train a neural network

You no longer have to write backpropagation logic!

This may have seemed like quite a bit of engineering effort, but it's about to pay off. Now, when you train a neural network, you don't have to write any backpropagation logic! As a toy example, here's a neural network to backprop by hand:

```python
import numpy
np.random.seed(0)

data = np.array([[0,0],[0,1],[1,0],[1,1]])
target = np.array([[0],[1],[0],[1]])

weights_0_1 = np.random.rand(2,3)
weights_1_2 = np.random.rand(3,1)

for i in range(10):

    layer_1 = data.dot(weights_0_1)                          # Predict
    layer_2 = layer_1.dot(weights_1_2)

    diff = (layer_2 - target)                                # Compare
    sqdiff = (diff * diff)
    loss = sqdiff.sum(0)                                     # Mean squared
                                                             # error loss
    layer_1_grad = diff.dot(weights_1_2.transpose())         # Learn; this is the
    weight_1_2_update = layer_1.transpose().dot(diff)        # backpropagation
    weight_0_1_update = data.transpose().dot(layer_1_grad)   # piece.

    weights_1_2 -= weight_1_2_update * 0.1
    weights_0_1 -= weight_0_1_update * 0.1
    print(loss[0])
```

```
0.4520108746468352
0.33267400101121475
0.25307308516725036
0.1969566997160743
0.15559900212801492
0.12410658864910949
0.09958132129923322
0.08019781265417164
0.06473333002675746
0.05232281719234398
```

You have to forward propagate in such a way that `layer_1`, `layer_2`, and `diff` exist as variables, because you need them later. You then have to backpropagate each gradient to its appropriate weight matrix and perform the weight update appropriately.

```
import numpy
np.random.seed(0)

data = Tensor(np.array([[0,0],[0,1],[1,0],[1,1]]), autograd=True)
target = Tensor(np.array([[0],[1],[0],[1]]), autograd=True)

w = list()
w.append(Tensor(np.random.rand(2,3), autograd=True))
w.append(Tensor(np.random.rand(3,1), autograd=True))

for i in range(10):

    pred = data.mm(w[0]).mm(w[1])                    ← Predict

    loss = ((pred - target)*(pred - target)).sum(0)  ← Compare

    loss.backward(Tensor(np.ones_like(loss.data)))   ← Learn

    for w_ in w:
        w_.data -= w_.grad.data * 0.1
        w_.grad.data *= 0

    print(loss)
```

But with the fancy new autograd system, the code is much simpler. You don't have to keep around any temporary variables (because the dynamic graph keeps track of them), and you don't have to implement any backpropagation logic (because the .backward() method handles that). Not only is this more convenient, but you're less likely to make silly mistakes in the backpropagation code, reducing the likelihood of bugs!

```
[0.58128304]
[0.48988149]
[0.41375111]
[0.34489412]
[0.28210124]
[0.2254484]
[0.17538853]
[0.1324231]
[0.09682769]
[0.06849361]
```

Before moving on, I'd like to point out one stylistic thing in this new implementation. Notice that I put all the parameters in a list, which I could iterate through when performing the weight update. This is a bit of foreshadowing for the next piece of functionality. When you have an autograd system, stochastic gradient descent becomes trivial to implement (it's just that for loop at the end). Let's try making this its own class as well.

Adding automatic optimization

Let's make a stochastic gradient descent optimizer.

At face value, creating something called a stochastic gradient descent optimizer may sound difficult, but it's just copying and pasting from the previous example with a bit of good, old-fashioned object-oriented programming:

```python
class SGD(object):

    def __init__(self, parameters, alpha=0.1):
        self.parameters = parameters
        self.alpha = alpha

    def zero(self):
        for p in self.parameters:
            p.grad.data *= 0

    def step(self, zero=True):

        for p in self.parameters:

            p.data -= p.grad.data * self.alpha

            if(zero):
                p.grad.data *= 0
```

The previous neural network is further simplified as follows, with exactly the same results as before:

```python
import numpy
np.random.seed(0)

data = Tensor(np.array([[0,0],[0,1],[1,0],[1,1]]), autograd=True)
target = Tensor(np.array([[0],[1],[0],[1]]), autograd=True)

w = list()
w.append(Tensor(np.random.rand(2,3), autograd=True))
w.append(Tensor(np.random.rand(3,1), autograd=True))

optim = SGD(parameters=w, alpha=0.1)

for i in range(10):

    pred = data.mm(w[0]).mm(w[1])                    ← Predict

    loss = ((pred - target)*(pred - target)).sum(0)  ← Compare

    loss.backward(Tensor(np.ones_like(loss.data)))   ← Learn
    optim.step()
```

Adding support for layer types
You may be familiar with layer types in Keras or PyTorch.

At this point, you've done the most complicated pieces of the new deep learning framework. Further work is mostly about adding new functions to the tensor and creating convenient higher-order classes and functions. Probably the most common abstraction among nearly all frameworks is the layer abstraction. It's a collection of commonly used forward propagation techniques packaged into an simple API with some kind of `.forward()` method to call them. Here's an example of a simple linear layer:

```python
class Layer(object):

    def __init__(self):
        self.parameters = list()

    def get_parameters(self):
        return self.parameters


class Linear(Layer):

    def __init__(self, n_inputs, n_outputs):
        super().__init__()
        W = np.random.randn(n_inputs, n_outputs)*np.sqrt(2.0/(n_inputs))
        self.weight = Tensor(W, autograd=True)
        self.bias = Tensor(np.zeros(n_outputs), autograd=True)

        self.parameters.append(self.weight)
        self.parameters.append(self.bias)

    def forward(self, input):
        return input.mm(self.weight)+self.bias.expand(0,len(input.data))
```

Nothing here is particularly new. The weights are organized into a class (and I added bias weights because this is a true linear layer). You can initialize the layer all together, such that both the weights and bias are initialized with the correct sizes, and the correct forward propagation logic is always employed.

Also notice that I created an abstract class `Layer`, which has a single getter. This allows for more-complicated layer types (such as layers containing other layers). All you need to do is override `get_parameters()` to control what tensors are later passed to the optimizer (such as the `SGD` class created in the previous section).

Layers that contain layers

Layers can also contain other layers.

The most popular layer is a sequential layer that forward propagates a list of layers, where each layer feeds its outputs into the inputs of the next layer:

```python
class Sequential(Layer):

    def __init__(self, layers=list()):
        super().__init__()

        self.layers = layers

    def add(self, layer):
        self.layers.append(layer)

    def forward(self, input):
        for layer in self.layers:
            input = layer.forward(input)
        return input

    def get_parameters(self):
        params = list()
        for l in self.layers:
            params += l.get_parameters()
        return params

data = Tensor(np.array([[0,0],[0,1],[1,0],[1,1]]), autograd=True)
target = Tensor(np.array([[0],[1],[0],[1]]), autograd=True)

model = Sequential([Linear(2,3), Linear(3,1)])

optim = SGD(parameters=model.get_parameters(), alpha=0.05)

for i in range(10):

    pred = model.forward(data)                    ◄──── Predict

    loss = ((pred - target)*(pred - target)).sum(0)   ◄──── Compare

    loss.backward(Tensor(np.ones_like(loss.data)))   ◄──── Learn
    optim.step()
    print(loss)
```

Loss-function layers

Some layers have no weights.

You can also create layers that are functions on the input. The most popular version of this kind of layer is probably the loss-function layer, such as mean squared error:

```python
class MSELoss(Layer):

    def __init__(self):
        super().__init__()

    def forward(self, pred, target):
        return ((pred - target)*(pred - target)).sum(0)

import numpy
np.random.seed(0)

data = Tensor(np.array([[0,0],[0,1],[1,0],[1,1]]), autograd=True)
target = Tensor(np.array([[0],[1],[0],[1]]), autograd=True)

model = Sequential([Linear(2,3), Linear(3,1)])
criterion = MSELoss()

optim = SGD(parameters=model.get_parameters(), alpha=0.05)

for i in range(10):

    pred = model.forward(data)               ←——— Predict

    loss = criterion.forward(pred, target)   ←——— Compare

    loss.backward(Tensor(np.ones_like(loss.data)))  ←——— Learn
    optim.step()
    print(loss)
```

```
[2.33428272]
[0.06743796]
      ...
[0.01153118]
[0.00889602]
```

If you'll forgive the repetition, again, nothing here is particularly new. Under the hood, the last several code examples all do the exact same computation. It's just that autograd is doing all the backpropagation, and the forward propagation steps are packaged in nice classes to ensure that the functionality executes in the correct order.

How to learn a framework

Oversimplified, frameworks are autograd + a list of prebuilt layers and optimizers.

You've been able to write (rather quickly) a variety of new layer types using the underlying autograd system, which makes it quite easy to piece together arbitrary layers of functionality. Truth be told, this is the main feature of modern frameworks, eliminating the need to handwrite each and every math operation for forward and backward propagation. Using frameworks greatly increases the speed with which you can go from idea to experiment and will reduce the number of bugs in your code.

Viewing a framework as merely an autograd system coupled with a big list of layers and optimizers will help you learn them. I expect you'll be able to pivot from this chapter into almost any framework fairly quickly, although the framework that's most similar to the API built here is PyTorch. Either way, for your reference, take a moment to peruse the lists of layers and optimizers in several of the big frameworks:

- https://pytorch.org/docs/stable/nn.html

- https://keras.io/layers/about-keras-layers

- https://www.tensorflow.org/api_docs/python/tf/layers

The general workflow for learning a new framework is to find the simplest possible code example, tweak it and get to know the autograd system's API, and then modify the code example piece by piece until you get to whatever experiment you care about.

```
def backward(self,grad=None, grad_origin=None):
    if(self.autograd):

        if(grad is None):
            grad = Tensor(np.ones_like(self.data))
```

One more thing before we move on. I'm adding a nice convenience function to `Tensor.backward()` that makes it so you don't have to pass in a gradient of 1s the first time you call `.backward()`. It's not, strictly speaking, necessary—but it's handy.

Nonlinearity layers

Let's add nonlinear functions to Tensor and then create some layer types.

For the next chapter, you'll need `.sigmoid()` and `.tanh()`. Let's add them to the `Tensor` class. You learned about the derivative for both quite some time ago, so this should be easy:

```python
def sigmoid(self):
    if(self.autograd):
        return Tensor(1 / (1 + np.exp(-self.data)),
                      autograd=True,
                      creators=[self],
                      creation_op="sigmoid")
    return Tensor(1 / (1 + np.exp(-self.data)))

def tanh(self):
    if(self.autograd):
        return Tensor(np.tanh(self.data),
                      autograd=True,
                      creators=[self],
                      creation_op="tanh")
    return Tensor(np.tanh(self.data))
```

The following code shows the backprop logic added to the `Tensor.backward()` method:

```python
if(self.creation_op == "sigmoid"):
    ones = Tensor(np.ones_like(self.grad.data))
    self.creators[0].backward(self.grad * (self * (ones - self)))

if(self.creation_op == "tanh"):
    ones = Tensor(np.ones_like(self.grad.data))
    self.creators[0].backward(self.grad * (ones - (self * self)))
```

Hopefully, this feels fairly routine. See if you can make a few more nonlinearities as well: try `HardTanh` or `relu`.

```python
class Tanh(Layer):                      class Sigmoid(Layer):
    def __init__(self):                     def __init__(self):
        super().__init__()                      super().__init__()

    def forward(self, input):               def forward(self, input):
        return input.tanh()                     return input.sigmoid()
```

Let's try out the new nonlinearities. New additions are in bold:

```
import numpy
np.random.seed(0)

data = Tensor(np.array([[0,0],[0,1],[1,0],[1,1]]), autograd=True)
target = Tensor(np.array([[0],[1],[0],[1]]), autograd=True)

model = Sequential([Linear(2,3), Tanh(), Linear(3,1), Sigmoid()])
criterion = MSELoss()

optim = SGD(parameters=model.get_parameters(), alpha=1)

for i in range(10):
    pred = model.forward(data)                          ← Predict

    loss = criterion.forward(pred, target)              ← Compare

    loss.backward(Tensor(np.ones_like(loss.data)))  ←——— Learn
    optim.step()
    print(loss)
```

```
[1.06372865]
[0.75148144]
[0.57384259]
[0.39574294]
[0.2482279]
[0.15515294]
[0.10423398]
[0.07571169]
[0.05837623]
[0.04700013]
```

As you can see, you can drop the new `Tanh()` and `Sigmoid()` layers into the input parameters to `Sequential()`, and the neural network knows exactly how to use them. Easy!

In the previous chapter, you learned about recurrent neural networks. In particular, you trained a model to predict the next word, given the previous several words. Before we finish this chapter, I'd like for you to translate that code into the new framework. To do this, you'll need three new layer types: an embedding layer that learns word embeddings, an RNN layer that can learn to model sequences of inputs, and a softmax layer that can predict a probability distribution over labels.

The embedding layer

An embedding layer translates indices into activations.

In chapter 11, you learned about word embeddings, which are vectors mapped to words that you can forward propagate into a neural network. Thus, if you have a vocabulary of 200 words, you'll also have 200 embeddings. This gives the initial spec for creating an embedding layer. First, initialize a list (of the right length) of word embeddings (of the right size):

```
class Embedding(Layer):

    def __init__(self, vocab_size, dim):
        super().__init__()

        self.vocab_size = vocab_size
        self.dim = dim

        weight = np.random.rand(vocab_size, dim) - 0.5) / dim
```

This initialization style is a convention from word2vec.

So far, so good. The matrix has a row (vector) for each word in the vocabulary. Now, how will you forward propagate? Well, forward propagation always starts with the question, "How will the inputs be encoded?" In the case of word embeddings, you obviously can't pass in the words themselves, because the words don't tell you which rows in `self.weight` to forward propagate with. Instead, as you hopefully remember from chapter 11, you forward propagate indices. Fortunately, NumPy supports this operation:

```
identity = np.eye(5)
print(identity)
```
→
```
array([[1., 0., 0., 0., 0.],
       [0., 1., 0., 0., 0.],
       [0., 0., 1., 0., 0.],
       [0., 0., 0., 1., 0.],
       [0., 0., 0., 0., 1.]])
```

```
print(identity[np.array([[1,2,3,4],
                         [2,3,4,0]])])
```
→
```
[[[0. 1. 0. 0. 0.]
  [0. 0. 1. 0. 0.]
  [0. 0. 0. 1. 0.]
  [0. 0. 0. 0. 1.]]

 [[0. 0. 1. 0. 0.]
  [0. 0. 0. 1. 0.]
  [0. 0. 0. 0. 1.]
  [1. 0. 0. 0. 0.]]]
```

Notice how, when you pass a matrix of integers into a NumPy matrix, it returns the same matrix, but with each integer replaced with the row the integer specified. Thus a 2D matrix of indices turns into a 3D matrix of embeddings (rows). This is perfect!

Adding indexing to autograd

Before you can build the embedding layer, autograd needs to support indexing.

In order to support the new embedding strategy (which assumes words are forward propagated as matrices of indices), the indexing you played around with in the previous section must be supported by autograd. This is a pretty simple idea. You need to make sure that during backpropagation, the gradients are placed in the same rows as were indexed into for forward propagation. This requires that you keep around whatever indices were passed in, so you can place each gradient in the appropriate location during backpropagation with a simple for loop:

```
def index_select(self, indices):

    if(self.autograd):
        new = Tensor(self.data[indices.data],
                    autograd=True,
                    creators=[self],
                    creation_op="index_select")
        new.index_select_indices = indices
        return new
    return Tensor(self.data[indices.data])
```

First, use the NumPy trick you learned in the previous section to select the correct rows:

```
if(self.creation_op == "index_select"):
    new_grad = np.zeros_like(self.creators[0].data)
    indices_ = self.index_select_indices.data.flatten()
    grad_ = grad.data.reshape(len(indices_), -1)
    for i in range(len(indices_)):
        new_grad[indices_[i]] += grad_[i]
    self.creators[0].backward(Tensor(new_grad))
```

Then, during backprop(), initialize a new gradient of the correct size (the size of the original matrix that was being indexed into). Second, flatten the indices so you can iterate through them. Third, collapse grad_ to a simple list of rows. (The subtle part is that the list of indices in indices_ and the list of vectors in grad_ will be in the corresponding order.) Then, iterate through each index, add it into the correct row of the new gradient you're creating, and backpropagate it into self.creators[0]. As you can see, grad_[i] correctly updates each row (adds a vector of 1s, in this case) in accordance with the number of times the index is used. Indices 2 and 3 update twice (in bold):

```
x = Tensor(np.eye(5), autograd=True)                    [[0. 0. 0. 0. 0.]
x.index_select(Tensor([[1,2,3],                          [1. 1. 1. 1. 1.]
                    [2,3,4]])).backward()   ──────▶      [2. 2. 2. 2. 2.]
print(x.grad)                                            [2. 2. 2. 2. 2.]
                                                         [1. 1. 1. 1. 1.]]
```

The embedding layer (revisited)

Now you can finish forward propagation using the new .index_select() method.

For forward prop, call `.index_select()`, and autograd will handle the rest:

```
class Embedding(Layer):

    def __init__(self, vocab_size, dim):
        super().__init__()

        self.vocab_size = vocab_size
        self.dim = dim

        weight = np.random.rand(vocab_size, dim) - 0.5) / dim
        self.weight = Tensor((weight, autograd=True)

        self.parameters.append(self.weight)

    def forward(self, input):
        return self.weight.index_select(input)
```

This initialization style is a convention from word2vec.

```
data = Tensor(np.array([1,2,1,2]), autograd=True)
target = Tensor(np.array([[0],[1],[0],[1]]), autograd=True)

embed = Embedding(5,3)
model = Sequential([embed, Tanh(), Linear(3,1), Sigmoid()])
criterion = MSELoss()

optim = SGD(parameters=model.get_parameters(), alpha=0.5)

for i in range(10):

    pred = model.forward(data)                         Predict

    loss = criterion.forward(pred, target)             Compare

    loss.backward(Tensor(np.ones_like(loss.data)))     Learn
    optim.step()
    print(loss)
```

```
[0.98874126]
[0.6658868]
[0.45639889]
   ...
[0.08731868]
[0.07387834]
```

In this neural network, you learn to correlate input indices 1 and 2 with the prediction 0 and 1. In theory, indices 1 and 2 could correspond to words (or some other input object), and in the final example, they will. This example was to show the embedding working.

The cross-entropy layer

Let's add cross entropy to the autograd and create a layer.

Hopefully, at this point you're starting to feel comfortable with how to create new layer types. Cross entropy is a pretty standard one that you've seen many times throughout this book. Because we've already walked through how to create several new layer types, I'll leave the code here for your reference. Attempt to do it yourself before copying this code.

```python
def cross_entropy(self, target_indices):

    temp = np.exp(self.data)
    softmax_output = temp / np.sum(temp,
                                   axis=len(self.data.shape)-1,
                                   keepdims=True)

    t = target_indices.data.flatten()
    p = softmax_output.reshape(len(t),-1)
    target_dist = np.eye(p.shape[1])[t]
    loss = -(np.log(p) * (target_dist)).sum(1).mean()

    if(self.autograd):
        out = Tensor(loss,
                     autograd=True,
                     creators=[self],
                     creation_op="cross_entropy")
        out.softmax_output = softmax_output
        out.target_dist = target_dist
        return out

    return Tensor(loss)



            if(self.creation_op == "cross_entropy"):
                dx = self.softmax_output - self.target_dist
                self.creators[0].backward(Tensor(dx))



class CrossEntropyLoss(object):

    def __init__(self):
        super().__init__()

    def forward(self, input, target):
        return input.cross_entropy(target)
```

```
import numpy
np.random.seed(0)

# data indices
data = Tensor(np.array([1,2,1,2]), autograd=True)

# target indices
target = Tensor(np.array([0,1,0,1]), autograd=True)

model = Sequential([Embedding(3,3), Tanh(), Linear(3,4)])
criterion = CrossEntropyLoss()

optim = SGD(parameters=model.get_parameters(), alpha=0.1)

for i in range(10):

    pred = model.forward(data)                        ◀───── Predict

    loss = criterion.forward(pred, target)            ◀───── Compare

    loss.backward(Tensor(np.ones_like(loss.data)))    ◀───── Learn
    optim.step()
    print(loss)
```

```
1.3885032434928422
0.9558181509266037
0.6823083585795604
0.5095259967493119
0.39574491472895856
0.31752527285348264
0.2617222861964216
0.22061283923954234
0.18946427334830068
0.16527389263866668
```

Using the same cross-entropy logic employed in several previous neural networks, you now have a new loss function. One noticeable thing about this loss is different from others: both the final softmax and the computation of the loss are within the loss class. This is an extremely common convention in deep neural networks. Nearly every framework will work this way. When you want to finish a network and train with cross entropy, you can leave off the softmax from the forward propagation step and call a cross-entropy class that will automatically perform the softmax as a part of the loss function.

The reason these are combined so consistently is performance. It's much faster to calculate the gradient of softmax and negative log likelihood together in a cross-entropy function than to forward propagate and backpropagate them separately in two different modules. This has to do with a shortcut in the gradient math.

The recurrent neural network layer

By combining several layers, you can learn over time series.

As the last exercise of this chapter, let's create one more layer that's the composition of multiple smaller layer types. The point of this layer will be to learn the task you finished at the end of the previous chapter. This layer is the *recurrent layer*. You'll construct it using three linear layers, and the .forward() method will take both the output from the previous hidden state and the input from the current training data:

```
class RNNCell(Layer):

    def __init__(self, n_inputs,n_hidden,n_output,activation='sigmoid'):
        super().__init__()

        self.n_inputs = n_inputs
        self.n_hidden = n_hidden
        self.n_output = n_output

        if(activation == 'sigmoid'):
            self.activation = Sigmoid()
        elif(activation == 'tanh'):
            self.activation == Tanh()
        else:
            raise Exception("Non-linearity not found")

        self.w_ih = Linear(n_inputs, n_hidden)
        self.w_hh = Linear(n_hidden, n_hidden)
        self.w_ho = Linear(n_hidden, n_output)

        self.parameters += self.w_ih.get_parameters()
        self.parameters += self.w_hh.get_parameters()
        self.parameters += self.w_ho.get_parameters()

    def forward(self, input, hidden):
        from_prev_hidden = self.w_hh.forward(hidden)
        combined = self.w_ih.forward(input) + from_prev_hidden
        new_hidden = self.activation.forward(combined)
        output = self.w_ho.forward(new_hidden)
        return output, new_hidden

    def init_hidden(self, batch_size=1):
        return Tensor(np.zeros((batch_size,self.n_hidden)),autograd=True)
```

It's out of scope for this chapter to reintroduce RNNs, but it's worth pointing out the pieces that should be familiar already. RNNs have a state vector that passes from timestep to timestep. In this case, it's the variable hidden, which is both an input parameter and output variable to the forward function. RNNs also have several different weight matrices: one that maps input vectors to hidden vectors (processing input data), one that maps from hidden to hidden (which updates each hidden vector based on the previous), and optionally a hidden-to-output layer that learns to make predictions based on the hidden vector. This RNNCell implementation includes all three. The `self.w_ih` layer is the input-to-hidden layer, `self.w_hh` is the hidden-to-hidden layer, and `self.w_ho` is the hidden-to-output layer. Note the dimensionality of each. The input size of `self.w_ih` and the output size of `self.w_ho` are both the size of the vocabulary. All other dimensions are configurable based on the `n_hidden` parameter.

Finally, an `activation` input parameter defines which nonlinearity is applied to hidden vectors at each timestep. I've added two possibilities (`Sigmoid` and `Tanh`), but there are many options to choose from. Let's train a network:

```
import sys,random,math
from collections import Counter
import numpy as np

f = open('tasksv11/en/qa1_single-supporting-fact_train.txt','r')
raw = f.readlines()
f.close()

tokens = list()
for line in raw[0:1000]:
    tokens.append(line.lower().replace("\n","").split(" ")[1:])

new_tokens = list()
for line in tokens:
    new_tokens.append((['-'] * (6 - len(line))) + line)
tokens = new_tokens

vocab = set()
for sent in tokens:
    for word in sent:
        vocab.add(word)

vocab = list(vocab)

word2index = {}
for i,word in enumerate(vocab):
    word2index[word]=i

def words2indices(sentence):
    idx = list()
    for word in sentence:
        idx.append(word2index[word])
    return idx

indices = list()
for line in tokens:
    idx = list()
    for w in line:
        idx.append(word2index[w])
    indices.append(idx)

data = np.array(indices)
```

You can learn to fit the task you previously accomplished in the preceding chapter.

Now you can initialize the recurrent layer with an embedding input and train a network to solve the same task as in the previous chapter. Note that this network is slightly more complex (it has one extra layer) despite the code being much simpler, thanks to the little framework.

```
embed = Embedding(vocab_size=len(vocab),dim=16)
model = RNNCell(n_inputs=16, n_hidden=16, n_output=len(vocab))

criterion = CrossEntropyLoss()
params = model.get_parameters() + embed.get_parameters()
optim = SGD(parameters=params, alpha=0.05)
```

First, define the input embeddings and then the recurrent cell. (Note that *cell* is a conventional name given to recurrent layers when they're implementing only a single recurrence. If you created another layer that provided the ability to configure arbitrary numbers of cells together, it would be called an RNN, and n_layers would be an input parameter.)

```
for iter in range(1000):
    batch_size = 100
    total_loss = 0

    hidden = model.init_hidden(batch_size=batch_size)

    for t in range(5):
        input = Tensor(data[0:batch_size,t], autograd=True)
        rnn_input = embed.forward(input=input)
        output, hidden = model.forward(input=rnn_input, hidden=hidden)

    target = Tensor(data[0:batch_size,t+1], autograd=True)
    loss = criterion.forward(output, target)
    loss.backward()
    optim.step()
    total_loss += loss.data
    if(iter % 200 == 0):
        p_correct = (target.data == np.argmax(output.data,axis=1)).mean()
        print_loss = total_loss / (len(data)/batch_size)
        print("Loss:",print_loss,"% Correct:",p_correct)
```

```
Loss: 0.47631100976371393 % Correct: 0.01
Loss: 0.17189538896184856 % Correct: 0.28
Loss: 0.1460940222788725 % Correct: 0.37
Loss: 0.13845863915406884 % Correct: 0.37
Loss: 0.135574472565278 % Correct: 0.37
```

```
batch_size = 1
hidden = model.init_hidden(batch_size=batch_size)
for t in range(5):
    input = Tensor(data[0:batch_size,t], autograd=True)
    rnn_input = embed.forward(input=input)
    output, hidden = model.forward(input=rnn_input, hidden=hidden)

target = Tensor(data[0:batch_size,t+1], autograd=True)
loss = criterion.forward(output, target)

ctx = ""
for idx in data[0:batch_size][0][0:-1]:
    ctx += vocab[idx] + " "
print("Context:",ctx)
print("Pred:", vocab[output.data.argmax()])
```

```
Context: - mary moved to the
Pred: office.
```

As you can see, the neural network learns to predict the first 100 examples of the training dataset with an accuracy of around 37% (near perfect, for this toy task). It predicts a plausible location for Mary to be moving toward, much like at the end of chapter 12.

Summary

Frameworks are efficient, convenient abstractions of forward and backward logic.

I hope this chapter's exercise has given you an appreciation for how convenient frameworks can be. They can make your code more readable, faster to write, faster to execute (through built-in optimizations), and much less buggy. More important, this chapter will prepare you for using and extending industry standard frameworks like PyTorch and TensorFlow. Whether debugging existing layer types or prototyping your own, the skills you've learned here will be some of the most important you acquire in this book, because they bridge the abstract knowledge of deep learning from previous chapters with the design of real-world tools you'll use to implement models in the future.

The framework that's most similar to the one built here is PyTorch, and I highly recommend diving into it when you complete this book. It will likely be the framework that feels most familiar.

learning to write like Shakespeare: long short-term memory | 14

In this chapter

- Character language modeling

- Truncated backpropagation

- Vanishing and exploding gradients

- A toy example of RNN backpropagation

- Long short-term memory (LSTM) cells

> 66 Lord, what fools these mortals be! 99
>
> —William Shakespeare
> A Midsummer Night's Dream

Character language modeling

Let's tackle a more challenging task with the RNN.

At the end of chapters 12 and 13, you trained vanilla recurrent neural networks (RNNs) that learned a simple series prediction problem. But you were training over a toy dataset of phrases that were synthetically generated using rules.

In this chapter, you'll attempt language modeling over a much more challenging dataset: the works of Shakespeare. And instead of learning to predict the next word given the previous words (as in the preceding chapter), the model will train on characters. It needs to learn to predict the next character given the previous characters observed. Here's what I mean:

```python
import sys,random,math
from collections import Counter
import numpy as np
import sys

np.random.seed(0)

f = open('shakespear.txt','r')
raw = f.read()          From http://karpathy.github.io/2015/05/21/rnn-effectiveness/
f.close()

vocab = list(set(raw))
word2index = {}
for i,word in enumerate(vocab):
    word2index[word]=i
indices = np.array(list(map(lambda x:word2index[x], raw)))
```

Whereas in chapters 12 and 13 the vocabulary was made up of the words from the dataset, now the vocabulary is made up the characters in the dataset. As such, the dataset is also transformed into a list of indices corresponding to characters instead of words. Above this is the `indices` NumPy array:

```python
embed = Embedding(vocab_size=len(vocab),dim=512)
model = RNNCell(n_inputs=512, n_hidden=512, n_output=len(vocab))

criterion = CrossEntropyLoss()
optim = SGD(parameters=model.get_parameters() + embed.get_parameters(),
            alpha=0.05)
```

This code should all look familiar. It initializes the embeddings to be of dimensionality 8 and the RNN hidden state to be of size 512. The output weights are initialized as 0s (not a rule, but I found it worked a bit better). Finally, you initialize the cross-entropy loss and stochastic gradient descent optimizer.

The need for truncated backpropagation

Backpropagating through 100,000 characters is intractable.

One of the more challenging aspects of reading code for RNNs is the mini-batching logic for feeding in data. The previous (simpler) neural network had an inner `for` loop like this (the **bold** part):

```
for iter in range(1000):
    batch_size = 100
    total_loss = 0

    hidden = model.init_hidden(batch_size=batch_size)

    for t in range(5):
        input = Tensor(data[0:batch_size,t], autograd=True)
        rnn_input = embed.forward(input=input)
        output, hidden = model.forward(input=rnn_input, hidden=hidden)

    target = Tensor(data[0:batch_size,t+1], autograd=True)
    loss = criterion.forward(output, target)
    loss.backward()
    optim.step()
    total_loss += loss.data
    if(iter % 200 == 0):
        p_correct = (target.data == np.argmax(output.data,axis=1)).mean()
        print_loss = total_loss / (len(data)/batch_size)
        print("Loss:",print_loss,"% Correct:",p_correct)
```

You might ask, "Why iterate to 5?" As it turns out, the previous dataset didn't have any example longer than six words. It read in five words and then attempted to predict the sixth.

Even more important is the backpropagation step. Consider when you did a simple feedforward network classifying MNIST digits: the gradients always backpropagated all the way through the network, right? They kept backpropagating until they reached the input data. This allowed the network to adjust every weight to try to learn how to correctly predict given the entire input example.

The recurrent example here is no different. You forward propagate through five input examples and then, when you later call `loss.backward()`, it backpropagates gradients all the way back through the network to the input datapoints. You can do this because you aren't feeding in that many input datapoints at a time. But the Shakespeare dataset has 100,000 characters! This is way too many to backpropagate through for every prediction. What do you do?

You don't! You backpropagate for a fixed number of steps into the past and then stop. This is called *truncated backpropagation*, and it's the industry standard. The length you backprop becomes another tunable parameter (like batch size or alpha).

Truncated backpropagation

Technically, it weakens the theoretical maximum of the neural network.

The downside of using truncated backpropagation is that it shortens the distance a neural network can learn to remember things. Basically, cutting off gradients after, say, five timesteps, means the neural network can't learn to remember events that are longer than five timesteps in the past.

Strictly speaking, it's more nuanced than this. There can accidentally be residual information in an RNN's hidden layer from more than five timesteps in the past, but the neural network can't use gradients to specifically request that the model keep information around from six timesteps in the past to help with the current prediction. Thus, in practice, neural networks won't learn to make predictions based on input signal from more than five timesteps in the past (if truncation is set at five timesteps). In practice, for language modeling, the truncation variable is called bptt, and it's usually set somewhere between 16 and 64:

```
batch_size = 32
bptt = 16
n_batches = int((indices.shape[0] / (batch_size)))
```

The other downside of truncated backpropagation is that it makes the mini-batching logic a bit more complex. To use truncated backpropagation, you pretend that instead of having one big dataset, you have a bunch of small datasets of size bptt. You need to group the datasets accordingly:

```
trimmed_indices = indices[:n_batches*batch_size]
batched_indices = trimmed_indices.reshape(batch_size, n_batches)
batched_indices = batched_indices.transpose()

input_batched_indices = batched_indices[0:-1]
target_batched_indices = batched_indices[1:]

n_bptt = int(((n_batches-1) / bptt))
input_batches = input_batched_indices[:n_bptt*bptt]
input_batches = input_batches.reshape(n_bptt,bptt,batch_size)
target_batches = target_batched_indices[:n_bptt*bptt]
target_batches = target_batches.reshape(n_bptt, bptt, batch_size)
```

There's a lot going on here. The top line makes the dataset an even multiple between the batch_size and n_batches. This is so that when you group it into tensors, it's square (alternatively, you could pad the dataset with 0s to make it square). The second and third lines reshape the dataset so each column is a section of the initial indices array. I'll show you that part, as if batch_size was set to 8 (for readability):

```
print(raw[0:5])
print(indices[0:5])
```

```
'That,'
array([ 9, 14,  2, 10, 57])
```

Those are the first five characters in the Shakespeare dataset. They spell out the string "That,". Following are the first five rows of the output of the transformation contained within `batched_indices`:

```
print(batched_indices[0:5])
```

```
array([[ 9, 43, 21, 10, 10, 23, 57, 46],
       [14, 44, 39, 21, 43, 14,  1, 10],
       [ 2, 41, 39, 54, 37, 21, 26, 57],
       [10, 39, 57, 48, 21, 54, 38, 43],
       [57, 39, 43,  1, 10, 21, 21, 33]])
```

I've highlighted the first column in bold. See how the indices for the phrase "That," are in the first column on the left? This is a standard construction. The reason there are eight columns is that the `batch_size` is 8. This tensor is then used to construct a list of smaller datasets, each of length `bptt`.

You can see here how the input and target are constructed. Notice that the target indices are the input indices offset by one row (so the network predicts the next character). Note again that `batch_size` is 8 in this printout so it's easier to read, but you're really setting it to 32.

```
print(input_batches[0][0:5])
```

```
print(target_batches[0][0:5])
```

```
array([[ 9, 43, 21, 10, 10, 23, 57, 46],
       [14, 44, 39, 21, 43, 14,  1, 10],
       [ 2, 41, 39, 54, 37, 21, 26, 57],
       [10, 39, 57, 48, 21, 54, 38, 43],
       [57, 39, 43,  1, 10, 21, 21, 33]])
```

```
array([[14, 44, 39, 21, 43, 14,  1, 10],
       [ 2, 41, 39, 54, 37, 21, 26, 57],
       [10, 39, 57, 48, 21, 54, 38, 43],
       [57, 39, 43,  1, 10, 21, 21, 33],
       [43, 43, 41, 60, 52, 12, 54,  1]])
```

Don't worry if this doesn't make sense to you yet. It doesn't have much to do with deep learning theory; it's just a particularly complex part of setting up RNNs that you'll run into from time to time. I thought I'd spend a couple of pages explaining it.

Let's see how to iterate using truncated backpropagation.

The following code shows truncated backpropagation in practice. Notice that it looks very similar to the iteration logic from chapter 13. The only real difference is that you generate a `batch_loss` at each step; and after every `bptt` steps, you backpropagate and perform a weight update. Then you keep reading through the dataset like nothing happened (even using the same hidden state from before, which only gets reset with each epoch):

```
def train(iterations=100):
    for iter in range(iterations):
        total_loss = 0
        n_loss = 0

        hidden = model.init_hidden(batch_size=batch_size)
        for batch_i in range(len(input_batches)):

            hidden = Tensor(hidden.data, autograd=True)
            loss = None
            losses = list()
            for t in range(bptt):
                input = Tensor(input_batches[batch_i][t], autograd=True)
                rnn_input = embed.forward(input=input)
                output, hidden = model.forward(input=rnn_input,
                                               hidden=hidden)
                target = Tensor(target_batches[batch_i][t], autograd=True)
                batch_loss = criterion.forward(output, target)
                losses.append(batch_loss)
                if(t == 0):
                    loss = batch_loss
                else:
                    loss = loss + batch_loss
            for loss in losses:
                ""
            loss.backward()
            optim.step()
            total_loss += loss.data
            log = "\r Iter:" + str(iter)
            log += " - Batch "+str(batch_i+1)+"/"+str(len(input_batches))
            log += " - Loss:" + str(np.exp(total_loss / (batch_i+1)))
            if(batch_i == 0):
                log += " - " + generate_sample(70,'\n').replace("\n"," ")
            if(batch_i % 10 == 0 or batch_i-1 == len(input_batches)):
                sys.stdout.write(log)
        optim.alpha *= 0.99
        print()
train()
```

```
Iter:0 - Batch 191/195 - Loss:148.00388828554404
Iter:1 - Batch 191/195 - Loss:20.588816924127116 mhnethet tttttt t t t
                                ....
Iter:99 - Batch 61/195 - Loss:1.0533843281265225 I af the mands your
```

A sample of the output

By sampling from the predictions of the model, you can write Shakespeare!

The following code uses a subset of the training logic to make predictions using the model. You store the predictions in a string and return the string version as output to the function. The sample that's generated looks quite Shakespearian and even includes characters talking:

```
def generate_sample(n=30, init_char=' '):
    s = ""
    hidden = model.init_hidden(batch_size=1)
    input = Tensor(np.array([word2index[init_char]]))
    for i in range(n):
        rnn_input = embed.forward(input)
        output, hidden = model.forward(input=rnn_input, hidden=hidden)
        output.data *= 10                          Temperature for sampling;
        temp_dist = output.softmax()               higher = greedier
        temp_dist /= temp_dist.sum()

        m = (temp_dist > np.random.rand()).argmax()    Samples
        c = vocab[m]                                    from pred
        input = Tensor(np.array([m]))
        s += c
    return s
print(generate_sample(n=2000, init_char='\n'))
```

```
I war ded abdons would.

CHENRO:
Why, speed no virth to her,
Plirt, goth Plish love,
Befion
 hath if be fe woulds is feally your hir, the confectife to the nightion
As   rent Ron my hath iom
the worse, my goth Plish love,
Befion
Ass untrucerty of my fernight this we namn?

ANG, makes:
That's bond confect fe comes not commonour would be forch the conflill
As   poing from your jus  eep of m look o perves, the worse, my goth
Thould be good lorges ever word

DESS:
Where exbinder: if not conflill, the confectife to the nightion
As co move, sir, this we namn?

ANG VINE PAET:
There was courter hower how, my goth Plish lo res
Toures
ever wo formall, have abon, with a good lorges ever word.
```

Vanishing and exploding gradients

Vanilla RNNs suffer from vanishing and exploding gradients.

You may recall this image from when you first put together a RNN. The idea was to be able to combine the word embeddings in a way that order mattered. You did this by learning a matrix that transformed each embedding to the next timestep. Forward propagation then became a two-step process: start with the first word embedding (the embedding for "Red" in the following example), multiply by the weight matrix, and add the next embedding ("Sox"). You then take the resulting vector, multiply it by the same weight matrix, and then add in the next word, repeating until you've read in the entire series of words.

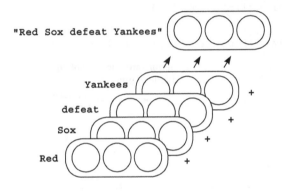

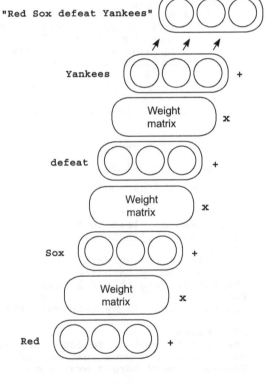

But as you know, an additional nonlinearity was added to the hidden state-generation process. Thus, forward propagation becomes a three-step process: matrix multiply the previous hidden state by a weight matrix, add in the next word's embedding, and apply a nonlinearity.

Note that this nonlinearity plays an important role in the stability of the network. No matter how long the sequence of words is, the hidden states (which could in theory grow larger and larger over time) are forced to stay between the values of the nonlinearity (between 0 and 1, in the case of a sigmoid). But backpropagation happens in a slightly different way than forward propagation, which doesn't have this nice property. Backpropagation tends to lead to either extremely large or extremely small values. Large values can cause divergence (lots of not-a-numbers [NaNs]), whereas extremely small values keep the network from learning. Let's take a closer look at RNN backpropagation.

A toy example of RNN backpropagation

To see vanishing/exploding gradients firsthand, let's synthesize an example.

The following code shows a recurrent backpropagation loop for `sigmoid` and `relu` activations. Notice how the gradients become very small/large for `sigmoid`/`relu`, respectively. During backprop, they become large as the result of the matrix multiplication, and small as a result of the `sigmoid` activation having a very flat derivative at its tails (common for many nonlinearities).

```
(sigmoid,relu)=(lambda x:1/(1+np.exp(-x)), lambda x:(x>0).astype(float)*x)
weights = np.array([[1,4],[4,1]])
activation = sigmoid(np.array([1,0.01]))

print("Sigmoid Activations")
activations = list()
for iter in range(10):
    activation = sigmoid(activation.dot(weights))
    activations.append(activation)
    print(activation)
print("\nSigmoid Gradients")
gradient = np.ones_like(activation)
for activation in reversed(activations):
    gradient = (activation * (1 - activation) * gradient)
    gradient = gradient.dot(weights.transpose())
    print(gradient)

print("Activations")
activations = list()
for iter in range(10):
    activation = relu(activation.dot(weights))
    activations.append(activation)
    print(activation)
print("\nGradients")
gradient = np.ones_like(activation)
for activation in reversed(activations):
    gradient = ((activation > 0) * gradient).dot(weights.transpose())
    print(gradient)
```

The derivative of sigmoid causes very small gradients when activation is very near 0 or 1 (the tails).

The matrix multiplication causes exploding gradients that don't get squished by a nonlinearity (as in sigmoid).

Sigmoid Activations	Relu Activations
[0.93940638 0.96852968]	[23.71814585 23.98025559]
[0.9919462 0.99121735]	[119.63916823 118.852839]
[0.99301385 0.99302901]	[595.05052421 597.40951192]
. . .	. . .
[0.99307291 0.99307291]	[46583049.71437107 46577890.60826711]

Sigmoid Gradients	Relu Gradients
[0.03439552 0.03439552]	[5. 5.]
[0.00118305 0.00118305]	[25. 25.]
[4.06916726e-05 4.06916726e-05]	[125. 125.]
. . .	. . .
[1.45938177e-14 2.16938983e-14]	[9765625. 9765625.]

Long short-term memory (LSTM) cells

LSTMs are the industry standard model to counter vanishing/exploding gradients.

The previous section explained how vanishing/exploding gradients result from the way hidden states are updated in a RNN. The problem is the combination of matrix multiplication and nonlinearity being used to form the next hidden state. The solution that LSTMs provide is surprisingly simple.

> **The gated copy trick**
>
> LSTMs create the next hidden state by copying the previous hidden state and then adding or removing information as necessary. The mechanisms the LSTM uses for adding and removing information are called *gates*.

```
def forward(self, input, hidden):
    from_prev_hidden = self.w_hh.forward(hidden)
    combined = self.w_ih.forward(input) + from_prev_hidden
    new_hidden = self.activation.forward(combined)
    output = self.w_ho.forward(new_hidden)
    return output, new_hidden
```

The previous code is the forward propagation logic for the RNN cell. Following is the new forward propagation logic for the LSTM cell. The LSTM has two hidden state vectors: h (for hidden) and `cell`.

The one you care about is `cell`. Notice how it's updated. Each new cell is the previous cell plus u, weighted by i and f. f is the "forget" gate. If it takes a value of 0, the new cell will erase what it saw previously. If i is 1, it will fully add in the value of u to create the new cell. o is an output gate that controls how much of the cell's state the output prediction is allowed to see. For example, if o is all zeros, then the `self.w_ho.forward(h)` line will make a prediction ignoring the cell state entirely.

```
def forward(self, input, hidden):

    prev_hidden, prev_cell = (hidden[0], hidden[1])

    f = (self.xf.forward(input) + self.hf.forward(prev_hidden)).sigmoid()
    i = (self.xi.forward(input) + self.hi.forward(prev_hidden)).sigmoid()
    o = (self.xo.forward(input) + self.ho.forward(prev_hidden)).sigmoid()
    u = (self.xc.forward(input) + self.hc.forward(prev_hidden)).tanh()
    cell = (f * prev_cell) + (i * u)
    h = o * cell.tanh()
    output = self.w_ho.forward(h)
    return output, (h, cell)
```

Some intuition about LSTM gates

LSTM gates are semantically similar to reading/writing from memory.

So there you have it! There are three gates—f, i, o—and a cell-update vector u; think of these as forget, input, output, and update, respectively. They work together to ensure that any information to be stored or manipulated in c can be so without requiring each update of c to have any matrix multiplications or nonlinearities applied to it. In other words, you're avoiding ever calling `nonlinearity(c)` or `c.dot(weights)`.

This is what allows the LSTM to store information across a time series without worrying about vanishing or exploding gradients. Each step is a copy (assuming f is nonzero) plus an update (assuming i is nonzero). The hidden value h is then a masked version of the cell that's used for prediction.

Notice further that each of the three gates is formed the same way. They have their own weight matrices, but each of them conditions on the input and the previous hidden state, passed through a `sigmoid`. It's this `sigmoid` nonlinearity that makes them so useful as gates, because it saturates at 0 and 1:

```
f = (self.xf.forward(input) + self.hf.forward(prev_hidden)).sigmoid()
i = (self.xi.forward(input) + self.hi.forward(prev_hidden)).sigmoid()
o = (self.xo.forward(input) + self.ho.forward(prev_hidden)).sigmoid()
```

One last possible critique is about h. Clearly it's still prone to vanishing and exploding gradients, because it's basically being used the same as the vanilla RNN. First, because the h vector is always created using a combination of vectors that are squished with `tanh` and `sigmoid`, exploding gradients aren't really a problem—only vanishing gradients. But this ends up being OK because h is conditioned on c, which can carry long-range information: the kind of information vanishing gradients can't learn to carry. Thus, all long-range information is transported using c, and h is only a localized interpretation of c, useful for making an output prediction and constructing gate activations at the following timestep. In short, c can learn to transport information over long distances, so it doesn't matter if h can't.

The long short-term memory layer

You can use the autograd system to implement an LSTM.

```python
class LSTMCell(Layer):

    def __init__(self, n_inputs, n_hidden, n_output):
        super().__init__()

        self.n_inputs = n_inputs
        self.n_hidden = n_hidden
        self.n_output = n_output

        self.xf = Linear(n_inputs, n_hidden)
        self.xi = Linear(n_inputs, n_hidden)
        self.xo = Linear(n_inputs, n_hidden)
        self.xc = Linear(n_inputs, n_hidden)
        self.hf = Linear(n_hidden, n_hidden, bias=False)
        self.hi = Linear(n_hidden, n_hidden, bias=False)
        self.ho = Linear(n_hidden, n_hidden, bias=False)
        self.hc = Linear(n_hidden, n_hidden, bias=False)

        self.w_ho = Linear(n_hidden, n_output, bias=False)

        self.parameters += self.xf.get_parameters()
        self.parameters += self.xi.get_parameters()
        self.parameters += self.xo.get_parameters()
        self.parameters += self.xc.get_parameters()
        self.parameters += self.hf.get_parameters()
        self.parameters += self.hi.get_parameters()
        self.parameters += self.ho.get_parameters()
        self.parameters += self.hc.get_parameters()

        self.parameters += self.w_ho.get_parameters()

    def forward(self, input, hidden):

        prev_hidden = hidden[0]
        prev_cell = hidden[1]

        f=(self.xf.forward(input)+self.hf.forward(prev_hidden)).sigmoid()
        i=(self.xi.forward(input)+self.hi.forward(prev_hidden)).sigmoid()
        o=(self.xo.forward(input)+self.ho.forward(prev_hidden)).sigmoid()
        g = (self.xc.forward(input) +self.hc.forward(prev_hidden)).tanh()
        c = (f * prev_cell) + (i * g)
        h = o * c.tanh()

        output = self.w_ho.forward(h)
        return output, (h, c)

    def init_hidden(self, batch_size=1):
        h = Tensor(np.zeros((batch_size, self.n_hidden)), autograd=True)
        c = Tensor(np.zeros((batch_size, self.n_hidden)), autograd=True)
        h.data[:,0] += 1
        c.data[:,0] += 1
        return (h, c)
```

Upgrading the character language model

Let's swap out the vanilla RNN with the new LSTM cell.

Earlier in this chapter, you trained a character language model to predict Shakespeare. Now let's train an LSTM-based model to do the same. Fortunately, the framework from the preceding chapter makes this easy to do (the complete code from the book's website, www. manning.com/books/grokking-deep-learning; or on GitHub at https://github.com/iamtrask/ grokking-deep-learning). Here's the new setup code. All edits from the vanilla RNN code are in bold. Notice that hardly anything has changed about how you set up the neural network:

```
import sys,random,math
from collections import Counter
import numpy as np
import sys

np.random.seed(0)

f = open('shakespear.txt','r')
raw = f.read()
f.close()

vocab = list(set(raw))
word2index = {}
for i,word in enumerate(vocab):
    word2index[word]=i
indices = np.array(list(map(lambda x:word2index[x], raw)))

embed = Embedding(vocab_size=len(vocab),dim=512)
model = LSTMCell(n_inputs=512, n_hidden=512, n_output=len(vocab))
model.w_ho.weight.data *= 0

criterion = CrossEntropyLoss()
optim = SGD(parameters=model.get_parameters() + embed.get_parameters(),
            alpha=0.05)

batch_size = 16
bptt = 25
n_batches = int((indices.shape[0] / (batch_size)))

trimmed_indices = indices[:n_batches*batch_size]
batched_indices = trimmed_indices.reshape(batch_size, n_batches)
batched_indices = batched_indices.transpose()

input_batched_indices = batched_indices[0:-1]
target_batched_indices = batched_indices[1:]

n_bptt = int(((n_batches-1) / bptt))
input_batches = input_batched_indices[:n_bptt*bptt]
input_batches = input_batches.reshape(n_bptt,bptt,batch_size)
target_batches = target_batched_indices[:n_bptt*bptt]
target_batches = target_batches.reshape(n_bptt, bptt, batch_size)
min_loss = 1000
```

This seemed to help training.

Training the LSTM character language model

The training logic also hasn't changed much.

The only real change you have to make from the vanilla RNN logic is the truncated backpropagation logic, because there are two hidden vectors per timestep instead of one. But this is a relatively minor fix (in bold). I've also added a few bells and whistles that make training easier (`alpha` slowly decreases over time, and there's more logging):

```
for iter in range(iterations):
    total_loss, n_loss = (0, 0)

    hidden = model.init_hidden(batch_size=batch_size)
    batches_to_train = len(input_batches)

    for batch_i in range(batches_to_train):

        hidden = (Tensor(hidden[0].data, autograd=True),
                  Tensor(hidden[1].data, autograd=True))
        losses = list()

        for t in range(bptt):
            input = Tensor(input_batches[batch_i][t], autograd=True)
            rnn_input = embed.forward(input=input)
            output, hidden = model.forward(input=rnn_input, hidden=hidden)

            target = Tensor(target_batches[batch_i][t], autograd=True)
            batch_loss = criterion.forward(output, target)

            if(t == 0):
                losses.append(batch_loss)
            else:
                losses.append(batch_loss + losses[-1])
        loss = losses[-1]

        loss.backward()
        optim.step()

        total_loss += loss.data / bptt
        epoch_loss = np.exp(total_loss / (batch_i+1))
        if(epoch_loss < min_loss):
            min_loss = epoch_loss
            print()
        log = "\r Iter:" + str(iter)
        log += " - Alpha:" + str(optim.alpha)[0:5]
        log += " - Batch "+str(batch_i+1)+"/"+str(len(input_batches))
        log += " - Min Loss:" + str(min_loss)[0:5]
        log += " - Loss:" + str(epoch_loss)
        if(batch_i == 0):
            s = generate_sample(n=70, init_char='T').replace("\n"," ")
            log += " - " + s
        sys.stdout.write(log)
    optim.alpha *= 0.99
```

Tuning the LSTM character language model

I spent about two days tuning this model, and it trained overnight.

Here's some of the training output for this model. Note that it took a very long time to train (there are a *lot* of parameters). I also had to train it many times in order to find a good tuning (learning rate, batch size, and so on) for this task, and the final model trained overnight (8 hours). In general, the longer you train, the better your results will be.

```
I:0 - Alpha:0.05 - Batch 1/249 - Min Loss:62.00 - Loss:62.00 - eeeeeeeee
                             ...
I:7 - Alpha:0.04 - Batch 140/249 - Min Loss:10.5 - Loss:10.7 - heres, and
                             ...
I:91 - Alpha:0.016 - Batch 176/249 - Min Loss:9.900 - Loss:11.9757225699
```

```
def generate_sample(n=30, init_char=' '):
    s = ""
    hidden = model.init_hidden(batch_size=1)
    input = Tensor(np.array([word2index[init_char]]))
    for i in range(n):
        rnn_input = embed.forward(input)
        output, hidden = model.forward(input=rnn_input, hidden=hidden)
        output.data *= 15
        temp_dist = output.softmax()
        temp_dist /= temp_dist.sum()

        m = output.data.argmax()         ← Takes the max
        c = vocab[m]                        prediction
        input = Tensor(np.array([m]))
        s += c
    return s
print(generate_sample(n=500, init_char='\n'))
```

```
Intestay thee.

SIR:
It thou my thar the sentastar the see the see:
Imentary take the subloud I
Stall my thentaring fook the senternight pead me, the gakentlenternot
they day them.

KENNOR:
I stay the see talk :
Non the seady!

Sustar thou shour in the suble the see the senternow the antently the see
the seaventlace peake,
I sentlentony my thent:
I the sentastar thamy this not thame.
```

Summary

LSTMs are incredibly powerful models.

The distribution of Shakespearian language that the LSTM learned to generate isn't to be taken lightly. Language is an incredibly complex statistical distribution to learn, and the fact that LSTMs can do so well (at the time of writing, they're the state-of-the-art approach by a wide margin) still baffles me (and others as well). Small variants on this model either are or have recently been the state of the art in a wide variety of tasks and, alongside word embeddings and convolutional layers, will undoubtedly be one of our go-to tools for a long time to come.

deep learning on unseen data: introducing federated learning | 15

In this chapter

- The problem of privacy in deep learning

- Federated learning

- Learning to detect spam

- Hacking into federated learning

- Secure aggregation

- Homomorphic encryption

- Homomorphically encrypted federated learning

> " Friends don't spy; true friendship is about privacy, too. "
>
> —Stephen King, *Hearts in Atlantis* (1999)

The problem of privacy in deep learning

Deep learning (and tools for it) often means you have access to your training data.

As you're keenly aware by now, deep learning, being a subfield of machine learning, is all about learning from data. But often, the data being learned from is incredibly personal. The most meaningful models interact with the most personal information about human lives and tell us things about ourselves that might have been difficult to know otherwise. To paraphrase, a deep learning model can study thousands of lives to help you better understand your own.

The primary natural resource for deep learning is training data (either synthetic or natural). Without it, deep learning can't learn; and because the most valuable use cases often interact with the most personal datsets, deep learning is often a reason behind companies seeking to aggregate data. They need it in order to solve a particular use case.

But in 2017, Google published a very exciting paper and blog post that made a significant dent in this conversation. Google proposed that we don't need to centralize a dataset in order to train a model over it. The company proposed this question: what if instead of bringing all the data to one place, we could bring the model to the data? This is a new, exciting subfield of machine learning called *federated learning*, and it's what this chapter is about.

> What if instead of bringing the corpus of training data to one place to train a model, you could bring the model to the data wherever it's generated?

This simple reversal is extremely important. First, it means in order to participate in the deep learning supply chain, people don't technically have to send their data to anyone. Valuable models in healthcare, personal management, and other sensitive areas can be trained without requiring anyone to disclose information about themselves. In theory, people could retain control over the only copy of their personal data (at least as far as deep learning is concerned).

This technique will also have a huge impact on the competitive landscape of deep learning in corporate competition and entrepreneurship. Large enterprises that previously wouldn't (or couldn't, for legal reasons) share data about their customers can potentially still earn revenue from that data. There are some problem domains where the sensitivity and regulatory constraints surrounding the data have been a headwind to progress. Healthcare is one example where datasets are often locked up tight, making research challenging.

Federated learning

You don't have to have access to a dataset in order to learn from it.

The premise of federated learning is that many datasets contain information that's useful for solving problems (for example, identifying cancer in an MRI), but it's hard to access these relevant datasets in large enough quantities to train a suitably strong deep learning model. The main concern is that, even though the dataset has information sufficient to train a deep learning model, it also has information that (presumably) has nothing to do with learning the task but could potentially harm someone if it were revealed.

Federated learning is about a model going into a secure environment and learning how to solve a problem without needing the data to move anywhere. Let's jump into an example.

```python
import numpy as np
from collections import Counter
import random
import sys
import codecs
np.random.seed(12345)
with codecs.open('spam.txt',"r",encoding='utf-8',errors='ignore') as f:
    raw = f.readlines()

vocab, spam, ham = (set(["<unk>"]), list(), list())
for row in raw:
    spam.append(set(row[:-2].split(" ")))
    for word in spam[-1]:
        vocab.add(word)

with codecs.open('ham.txt',"r",encoding='utf-8',errors='ignore') as f:
    raw = f.readlines()

for row in raw:
    ham.append(set(row[:-2].split(" ")))
    for word in ham[-1]:
        vocab.add(word)

vocab, w2i = (list(vocab), {})
for i,w in enumerate(vocab):
    w2i[w] = i

def to_indices(input, l=500):
    indices = list()
    for line in input:
        if(len(line) < l):
            line = list(line) + ["<unk>"] * (l - len(line))
            idxs = list()
            for word in line:
                idxs.append(w2i[word])
            indices.append(idxs)
    return indices
```

Dataset from http://www2.aueb.gr/users/ion/data/enron-spam/

Learning to detect spam

Let's say you want to train a model across people's emails to detect spam.

The use case we'll talk about is email classification. The first model will be trained on a publicly available dataset called the Enron dataset, which is a large corpus of emails released from the famous Enron lawsuit (now an industry standard email analytics corpus). Fun fact: I used to know someone who read/annotated this dataset professionally, and people emailed all sorts of crazy stuff to each other (much of it very personal). But because it was all released to the public in the court case, it's free to use now.

The code in the previous section and this section is just the preprocessing. The input data files (ham.txt and spam.txt) are available on the book's website, www.manning.com/books/grokking-deep-learning; and on GitHub at https://github.com/iamtrask/Grokking-Deep-Learning. You preprocess it to get it ready to forward propagate into the embedding class created in chapter 13 when you created a deep learning framework. As before, all the words in this corpus are turned into lists of indices. You also make all the emails exactly 500 words long by either trimming the email or padding it with <unk> tokens. Doing so makes the final dataset square.

```
spam_idx = to_indices(spam)
ham_idx = to_indices(ham)

train_spam_idx = spam_idx[0:-1000]
train_ham_idx = ham_idx[0:-1000]

test_spam_idx = spam_idx[-1000:]
test_ham_idx = ham_idx[-1000:]

train_data = list()
train_target = list()

test_data = list()
test_target = list()

for i in range(max(len(train_spam_idx),len(train_ham_idx))):
    train_data.append(train_spam_idx[i%len(train_spam_idx)])
    train_target.append([1])

    train_data.append(train_ham_idx[i%len(train_ham_idx)])
    train_target.append([0])

for i in range(max(len(test_spam_idx),len(test_ham_idx))):
    test_data.append(test_spam_idx[i%len(test_spam_idx)])
    test_target.append([1])

    test_data.append(test_ham_idx[i%len(test_ham_idx)])
    test_target.append([0])
```

```
def train(model, input_data, target_data, batch_size=500, iterations=5):
    n_batches = int(len(input_data) / batch_size)
    for iter in range(iterations):
        iter_loss = 0
        for b_i in range(n_batches):

            # padding token should stay at 0
            model.weight.data[w2i['<unk>']] *= 0
            input = Tensor(input_data[b_i*bs:(b_i+1)*bs], autograd=True)
            target = Tensor(target_data[b_i*bs:(b_i+1)*bs], autograd=True)

            pred = model.forward(input).sum(1).sigmoid()
            loss = criterion.forward(pred,target)
            loss.backward()
            optim.step()

            iter_loss += loss.data[0] / bs

            sys.stdout.write("\r\tLoss:" + str(iter_loss / (b_i+1)))
        print()
    return model


def test(model, test_input, test_output):

    model.weight.data[w2i['<unk>']] *= 0

    input = Tensor(test_input, autograd=True)
    target = Tensor(test_output, autograd=True)

    pred = model.forward(input).sum(1).sigmoid()
    return ((pred.data > 0.5) == target.data).mean()
```

With these nice `train()` and `test()` functions, you can initialize a neural network and train it using the following few lines. After only three iterations, the network can already classify on the test dataset with 99.45% accuracy (the test dataset is balanced, so this is quite good):

```
model = Embedding(vocab_size=len(vocab), dim=1)
model.weight.data *= 0
criterion = MSELoss()
optim = SGD(parameters=model.get_parameters(), alpha=0.01)


for i in range(3):
    model = train(model, train_data, train_target, iterations=1)
    print("% Correct on Test Set: " + \
            str(test(model, test_data, test_target)*100))
```

```
        Loss:0.037140416860871446
% Correct on Test Set: 98.65
        Loss:0.011258669226059114
% Correct on Test Set: 99.15
        Loss:0.008068268387986223
% Correct on Test Set: 99.45
```

Let's make it federated

The previous example was plain vanilla deep learning. Let's protect privacy.

In the previous section, you got the email example. Now, let's put all the emails in one place. This is the old-school way of doing things (which is still far too common in the world). Let's start by simulating a federated learning environment that has multiple different collections of emails:

```
bob = (train_data[0:1000], train_target[0:1000])
alice = (train_data[1000:2000], train_target[1000:2000])
sue = (train_data[2000:], train_target[2000:])
```

Easy enough. Now you can do the same training as before, but across each person's email database all at the same time. After each iteration, you'll average the values of the models from Bob, Alice, and Sue and evaluate. Note that some methods of federated learning aggregate after each batch (or collection of batches); I'm keeping it simple:

```
for i in range(3):
    print("Starting Training Round...")
    print("\tStep 1: send the model to Bob")
    bob_model = train(copy.deepcopy(model), bob[0], bob[1], iterations=1)

    print("\n\tStep 2: send the model to Alice")
    alice_model = train(copy.deepcopy(model),
                        alice[0], alice[1], iterations=1)

    print("\n\tStep 3: Send the model to Sue")
    sue_model = train(copy.deepcopy(model), sue[0], sue[1], iterations=1)

    print("\n\tAverage Everyone's New Models")
    model.weight.data = (bob_model.weight.data + \
                         alice_model.weight.data + \
                         sue_model.weight.data)/3

    print("\t% Correct on Test Set: " + \
          str(test(model, test_data, test_target)*100))

    print("\nRepeat!!\n")
```

The next section shows the results. The model learns to nearly the same performance as before, and in theory you didn't have access to the training data—or did you? After all, each person is changing the model somehow, right? Can you really not discover anything about their dataset?

```
Starting Training Round...
   Step 1: send the model to Bob
   Loss:0.21908166249699718

            . . . . . .

   Step 3: Send the model to Sue
   Loss:0.015368461608470256

   Average Everyone's New Models
   % Correct on Test Set: 98.8
```

Hacking into federated learning

Let's use a toy example to see how to still learn the training dataset.

Federated learning has two big challenges, both of which are at their worst when each person in the training dataset has only a small handful of training examples. These challenges are performance and privacy. As it turns out, if someone has only a few training examples (or the model improvement they send you uses only a few examples: a training batch), you can still learn quite a bit about the data. Given 10,000 people (each with a little data), you'll spend most of your time sending the model back and forth and not much time training (especially if the model is really big).

But we're getting ahead of ourselves. Let's see what you can learn when a user performs a weight update over a single batch:

```
import copy

bobs_email = ["my", "computer", "password", "is", "pizza"]

bob_input = np.array([[w2i[x] for x in bobs_email]])
bob_target = np.array([[0]])

model = Embedding(vocab_size=len(vocab), dim=1)
model.weight.data *= 0

bobs_model = train(copy.deepcopy(model),
                   bob_input, bob_target, iterations=1, batch_size=1)
```

Bob is going to create an update to the model using an email in his inbox. But Bob saved his password in an email to himself that says, "My computer password is pizza." Silly Bob. By looking at which weights changed, you can figure out the vocabulary (and infer the meaning) of Bob's email:

```
for i, v in enumerate(bobs_model.weight.data - model.weight.data):
    if(v != 0):
        print(vocab[i])
```

```
is
pizza
computer
password
my
```

And just like that, you learned Bob's super-secret password (and probably his favorite food, too). What's to be done? How can you use federated learning if it's so easy to tell what the training data was from the weight update?

Secure aggregation

Let's average weight updates from zillions of people before anyone can see them.

The solution is to never let Bob put a gradient out in the open like that. How can Bob contribute his gradient if people shouldn't see it? The social sciences use an interesting technique called *randomized response*.

It goes like this. Let's say you're conducting a survey, and you want to ask 100 people whether they've committed a heinous crime. Of course, all would answer "No" even if you promised them you wouldn't tell. Instead, you have them flip a coin twice (somewhere you can't see), and tell them that if the first coin flip is heads, they should answer honestly; and if it's tails, they should answer "Yes" or "No" according to the second coin flip.

Given this scenario, you never actually ask people to tell you whether they committed crimes. The true answers are hidden in the random noise of the first and second coin flips. If 60% of people say "Yes," you can determine (using simple math) that about 70% of the people you surveyed committed heinous crimes (give or take a few percentage points). The idea is that the random noise makes it plausible that any information you learn about the person came from the noise instead of from them.

> ### Privacy via plausible deniability
>
> The level of chance that a particular answer came from random noise instead of an individual protects their privacy by giving them plausible deniability. This forms the basis for secure aggregation and, more generally, much of differential privacy.

You're looking only at aggregate statistics overall. (You never see anyone's answer directly; you see only pairs of answers or perhaps larger groupings.) Thus, the more people you can aggregate before adding noise, the less noise you have to add to hide them (and the more accurate the findings are).

In the context of federated learning, you could (if you wanted) add a ton of noise, but this would hurt training. Instead, first sum all the gradients from all the participants in such a way that no one can see anyone's gradient but their own. The class of problems for doing this is called *secure aggregation*, and in order to do it, you'll need one more (very cool) tool: *homomorphic encryption*.

Homomorphic encryption

You can perform arithmetic on encrypted values.

One of the most exciting frontiers of research is the intersection of artificial intelligence (including deep learning) and cryptography. Front and center in this exciting intersection is a very cool technology called homomorphic encryption. Loosely stated, homomorphic encryption lets you perform computation on encrypted values without decrypting them.

In particular, we're interested in performing addition over these values. Explaining exactly how it works would take an entire book on its own, but I'll show you how it works with a few definitions. First, a *public key* lets you encrypt numbers. A *private key* lets you decrypt encrypted numbers. An encrypted value is called a *ciphertext*, and an unencrypted value is called a *plaintext*.

Let's see an example of homomorphic encryption using the phe library. (To install the library, run `pip install phe` or download it from GitHub at https://github.com/n1analytics/python-paillier):

```
import phe

public_key, private_key = phe.generate_paillier_keypair(n_length=1024)

x = public_key.encrypt(5)  ◄──────────  Encrypts the number 5

y = public_key.encrypt(3)  ◄──────────  Encrypts the number 3

z = x + y  ◄──────────────────────  Adds the two encrypted values

z_ = private_key.decrypt(z)  ◄────────  Decrypts the result
print("The Answer: " + str(z_))
```

```
The Answer: 8
```

This code encrypts two numbers (5 and 3) and adds them together while they're still encrypted. Pretty neat, eh? There's another technique that's a sort-of cousin to homomorphic encryption: *secure multi-party computation*. You can learn about it at the "Cryptography and Machine Learning" blog (https://mortendahl.github.io).

Now, let's return to the problem of secure aggregation. Given your new knowledge that you can add together numbers you can't see, the answer becomes plain. The person who initializes the model sends a `public_key` to Bob, Alice, and Sue so they can each encrypt their weight updates. Then, Bob, Alice, and Sue (who don't have the private key) talk directly to each other and accumulate all their gradients into a single, final update that's sent back to the model owner, who decrypts it with the `private_key`.

Homomorphically encrypted federated learning

Let's use homomorphic encryption to protect the gradients being aggregated.

```
model = Embedding(vocab_size=len(vocab), dim=1)
model.weight.data *= 0

# note that in production the n_length should be at least 1024
public_key, private_key = phe.generate_paillier_keypair(n_length=128)

def train_and_encrypt(model, input, target, pubkey):
    new_model = train(copy.deepcopy(model), input, target, iterations=1)

    encrypted_weights = list()
    for val in new_model.weight.data[:,0]:
        encrypted_weights.append(public_key.encrypt(val))
    ew = np.array(encrypted_weights).reshape(new_model.weight.data.shape)

    return ew


for i in range(3):
    print("\nStarting Training Round...")
    print("\tStep 1: send the model to Bob")
    bob_encrypted_model = train_and_encrypt(copy.deepcopy(model),
                                      bob[0], bob[1], public_key)

    print("\n\tStep 2: send the model to Alice")
    alice_encrypted_model=train_and_encrypt(copy.deepcopy(model),
                                      alice[0],alice[1],public_key)

    print("\n\tStep 3: Send the model to Sue")
    sue_encrypted_model = train_and_encrypt(copy.deepcopy(model),
                                      sue[0], sue[1], public_key)

    print("\n\tStep 4: Bob, Alice, and Sue send their")
    print("\tencrypted models to each other.")
    aggregated_model = bob_encrypted_model + \
                       alice_encrypted_model + \
                       sue_encrypted_model

    print("\n\tStep 5: only the aggregated model")
    print("\tis sent back to the model owner who")
    print("\t can decrypt it.")
    raw_values = list()
    for val in sue_encrypted_model.flatten():
        raw_values.append(private_key.decrypt(val))
    new = np.array(raw_values).reshape(model.weight.data.shape)/3
    model.weight.data = new

    print("\t% Correct on Test Set: " + \
            str(test(model, test_data, test_target)*100))
```

Now you can run the new training scheme, which has an added step. Alice, Bob, and Sue add up their homomorphically encrypted models before sending them back to you, so you never see which updates came from which person (a form of plausible deniability). In production, you'd also add some additional random noise sufficient to meet a certain privacy threshold required by Bob, Alice, and Sue (according to their personal preferences). More on that in future work.

```
Starting Training Round...
  Step 1: send the model to Bob
  Loss:0.21908166249699718

  Step 2: send the model to Alice
  Loss:0.2937106899184867

          ...
          ...
          ...

% Correct on Test Set: 99.15
```

Summary

Federated learning is one of the most exciting breakthroughs in deep learning.

I firmly believe that federated learning will change the landscape of deep learning in the coming years. It will unlock new datasets that were previously too sensitive to work with, creating great social good as a result of this newly available entrepreneurial opportunities. This is part of a broader convergence between encryption and artificial intelligence research that, in my opinion, is the most exciting convergence of the decade.

The main thing holding back these techniques from practical use is their lack of availability in modern deep learning toolkits. The tipping point will be when anyone can run `pip install...` and then have access to deep learning frameworks where privacy and security are first-class citizens, and where techniques such as federated learning, homomorphic encryption, differential privacy, and secure multi-party computation are all built in (and you don't have to be an expert to use them).

Out of this belief, I've been working with a team of open source volunteers as a part of the OpenMined project for the past year, extending major deep learning frameworks with these primitives. If you believe in the importance of these tools to the future of privacy and security, come check us out at http://openmined.org or at the GitHub repository (https://github.com/OpenMined). Show your support, even if it's only starring a few repos; and do join if you can (slack.openmined.org is the chat room).

In this chapter

- Step 1: Start learning PyTorch

- Step 2: Start another deep learning course

- Step 3: Grab a mathy deep learning textbook

- Step 4: Start a blog, and teach deep learning

- Step 5: Twitter

- Step 6: Implement academic papers

- Step 7: Acquire access to a GPU

- Step 8: Get paid to practice

- Step 9: Join an open source project

- Step 10: Develop your local community

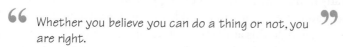

> " Whether you believe you can do a thing or not, you
> are right.
>
> —Henry Ford, automobile manufacturer

Congratulations!

If you're reading this, you've made it through nearly 300 pages of deep learning.

You did it! This was a lot of material. I'm proud of you, and you should be proud of yourself. Today should be a cause for celebration. At this point, you understand the basic concepts behind artificial intelligence, and should feel quite confident in your abilities to speak about them as well as your abilities to learn advanced concepts.

This last chapter includes a few short sections discussing appropriate next steps for you, especially if this is your first resource in the field of deep learning. My general assumption is that you're interested in pursuing a career in the field or at least continuing to dabble on the side, and I hope my general comments will help guide you in the right direction (although they're only very general guidelines that may or may not directly apply to you).

Step 1: Start learning PyTorch

The deep learning framework you made most closely resembles PyTorch.

You've been learning deep learning using NumPy, which is a basic matrix library. You then built your own deep learning toolkit, and you've used that quite a bit as well. But from this point forward, except when learning about a new architecture, you should use an actual framework for your experiments. It will be less buggy. It will run (*way*) faster, and you'll be able to inherit/study other people's code.

Why should you choose PyTorch? There are many good options, but if you're coming from a NumPy background, PyTorch will feel the most familiar. Furthermore, the framework you built in chapter 13 closely resembles the API of PyTorch. I did it this way specifically with the intent of preparing you for an actual framework. If you choose PyTorch, you'll feel right at home. That said, choosing a deep learning framework is sort of like joining a house at Hogwarts: they're all great (but PyTorch is definitely Gryffindor).

Now the next question: how should you learn PyTorch? The best way is to take a deep learning course that teaches you deep learning using the framework. This will jog your memory about the concepts you're already familiar with while showing you where each piece lives in PyTorch. (You'll review stochastic gradient descent while also learning about where it's located in PyTorch's API.) The best place to do this at the time of writing is either Udacity's deep learning Nanodegree (although I'm biased: I helped teach it) or fast.ai. In addition, https://pytorch.org/tutorials and https://github.com/pytorch/examples are golden resources.

Step 2: Start another deep learning course

I learned deep learning by relearning the same concepts over and over.

Although it would be nice to think that one book or course is sufficient for your entire deep learning education, it's not. Even if every concept was covered in this book (they aren't), hearing the same concepts from multiple perspectives is essential for you to really grok them (see what I did there?). I've taken probably a half-dozen different courses (or YouTube series) in my growth as a developer in addition to watching tons of YouTube videos and reading lots of blog posts describing basic concepts.

Look for online courses on YouTube from the big deep learning universities or AI labs (Stanford, MIT, Oxford, Montreal, NYU, and so on). Watch all the videos. Do all the exercises. Do fast.ai, and Udacity if you can. Relearn the same concepts over and over. Practice them. Become familiar with them. You want the fundamentals to be second nature in your head.

Step 3: Grab a mathy deep learning textbook

You can reverse engineer the math from your deep learning knowledge.

My undergraduate degree at university was in applied discrete mathematics, but I learned way more about algebra, calculus, and statistics from spending time in deep learning than I ever did in the classroom. Furthermore, and this might sound surprising, I learned by hacking together NumPy code and then going back to the math problems it implements to figure out how they worked. This is how I really learned the deep learning–related math at a deeper level. It's a nice trick I hope you'll take to heart.

If you're not sure which mathy book to go for, probably the best on the market at the time of writing is *Deep Learning* by Ian Goodfellow, Yoshua Bengio, and Aaron Courville (MIT Press, 2016). It's not insane on the math side, but it's the next step up from this book (and the math notation guide in the front of the book is golden).

Step 4: Start a blog, and teach deep learning

Nothing I've ever done has helped my knowledge or career more.

I probably should have put this as step 1, but here goes. Nothing has boosted my knowledge of deep learning (and my career in deep learning) more than teaching deep learning on my blog. Teaching forces you to explain everything as simply as possible, and the fear of public shaming will ensure that you do a good job.

Funny story: one of my first blog posts made it onto Hacker News, but it was horribly written, and a major researcher at a top AI lab totally destroyed me in the comments. It hurt my feelings and my confidence, but it also tightened up my writing. It made me realize that most of the time, when I read something and it's hard to understand, it's not my fault; the person who was writing it didn't take enough time to explain all the little pieces I needed to know to understand the full concepts. They didn't provide relatable analogies to help my understanding.

All that is to say, start a blog. Try to get on the Hacker News or ML Reddit front page. Start by teaching the basic concepts. Try to do it better than anyone else. Don't worry if the topic has already been covered. To this day, my most popular blog post is "A Neural Network in 11 Lines of Python," which teaches the most over-taught thing in deep learning: a basic feedforward neural network. But I was able to explain it in a new way, which helped some folks. The main reason it did was that I wrote the post in a way that helped *me* understand it. That's the ticket. Teach things the way you want to learn them.

And don't just do summaries of deep learning concepts! Summaries are boring, and no one wants to read them. Write tutorials. Every blog post you write should include a neural network that learns to do something—something the reader can download and run. Your blog should give a line-by-line account of what each piece does so that even a five-year-old could understand. That's the standard. You may want to give up when you've been working on a two-page blog post for three days, but that's not the time to turn back: that's the time to press on and make it amazing! One great blog post can change your life. Trust me.

If you want to apply to a job, masters, or PhD program to do AI, pick a researcher you want to work with in that program, and write tutorials about their work. Every time I've done that, it has led to later meeting that researcher. Doing this shows that you understand the concepts they're working with, which is a prerequisite to them wanting to work with you. This is much better than a cold email, because, assuming it gets on Reddit, Hacker News, or some other venue, someone else will send it to them first. Sometimes they'll even reach out to you.

Step 5: Twitter

A lot of AI conversation happens on Twitter.

I've met more researchers from around the world on Twitter than almost any other way, and I've learned about nearly every paper I read because I was following someone who tweeted about it. You want to be up-to-date on the latest changes; and, more important, you want to become part of the conversation. I started by finding some AI researchers I looked up to, following them, and then following the people they follow. That got my feed started, and it has helped me greatly. (Just don't let it become an addiction!)

Step 6: Implement academic papers

Twitter + your blog = tutorials on academic papers.

Watch your Twitter feed until you come across a paper that both sounds interesting and doesn't need an insane number of GPUs. Write a tutorial on it. You'll have to read the paper, decipher the math, and go through the motions of tuning that the original researchers also had to go through. There's no better exercise if you're interested in doing abstract research. My first published paper at the International Conference on Machine Learning (ICML) came out of me reading the paper for and subsequently reverse-engineering the code in word2vec. Eventually, you'll be reading along and go, "Wait! I think I can make this better!" And voila: you're a researcher.

Step 7: Acquire access to a GPU (or many)

The faster you can experiment, the faster you can learn.

It's no secret that GPUs give 10 to 100× faster training times, but the implication is that you can iterate through your own (good and bad) ideas 100× faster. This is unbelievably valuable for learning deep learning. One of the mistakes I made in my career was waiting too long to start working with GPUs. Don't be like me: go buy one from NVIDIA, or use the free K80s you can access in Google Colab notebooks. NVIDIA also occasionally lets students use theirs for free for certain AI competitions, but you have to watch out for them.

Step 8: Get paid to practice

The more time you have to do deep learning, the faster you'll learn.

Another pivot point in my career was when I got a job that let me explore deep learning tools and research. Become a data scientist, data engineer, or research engineer, or freelance as a consultant doing statistics. The point is, you want to find a way to get paid to keep learning during work hours. These jobs exist; it just takes some effort to find them.

Your blog is essential to getting a job like this. Whatever job you want to get, write at least two blog posts showing that you can do whatever it is they're looking to hire someone for. That's the perfect resume (better than a degree in math). The perfect candidate is someone who has already shown they can do the job.

Step 9: Join an open source project

The best way to network and career-build in AI is to become a core developer in an open source project.

Find a deep learning framework you like, and start implementing things. Before you know it, you'll be interacting with researchers at the top labs (who will be reading/approving your pull requests). I know of plenty of folks who have landed awesome jobs (seemingly from nowhere) using this approach.

That being said, you have to put in the time. No one is going to hold your hand. Read the code. Make friends. Start by adding unit tests and documentation explaining the code, then work on bugs, and eventually start in on bigger projects. It takes time, but it's an investment in your future. If you're not sure, go with a major deep learning framework like PyTorch, TensorFlow, or Keras, or you can come work with me at OpenMined (which I think is the coolest open source project around). We're very newbie friendly.

Step 10: Develop your local community

I really learned deep learning because I enjoyed hanging with friends who were.

I learned deep learning at Bongo Java, sitting next to my best friends who were also interested in it. A big part of me sticking with it when the bugs were hard to fix (it took me two days to find a single period once) or the concepts were hard to master was that I was spending time around the people I loved being with. Don't underestimate this. If you're in a place you like to be, with people you like to be with, you're going to work longer and advance faster. It's not rocket science, but you have to be intentional. Who knows? You might even have a little fun while you're at it!

index

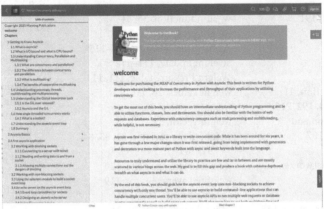

A new online reading experience

liveBook, our online reading platform, adds a new dimension to your Manning books, with features that make reading, learning, and sharing easier than ever. A liveBook version of your book is included FREE with every Manning book.

This next generation book platform is more than an online reader. It's packed with unique features to upgrade and enhance your learning experience.

- Add your own notes and bookmarks
- One-click code copy
- Learn from other readers in the discussion forum
- Audio recordings and interactive exercises
- Read all your purchased Manning content in any browser, anytime, anywhere

As an added bonus, you can search every Manning book and video in liveBook—even ones you don't yet own. Open any liveBook, and you'll be able to browse the content and read anything you like.*

Find out more at www.manning.com/livebook-program.

*Open reading is limited to 10 minutes per book daily